ALSO BY WALTER ABISH

DOUBLE VISION

DOUBLE VISION

Walter Abish

ALFRED A. KNOPF

NEW YORK

2004

THIS IS A BORZOI BOOK
PUBLISHED BY ALFRED A. KNOPF

www.aaknopf.com

Knopf, Borzoi Books, and the colophon are registered trademarks
of Random House, Inc.

Portions of this book have appeared in different
form in *Antaeus* and *Conjunctions.*

Library of Congress Cataloging-in-Publication Data
Abish, Walter.
Double vision / Walter Abish.—1st ed.
p.   cm.
ISBN 0-679-41868-7
1. Abish, Walter.   2. Abish, Walter—Childhood and youth.   3. Abish, Walter—
Journeys—Europe, German-speaking.   4. Novelists, American—20th century—
Biography.   5. Refugees, Jewish—United States—Biography.   6. Jewish
authors—United States—Biography.   7. Jewish families—Austria—Vienna.
8. Vienna (Austria)—Biography.   I. Title.

PS3551.B5Z465 2004
813'.54—dc21
[B]
2003047576

Manufactured in the United States of America
First Edition

This book is for Cecile,
and in memory of my aunt Adele.

It's possible to think of language as the most versatile, and maybe the original, form of deception, a sort of fortunate fall; I lie and am lied to, but the result of my lie is mental leaps, memory, knowledge. Portions of the world are caught in my psychic net. I become human, and increasingly more human, because the acrobatic gift of my lie turns into a truth of another sort. If each man contains all the possibilities of human nature, it is because language's acrobatic lie has thrown them in a busy dance about the ears.

—PAUL ZWEIG

Contents

Contents

PART ONE

THE WRITER-TO-BE

Vienna

That's why things happened the way they did. The oppressiveness of good manners. The emotional repression. My discontent. That's why my head is shaped the way it is. That's why my eyes are blue. We are talking about genes. About inherited traits. The way I smile—reluctantly. The way I reveal my anger. The reason I walk in a certain way. Is there no freedom at all from the family? The efficiently cool and remote mother and the energetic businessman father. Their distinctly separate worlds, their separate concerns collide uneasily in my brain. I would like to think that together, though each not communicating his or her desire to the other, they managed, if you will, to fabricate a writer. They, who essentially did not and could not know how a writer functions, by their approach, their passion, their view of everyday life, combined to turn me into one. It was their unspoken plan—a desire they had never voiced. Evidently a desire so secret that after I became a writer they continued to withhold their approval for fear that I might yet change my mind. "Ah, a writer!" My father glanced doubtfully at me, not wishing to say anything that might wound me. "A risky business!" On the other hand he couldn't restrain his enthusiastic approval at my driving skill—"You're a far better driver than Frank"—when, on one of his infrequent visits to New York in the early seventies, I picked him up at La Guardia and drove him to our home. It may have been the first time he had seen me at the wheel of a car. From him, this favorable comparison to Frank—a close friend of the family and, in the U.S., his business partner—was the ultimate compliment. Was it that he had never been led to expect much from me? Observing me drive well may have given him a little more confidence in my general capabilities. Driving was one thing he could judge me by. Clearly, in that respect I had passed with honors.

How readily I was able to identify with my sophisticated mother, and yet, in retrospect, it's my father I love unabashedly. No complications there. I love him, I have to admit, because he is so easy to love. He concealed his complications, if any. He didn't burden anyone with the intricacies of his thoughts. He hid everything but his overwhelming affection and generosity. His readiness to help, to give of himself: today he'd be labeled a softie. Not infrequently he was censured for this. All the same, for many he was exemplary—ideal, special. Yet, wasn't there also underlying this near-unanimous esteem and praise ("Ah, Herr Abish, a wonderful man!") a mild condescension? As if his conscientiousness and trustworthiness—or more likely, his reluctance to shine—implied a deficiency? Indeed, he disliked being the center of attention. Receiving gifts made him uncomfortable. He was easy to love. He was emotionally predictable—by that I mean he didn't ever seem to question or measure the degree to which he was fond of someone. There was a perseverance to his attachments. In his uncomplicated way he did not seem to waver in his commitments. Whereas for my mother, attachment, like so much else, was transitory. It had first to be examined for probable flaws, for defects. So much seemed to be at stake—above all, one's self-esteem, one's picture of oneself. My mother preferred to control the display of her emotions, control—to the degree this was possible—any expression or even sign of love. I suspect to heighten the love she might have felt, it needed to be made more tangible, it needed to be staged. Then, only then, like any well-rehearsed performance, it could be both exquisite and irresistible. For one thing, it enabled me, as the infrequent recipient of her love, to appreciate the setting in which the emotions were given their release—in order to what? Wasn't it to love as tentatively and as provisionally but with a kind of exquisite grace?

But why did they have me? I was the wrong child for them. I provided far too little satisfaction, far too little pleasure. Everything in me spelled out a meager diet. It was as if, all along, I had known that I was merely a capricious factor and not the ineluctable concept that fed their notion of a family. True, my presence permitted them to perform their roles more effectively. My presence—trying as it may have been at times—encouraged them to go on with their daily lives, safe in the knowledge that as "parents" they now would be free of criticism. I arrived to regulate their lives, to accentuate the "willed" normality of their coexistence. When I arrived, there was already a schedule awaiting me. Every possible eventuality was taken into consideration. Was it not from a need to avoid the unexpected? I neatly slipped into a niche, my everyday needs and expectations anticipated—or so it seemed. In turn my mother gracefully glided into a caring maternal role, while my father, lacking my mother's innate skill and intuition, adopted the role of father in the way he had come to accept business opportunities that came his way, gravely and responsibly. Not much personal involvement was required of him. To think that they accomplished this without any prior rehearsal, without any prior instructions! There must have been a Viennese Dr. Spock or Dr. Skinner to guide them. But did they prepare for me the way one apprehensively prepares for a relative who for months has threatened to visit—a visit that has no end in sight? They furnished my room—so confident were they of my arrival. Yes, shortly after their wedding, when the apartment was being redecorated, my future tastes were already being taken into consideration. My mother was preoccupied with the selection of an appropriate name for me. Was it to be Günther, Peter, Fritz, Georg, Ernst, Franz, Adalbert, Maximilian, Magnus? No easy matter, for did not the name define everything that was to take place? As far as my father was concerned, without his having to give the matter a great deal of thought, I was destined to step into his well-polished shoes and, in time, become a successful perfumer.

My mother, I surmise, may have had more elaborate and high-minded designs. Each contributed to what I presently am. Each contributed to the doubt and uncertainty that permeate the life of a writer.

I accepted them as parents and yet, in the innermost recess of my mind, I must have remained bewildered to see them together. United. For I sensed they were not—at any rate, not then. Later, much later, yes. What was it that I failed to recognize? I did not see them together often and long enough to recognize anything. What, then, did I find so disquieting? Was it the logic that dictated their shared agendas? The practical motives? The monotonous yet reassuring routine? The harmonious—isn't that the appropriate word?—routine of everyday life? Was there something about this pattern that enraged me? Was my spitefully divisive rebelliousness a prewriterly criticism of the then-prevailing bourgeois values: an awareness that the rules of conduct my parents observed so religiously were rules that would, if one permitted them, also flatten all joy in life? Maybe so. All my tantrums accomplished was to bring my parents closer together. My father regarded me with serious concern. He could not decipher the symptoms. And my mother? Ah, she decoded everything: every sidelong glance, every hesitant pause, each time I gritted my teeth, every time I clenched my fist.

I was their product. Their first and, it turned out, their sole product. They showed a total lack of interest in trying once more, if only in order to improve the model. "Certainly not!" my mother replied sharply to the gentleman who with great presumption had inquired (in my presence, no less) if she wasn't intending to have another child. I couldn't be sure if her marked look of distaste was directed at the man who had so tactlessly raised the question or if it might not be a natural reaction to the thought, the mere suspicion, that my identifying mark, my supercilious smirk, would be stamped like a trademark on the face of the next child. In any event, her terse response was entirely consistent with my prescient view of myself. Largely isolated from the company of other children, I daily breathed the air of my mother's sharp, uncompromising skepticism and my father's unreasonable optimism. It was an optimism that withstood our many challenges—the invincible optimism that continued to defy us, soaring high above our heads, my mother's and mine, flourishing there despite our ceaseless attempts to ground it. How fortunate my father was not to share our interests—not to speak our language! For was it not always a censorious and fault-finding language, a language replete with subtexts befitting a critic?

I was their only child. I was there to observe them, to watch their comings and goings. I was put there to fuel my mother's frustration. In that respect, each one of us managed to give a flawless performance. My enterprising father, in and out of the house like clockwork. Undemanding, unobservant. Alert only to what interested him. There was little in the house—my mother's domain—that held his attention. He preferred the tranquillity of his beloved Viennese cafes, these cozy retreats where he could read his newspapers and journals undisturbed. I suspect that the cafes ranked second in importance only to his business, to his treasured perfumes—those tiny, elegantly shaped bottles snugly encased in their pale yellow boxes bearing the name Molinard as well their poetic fragrances: Ambre, Iles d'Or, Habanita, Fleurettes, Orval. Whenever my father would pull out his handkerchief, the entire room, within seconds, was filled with the delicate fragrance of those evocative names. My mother did not conceal her preference for Guerlain. At what age did I understand her choice to be an outright rejection—what else?—of my father's taste?

In my role as writer-to-be, little escaped my attention. Did they sense it? I was grotesque, I was poisonous. How I came to hate the shrill, spiteful sound of my voice! From the age of three I was conscious of everything that impeded my freedom. I was continually prevented from doing what I wanted. I couldn't leave the house because it might be windy and cold. I couldn't play because it was time for my bath. I was encouraged to eat when I had little desire to. Forced to sleep when I didn't wish to. Compelled to take a walk when by far I would have preferred to do something else instead. Even my bowel movements were scrutinized the way the ancients studied the entrails in the hope of extracting from them my uncertain future—as if my scarce and reluctant output might be made to disclose my fate. *Ein Bemserl*, I'd gleefully report—a minimum requirement. Barely a passing grade. How could I possibly have apprehended that I was being rigorously trained to be a writer? And that, in turn, my unease and resistance to the unswerving rules imposed upon me might be viewed as nothing but a preparation for the obstructions to come. Was I not being trained in obduracy to wage war on the impediments, such as the blank pages I was to face years later? Was I not being trained to surmount the hurdles of the text? Did they not see it? How could they have missed it? It was so obvious. My writerly concerns were, after all, printed all over my hideously distorted face. Deceitful. Liar. A prig to boot. The price one is made to pay when one is developing into a writer.

Did I not detest myself as a result? No. Hardly. To escape self-hatred I learned to like myself the way an inept writer comes to delude himself that what he has written will stand up to criticism, comes to reassure himself by saying, "But this is not too bad!"

Already at an early age I was given to understand that *Geschichte* was the strand of intelligence that intricately ordered and conclusively connected all events. This weighty, double-edged German word, appropriately combining "story" and "history" (for isn't history a form of storytelling?), was still treated with near-reverence. The adults around me repeatedly alluded to their immediate past, as if to indicate their willing association to that ongoing pageantry of history—whereas I, a child, was still far apart from history. In fact, *Geschichte,* a compilation of small and large events, seemed to pose a definite threat. I knew I'd have to measure up. Is it any wonder I sought refuge in play? Under the circumstances, it seems hardly surprising that the few children I encountered seemed, like me, to be out-of-step misfits, dwarfs, midgets, little grownups that were dependent for all their wants on the adults and, like pet cocker spaniels, though pampered, tolerated, and protected, were essentially an irritant and occasional source of amusement.

How was I to understand the adults who spoke so wistfully of their childhood as the best time in their lives? The *best* time? Surely not? The games they had played, the fun they had, the friendships: had every grown-up lived a life so different from my own? From the way it was described to me, childhood was an almost chimerical poetic event, an unending dream. They spoke of it yearningly, intending to elicit some corresponding spark. Either they were out-and-out self-deceivers, I decided—and the look on my mother's face led me to conclude that to be the correct conclusion—or they belonged to another planet, a world I had never encountered, a world enviably free of constriction, of plans and schedules, a world free of tests.

My likes and dislikes were always clearly stated on my face. "You don't really like that, do you?" my mother would say, scanning my face, interpreting my all-too-evident dislike. She was a Rubin, and the Rubins judged what was deemed socially acceptable with the purposeful severity with which they evaluated each other.

A family. Uncles, aunts, a number of cousins, and a devoted white-haired grandmother named Omi, short for Omama. Now two boxes, tightly packed cardboard boxes of family photographs. Snapshots of relatives and close friends in Vienna, Salzburg, Nice, Paris, Rome, Shanghai, Sydney, Buenos Aires, Ra'anana, Tel Aviv, and finally Detroit and St. Petersburg, Florida. On vacation, at home, in small groups, or standing next to that American emblem, a Chevy, while gazing into the camera lens, enduring the taking of the photo. Stoically being recorded—what else?—by a history machine. Being documented. But what was being documented? Their aging? Now these photos have been preserved in boxes to age—to accumulate a history. I was astonished at my mother's seeming diffidence when, several years before her death, she casually mentioned that in the move from Detroit to St. Petersburg she had lost most of the family photographs. I didn't then understand that she was simply divesting herself of the cumbersome weight of the past.

However, when I speak of my family, my uncles, aunts, and

cousins, am I not referring to my mother's side of the family? For somehow my father's side of the family was never fully in evidence. I seem to know next to nothing about them. I still tend to view my father's sisters and his brother as simply his sisters and brother instead of the uncle and aunts they truly were. At home we were far too preoccupied with my mother's side of the family to pay much attention to them. My father's older brother, Oskar, an exceedingly shy and gentle man, a former *Baumeister*, was his bookkeeper. Did I call him Uncle? I may have out of politeness. But it didn't count, because one could see on Oskar's face that he wasn't able to fulfill his role convincingly. And my father's sisters, Adele and Rita? Adele owned a small perfumery on Schönbrunnstrasse, while Rita, the oldest, was a hatmaker, with a store on Dorotheagasse. Why is it that I have no memory of their visiting us? Weren't they made to feel at home? The mystery of families—an all-too-familiar mystery.

In any event, my mother's side of the family survived. I don't know how much of it was due to sheer luck. True they seemed more enterprising, and—when it came to that—more confident, more capable, more opinionated, more overbearing than my father's side of the family. They also appeared to have had more money. But how is it that I grew up knowing so little of my father's side of the family?

My father, thirteen years my mother's senior, was a friend of her brothers, Phoebus, Joseph, and in particular Fritz, the oldest, who was killed in World War I. Why do I find this difficult to accept at face value? Was my father so self-contained, so closed off, so uncommunicative that I couldn't ever picture him in any close relationship? Only when it came to business did he appear to shine. There he was at his enterprising best. Why should his having fought in the Austrian army fill me with surprise? Am I not trying to prescribe too narrow a role for him? As a *Sanitäter* on the Russian front, for administering a few drops of opium to alleviate his sergeant's acute stomach cramps, my father was transferred by an irate doctor to the Italian Alps, where he became a mortar unit's telephonist. Luckily he was on leave in Vienna when a direct hit wiped out the entire mortar crew. In

1916 he was wounded by artillery shrapnel. Deriving satisfaction from the memory, he recalled how as he was carried down the steep side of a three-thousand-meter-high mountain, one of the stretcher bearers couldn't contain his excitement at the panoramic magnitude of the then-ongoing battle, stopping every now and then to point out the action to my father. In the distance one could see the bursts of artillery shells. "It was far more drama than I cared to see," my father said drily. In the first-aid station, a *Sanitäter* he happened to know hurriedly slapped a bandage on his bleeding neck and, accommodatingly, tagged the shrapnel wound as a far more severe gunshot wound. This inaccurate tagging may well have saved his life, for it prolonged my father's recuperation in an understaffed hospital in Bricksen, Tyrol, where, once he had recouped somewhat, he promptly volunteered his services as a medic, finally attaining the lofty rank of *Ordinationsschreiber.*

In another story, my father described a visit to the ward by a senior officer accompanied by a patrician-looking woman who was loaded down with little wrapped gifties for the wounded. Under the officer's supervision, she walked from one cot to the next, dispensing the presents. Approaching my father's cot, she hesitated, glancing at the officer for guidance. When he unaccountably shook his head, she walked to the next cot. "Were they short of presents?" I asked. My father, somewhat embarrassed to make this admission, tapped the side of his nose—as if to indicate by this, to me, uncharacteristic but poignant gesture that being Jewish was sufficient reason. What my father lacked in ability as a storyteller, he more than made up with his combination of sincerity and—dare I call it incredulity? He told or retold his war experiences with a perpetual look of amazement. He was both the teller and the listener to his own story, quite unlike my ironic, self-deprecating uncle Phoebus, who, experienced storyteller that he was, lovingly shaped each tale, savoring his audience's expectations.

My father, the antithesis to the volatile Phoebus, was attentive only in matters that affected his business. Outwardly void of a strong ego, he didn't, as far as I could tell, ever feel the need to compare his accomplishments to others'. He was quite prepared to let them shine . . . certainly, as long as they didn't directly impede him. He tolerated Frank's obstreperous conduct as readily as he had previously tolerated Phoebus's vagaries. As a result, neither of these extremely contentious men derived much satisfaction in opposing my father. There was no triumph, no victory to claim.

As far as I can determine, my mother's family was pleased by the marriage. My father's family, I suspect, less so; for they must have foreseen that as a result of this union my father would gradually withdraw from them, though, to the end, he continued to support his parents financially. My parents moved to Königsegggasse 2, Sechster Bezirk, where my mother redesigned the spacious third-floor apartment: a new bathroom, a bedroom for me. I was already in the planning stage. I was to authenticate their union. My room, readied for my arrival, was separated from theirs by the large, gloomy dining room. After considerable deliberation my mother selected the name Walter. Why Walter? I was born on the twenty-fourth of December and was at once thrust into an orderly life. The walls of my room were a creamy yellow, and the beige furniture had an attractive rounded orange trim.

There is, I suppose, a certain satisfaction to be derived from the fact that my earliest memory is that of being bored: a prolonged agonizing boredom as I waited for something to relieve the tedium. It may not have been the first time I was bored, but as a memory, it serves as an introduction to the agonizingly long bouts of boredom that were to follow.

I recall waking in a room which at that hour in the morning was still shrouded in darkness. I sat up, wide awake, as the color of the drawn heavy silk drapes turned from a deep russet to a warm gold and out of the darkness shapes became identifiable. My parents, in their separate beds, under their down covers, slept unaware of my terrible impatience, my boredom, and oblivious of my muted humming sound of distress: *Mmmmmmmmhhh . . . Mmmmmmmmhhh . . .* What was I doing in their room, at the foot of my mother's bed? Perhaps I was coming down with one of my periodic colds and, as my mother would say, needed to be "observed." To dispel my boredom I kept aimlessly looking around the gradually brightening interior, and after taking inventory of the objects on my mother's light-speckled vanity desk with the large circular mirror, I turned to the now discernible floral-pattern wallpaper and, having exhausted that, finally settled on the individually bundled, immobile presence of my mother and father. The curtains blocked my view of the outside world. I was imprisoned in a world of sleep. Imprisoned in a wooden crib in a room that I had already come to recognize as foreign . . . a room in which the objects, unlike the objects in the other rooms, vigilantly identified this "foreign" space of my mother and father, accentuating an "other" life of my parents, an "other" life I could not yet understand or reach.

What else can I tear away from my childhood Vienna?

I remember the tiny Christmas tree near the entrance to our dining room. Decorated with tinsel and a few ornaments, it hardly merited the designation of tree. It was more of a shrub. Next to it on the floor were the well-intentioned gifts for me, since my birthday is on the twenty-fourth of December, and a gift for the maid. My parents watched discreetly from a distance. Was this, I wonder, my very first awareness of self-deception? I understood the tree as icon to be unauthentic—or rather, in every fiber of my body I was aware of a deceptiveness. I still can see the maid eyeing our tree—how could she not be aware of its symbol?—uncertain as how to behave, not knowing the procedure . . . On being handed her gift, she said "Danke schön" with a little curtsy and quickly left our presence.

What else?
 The Automat on Mariahilferstrasse, where, the instant a coin was dropped into one of the many slots, the selected triangular open-faced sandwich was promptly transported on a mirrored revolving tray from behind the protective glass in which it had been enclosed, while a disembodied, pale woman's hand swiftly

replaced it with its virtual replica. I couldn't tell what was more satisfying, eating the tidbit or, as I closely followed the process of replacing it, trying to match the disembodied white hand with one of the impassive faces visible behind the tall marble counter. On a Sunday, in one of our neighborhood restaurants, I was able to derive a similar gratification as I watched the gray-haired waiter ceremoniously pouring *Frittatensuppe* from the silver soup pitchers into our soup dishes.

How come there was a street so far below Gumpendorfer and Corneliusgasse? Like a beacon for those infinitely mysterious and disorienting broad steps leading downward, a display in the pharmacy window at the corner advertised a weight-loss product that had a large, rotund, red-faced man repeatedly entering a cardboard house only to exit from the other end, a split second later, metamorphosed into a slim, younger man. I could have remained glued to the window for hours.

My mother pressed the tiny button underneath the tabletop to summon the maid to remove the dishes or to serve the next course. She did it with complete assurance. So much so that, to me, the household represented a world governed not by emotions but by reason alone. My parents never quarreled, never argued. It was as if emotions had been banned from the household. The exception to the rule was my grandmother—who was frequently edgy, nervous, teary, and easily intimidated. A sign of disapproval, however slight, from my mother would send her unsteadily from one room to the next, as if trying to retrace her steps to repair the error or misjudgment for which she had been rebuked and thus erase all signs of this unpleasant incident.

What justification, if any, did my mother give when she mentioned that she had entered the maid's windowless room next to the kitchen? What prompted her to open the door in the first place? Had she entered to inspect the room or did she suspect something was amiss? According to her, the man who lay stretched out on the bed in his underwear was as startled as she.

My mother was outraged: "What are you doing here?!" A question to which she really did not even require an answer. Sitting up in bed, he feebly offered some lame excuse. Her anger, fueled by a suspicion of sordid sexual excesses under our very roof, was righteous and utterly pitiless. An undressed man in the room! Nothing could excuse his presence. The maid's excuses that the man was a relative were not heeded—and she was asked to pack her bags on the spot.

The torment of summer camp. I didn't last more than a few days. I was unprepared for the presence of so many exuberant, uninhibited children. Unlike them, I was not able to walk barefoot on the torturous gravel path to the lake. I marveled at the way the kids, all good-natured, all at home in this friendly environment, seemed inured to what I perceived as hardships. Unlike them, I couldn't swim, and a nap in the dormitory after the spartan meal was out of the question for me. I kept tossing and turning on the bare mattress, while the other boys and girls obediently slept the sleep of the just. The sound of their calm breathing filled the dormitory. Even in a room to myself I couldn't fall asleep. My mother came to take me away, not concealing her annoyance. Why was I being so difficult? Her look of exasperation is the look I remember best.

My swimming lesson—I can recall only one session—fared no better. It has left me with a longstanding aversion to swimming pools. Even my mother's presence in the huge white-tiled indoor pool was not the least bit reassuring. She stood next to the bare-chested instructor, who lowered me into the water from a rope attached to a pole, then, in a stentorian voice, a voice more fitting for the parade grounds, a voice I would hear over and over again when I visited Germany for the first time in 1982, yelled instructions . . . His commands supplanted my brain's function. In sheer terror, I tried to coordinate the motions of my legs and arms, slapping the water, not knowing what I dreaded more, drowning or the disapproval of the powerful individual towering above me, who, incidentally, resembled my uncle Phoebus. What was it that

I was unable to understand? Even the rope by which I was being raised and lowered did not reassure me. Why was I being so difficult? The instructor was becoming more and more annoyed by my obstructive behavior. One moment I was swallowing huge quantities of water; the next, contained by the harness, I was perilously hovering above the surface as he bellowed fresh instructions to me. I stopped listening. His words ceased to register. In 1987, when my wife, Cecile, and I visited Berlin's former Olympic stadium and the swimming pools nearby, I saw an instructor, a virtual twin of the one who had yelled at me in 1936 or '37, roaring instructions to a hapless girl in a harness attached by a rope to the pole in his hand. The young girl was somewhat older than I was at the time I was being taught and, from her smooth response, inured to the punishing voice.

My first theater experience, a matinee performance at the Burgtheater: as the houselights dim, the curtain rises majestically to reveal actors, men and women in a lively dispute. I watch uncomprehendingly, yet riveted by the artificial spectacle, the make-believe. What's going on? Though the action is hard to follow—at most I catch a word here and there—I'm fixated by the spectacle, the sheer theatricality of the performance, as actors storm about the stage in a state of permanent disagreement. A rush of applause greets the ending of each scene. In advance of every intermission, a young boy in a bright red tunic and matching pillbox hat, smiling cockily, walks the length of the stage in front of the lowered curtain, brandishing a placard to indicate a five-minute or fifteen-minute intermission. He's the one I am able to identify with. Eagerly I wait for him to reappear. The heavyset actor whose effort to placate his shrewish wife meets with little success keeps ducking as she tosses dish after dish in his direction. The audience savors this buffoonery. Their applause and laughter drown out the dialogue. In the final, the most memorable, scene, all lights are extinguished as the curtain is lowered. In the ensuing pitch darkness, the wife's by now familiar shrill imprecations are muffled by the sound of smashing furniture and shattering glass. When the curtain is raised one final time, it reveals the extent of the disaster: it's total! I use my mother's opera glasses to focus on the rotund husband perilously clinging to this enormous heap of wreckage that reaches to the top of the stage. Sustained applause, calls of bravo, and uproarious laughter.

My father smoked cigars, wore well-cut three-piece gray or brown business suits, and said as little as humanly possible. He simply didn't have any inclination to share his opinions. He was always, however, courteously prepared to listen to what people had to offer. I don't recall ever seeing him fidget or show signs of impatience. After dinner he'd take a nap in his favorite leather armchair. Another ritual was our Sunday-morning walk. My father, smoking a cigar, would absentmindedly hold my hand. He was daydreaming, but of what? I did most of the talking. In front of a closed toy store on Mariahilferstrasse, I'd point out the toys in the window display that I craved, and then—was it to counterbalance my perhaps excessive demands?—I'd point to the ones he needn't purchase: "Don't bother with that . . . I don't need that, either." Amiably, he listened, nodding in seeming agreement. Feeling that I had made my point, I was happy. As we retraced our steps along the cobblestone street, the tempting smell of chicken dinner wafting from each building along the way reinforced my sense of well-being. My father looked content as well.

I do recall my mother mentioning to a friend how on a Sunday morning shortly after their honeymoon, my father, not about to let marriage disrupt his daily ritual, without consulting her set off for his favorite cafe. Distraught, she consulted her sister-in-law, Annie, who advised her to speak up. Speak up she did—for my father never again went to a cafe by himself on a Sunday.

I sensed that I was in my mother's way. I was a minor inconvenience. An irritant. There was, however, always a genuine concern for my well-being, my health, my appetite—almost an exaggerated concern. I was made to feel delicate. I required constant attention, for the slightest mishap might irreparably damage me. I carefully avoided eating anything that had dropped to the floor. I was not permitted out when it rained for fear that I might catch a chill. And yet, despite the best intentions, I was frequently in bed with a fever and a cold. My illnesses, all minor, all insignificant, coincided, as if diabolically planned, with our intended vacations in winter and summer. "I think he does it out of spite," my mother said in exasperation, not minding in the least that I could hear what she was saying.

Each day was mapped out: my breakfast, my daily walk, my lunch, my afternoon tea, early dinner, my bath, then bed. Everything was clocked. Time for your bath. Time for bed. So many daily hurdles. If my room looked uncluttered, it was because nightly, before going to bed, I was made to deposit— "toss" would be more accurate—my toys into a huge cardboard bin. Most of the toys had been taken apart. Methodically! What was it that drove me to reduce each toy, almost from the moment I received it, to its basic components: not to destroy, merely to dismember? Given an opportunity, I would have turned my destructive attention on the furniture, the radio, and the gramophone on which my mother played Tauber, singing "Wien, Wien, nur du allein" and "Dein ist mein ganzes Herz."

On the walls several still lifes and bleak landscapes in heavy gilded frames. There's nothing decorative or frivolous about them. They look serious. I now realize that their function was to signify not art but normality. And I, despite the evenly paced life, despite the appearance of order, always registered a slight temperature.

My sixth-birthday gift was a Pelikan fountain pen and matching pencil in a green leather étui. My father had bought two sets, one for me and one for my mother, and unthinkingly handed me the larger. "I think not," my mother said in that icy voice I knew so well, swiftly correcting his blunder, taking the set out of my hand in exchange for the one she had received. Looking perturbed, my father fled the room as I, woebegone, clutching the smaller set with a look of disbelief, burst into tears.

My parents were sensible, levelheaded, rational—in other words, perfectly normal. Absolutely normal! I was the one who stood out. I was the one who shamelessly persisted, much to the amusement of the other dancers on the gleaming black dance floor, in wedging myself between them as they were dancing to the music of a small band in a cafe. "Look at that little boy," people said. "Isn't he cute!" Did I resent being left by myself at the table to watch them dance in a tight embrace? My mother did not conceal her annoyance at my behavior: "We simply can't take him along with us." Somehow, I didn't even mind the laughter, the ridicule. I felt betrayed, having been brought to a cafe only to be left to myself without a prior warning. But how to explain this resolve of mine to join them on the dance floor?

My mother, distant, beautiful, remote. I tried to read her face, not the face of my father, to determine what lay ahead. In turn, I believe, she didn't have to listen to what I said, but merely to read the expression on my face to see what I intended to do next.

In the world in which I grew up, people did not publicly embrace or kiss each other on the mouth or show unbecoming affection. To my mother's amusement, I would recoil whenever some misguided lady visitor folded me into a warm embrace. What was it that made me so dread being kissed on the mouth? Initially, I would struggle to avoid the contact of lips, lips that moreover would leave a proprietary red mark on my cheek. By the age of nine, I was able to stoically endure being embraced and kissed.

I never questioned my mother's aloofness. If anything, I considered her coolness reassuring. Her coolness was a measure of her equanimity. Her coolness preserved order and calm. It protected us, or strove to protect us, from the turbulence and unpredictable passion of people such as her brother Phoebus, my favorite uncle, the one I identified with limitless courage and recklessness. To my mind, the two, courage and recklessness, seemed to go hand in hand. Yet he too, like my mother, could be icy.

Once—I was five at the time—I observed my father hesitantly (or so it seemed to me) touch and then caress my mother's bare arm as they were standing at the window, their backs to me.

Mesmerized, I watched his hand fondle my mother—amazed that he was given license to approach her in such an intimate manner. She turned her head to look at him—they were expecting friends for dinner and she was upset by his late return home. Expressionless, she listened to his low, hesitant, apologetic voice. When my father spoke, it was to cover the absence of words. My mother understood that. Nothing escaped her. What went through my mind as I sat, unobserved, in my father's chair? One day, when I grow up, I too will be able to caress a woman's arm, I idly thought.

In the eighties I twice visited a psychiatrist with the hope that self-hypnosis—his specialty—could alleviate my incessant trigeminal headaches. At the first of two sessions he invited me to tell him something about myself, and I, pleased to have the opportunity, included the abovementioned Oedipal gem, feeling a writerly gratification when he promptly jotted it down in his notebook.

Somehow, I also associate my mother's composure with her uncanny ability to remember every grudge, every slight. Nothing was ever too petty to be forgotten. After the war, my mother's brother Uncle Joseph, who left China for the U.S., was entrusted with Omi's diamond earrings. Years later, when my parents requested that he return them to Omi, then living with us in Israel, he explained that he was unable to since my aunt had had the earrings converted into a ring. To this day I'm still mystified by the debatable excuse and dumbfounded by their action. How could they justify it to themselves? Clearly, it must have been my aunt's idea, I decided, unwilling to blame my uncle, whom to this day I identify with rectitude. After my aunt's death my uncle repeatedly attempted to give the diamond ring to my mother, but she wouldn't accept it—no, never. By then Omi, long dead, certainly no longer had any need for it. Now, my grandmother's ring, like so much else, is in my possession. It's not a ring, it's the bearer of a story.

But what was it about Mutti that would lead me to suspect that she didn't find her role of mother, an exacting role she performed with such assurance and competence, in any way pleasing or fulfilling?

Love, unquestioning, undivided, limitless love, came from Omi. My father's love, equally genuine, was more circumscribed. A highly emotional man, he kept pulling back like someone who, knowing the rules only vaguely, was apprehensive of being censured for overstepping them. As for my mother, she was always preoccupied, always doing something. Infrequently we played cards. My mother, competitive to the bone, would invariably win. My father, enjoying my mother's presence, freely gave his best cards away, carelessly feeding them to Mutti or me, the two players who were trying to win by any means, fair or foul—as if everything in the world hinged on it.

We'd vacation twice yearly, with summers spent in Semmering or Payerbach. Mostly it was just my mother and me. On this occasion, as we were being served our afternoon coffee (*Jause*) in the hotel garden, I observed the boy next to me at the table calmly pour water from a glass to cool his piping-hot coffee, openly flouting—in the presence of our mothers, no less—what I understood to be a fundamental rule. Furtively, expecting to be reprimanded, I followed suit. No one paid the least attention. My mother either didn't see or pretended not to.

In March 1938, days before Hitler's annexation of Austria, my mother and I were sitting on the rustic terrace of a large resort hotel in Semmering with the mountains in full view. She and my father had honeymooned there in February 1928. I, all of six, armed with a drawing pad and colored pencils, studiously sketched the tranquil pastoral scenery. My mother was drinking coffee and half-listening to a gentleman, a guest at the hotel, who, at great length, complimented me on my drawing ability. Today I realize that the man was far more interested in chatting up my mother. This was not the first time that my mother and I had spent the vacation by ourselves. Usually, in the evening, following dinner, my mother and then I would briefly speak to my father on the phone. I recall these exchanges as both warm and a little strained. This time, the startling radio announcement of Germany's annexation of Austria, the Anschluss, abruptly terminated our vacation. Though I was far too young to understand the significance of this sudden political drama, I could infer from Mutti's tense telephone exchange with Papa that something serious had occurred. On the train my mother was unusually uncommunicative. I kept looking from her set face to the other passengers to determine if any of them were equally as affected.

The Germans may have marched in, but I couldn't see any evidence of their presence. The only noticeable change in our household was that my mother—who now had even less time for me—was spending an inordinate amount of time on the phone. Phoebus, when he came by, was unusually high-strung. There was mention of travel abroad. My grandmother, if anything a little more jittery, looked after me, while my mother, when not busy attending a dressmaking course, was daily working on her paper cutout dress patterns.

How is it that being Jewish remained so ill defined? There was something perplexing about my father's attempts to convey his Jewishness. Surely, it wasn't due to a lack of conviction. As for me, even the paraphernalia of devotion—the silken prayer shawl, the skullcap, not to mention the silver candlesticks—seemed to carry in their very distinct design markings as foreign as those of Christianity. My mother, especially on the Jewish High Holidays, sought, if not to disassociate, then to distance herself from the Jewish ceremonies, as if to disclaim any personal link or responsibility to their past—a past that for many assimilated Viennese Jews proved vexing in the extreme . . . It was as if for the sake of my father, my mother, who evidently had come from a different planet, gracefully acquiesced to the occasion. Yet, the acute feeling of artificiality I experienced as we went through the motions of a seder was undeniable. My father, who was not unaware of my mother's discomfort with the ritual, felt a need to speak nostalgically of Passover when he was a child, but all he managed to convey to me was a lack of authority. On the rare occasion I was taken to visit my father in the temple on the High Holidays, I couldn't rid myself of a feeling of disquiet at the outright tumult, the emotional turbulence of the men praying—a commotion at odds with my circumscribed life.

My visits, not more than two or three, to my father's parents fared no better. My grandfather's immense untrimmed beard alone was unsettling. From the few guarded comments my mother made on our trip home, I could infer her displeasure—for she, like many middle-class Austrian and German Jews, may have felt threatened by a likeness or history that was too proximate for comfort. My father pretended not to register her acute discomfort. As soon as I had determined Jehovah to be the name of the Almighty, I tested my grandmother, mischievously calling out the name Jehovah. "You mustn't say that name aloud," she pleaded. I chortled at her superstition, mockingly repeating "Jehovah, Jehovah" over and over again, gratified by her distress. Could I, at the age of five, have come to identify the Jewish religion and the eventful if grim Jewish past with abject powerlessness? The God I prayed to—and I vaguely recall saying an evening prayer—was to my mind a kind of nonreligious Almighty, a deity divested of everything Jewish or Christian.

Was I kept in complete ignorance of the almost ritualized humiliation inflicted on the Viennese Jews? Many were incarcerated, a sizable number killed. I didn't see the photos of men and women on their knees scrubbing Vienna's sidewalks with toothbrushes to the evidently gleeful and sardonic approval of the onlookers until years later. I suspect the eventuality of a dividend, a payoff, as a result of this state-generated public debasement wasn't lost on the gleeful spectators. How could the trickle-down rewards—in the form of academic advancement, the elimination of business competition, the forced sale of businesses, not to mention the vacated apartments, the auctions of the possessions the Viennese Jews were forced to leave behind—not animate the society? On November 9, the neighborhood synagogue, the one my father always attended on the High Holidays, was set ablaze. My father was one of the few lucky ones. Was it that he didn't have enemies? That he didn't clash with people? Was that the reason for his success? He avoided disputes like the plague. He did mention his one court victory against a Czechoslovakian cosmetic manufacturer who sued him and lost. On the day after Kristallnacht my father remained closeted in his office, even though—in a curious reversal of roles—Phoebus, hitherto the risk taker, kept calling in a high state of alarm to urge my mother to persuade her foolhardy husband to come home and be with us. My father, oblivious to the danger, explained that he had to prepare a number of shipments for the following day. He maintained that with his entrance padlocked he felt quite safe. His luck didn't hold, for the following day he was arrested and taken to the local police station, which also served as SA headquarters. After being kept waiting for hours, he was summoned by an official, only to be released when one of the senior NSDAP officials present, a businessman who owed my father a substantial amount of money, promptly intervened: "Let Abish go—he's okay." In what was a time for personal score settling, my father was fortunate in that he'd never, as he later explained, badgered the man for his money, having long ago written it off as a bad debt.

How could I fail to comprehend what was going on? Didn't my parents' unease rub off on me? The one day I vividly recall at the Jewish school, the only school I was permitted to attend, was the final day. At first the clamor from the street was barely audible. As the noise increased, our apprehensive teachers kept consulting each other, not knowing what to do. Despite the escalating commotion on the street below, we left the school at the customary hour without receiving any warning. Not that it would have made any difference. As we exited the school, I recall a sprinkling of uniformed SA wearing their power-affirming swastika armbands standing by impassively as a swarm of jeering, screeching women and truculent neighborhood kids, catching sight of us, surged forward. If anything, the SA's presence sanctioned the melee. Unflustered by the crowd, which in that inimitable Viennese dialect jeered every adult who had come to pick up a child, our invincible maid stepped forward, holding my raincoat—for it was raining—with an expression of someone not to be trifled with. As she took hold of my hand, steering me to safety, a woman, face distorted with rage, darted toward me, screaming at me from up close. Our maid's reaction was instantaneous. Her fury more than matched that of my antagonist, who by her quick retreat acknowledged not only our maid's resolve but, above all, our maid's right as a coequal to retaliate.

As always, a daily stroll with Omi to our neighborhood park, my favorite playground, Loquai Park. She adapting her steps to my pace. While playing with several boys, I recall, one of them gravely asked: "Bist du närrisch?" When I inquired at home, my parents were amused at my having confused *arisch,* which means Aryan, with *närrisch,* meaning daft or nuts. The incident hardly registered until a few weeks later, when several grim-faced SA enforcers, driven by self-righteous anger, invaded the tiny enclave, screaming, "Juden raus!" In panic, my grandmother and I along with several other women and children raced for the nearest exit, while everyone else stopped in their tracks to watch our precipitous getaway. Was the decision to clear children from a playground reached at the local SA headquarters? On my first visit back in 1982, as I retraced our steps from the small park, I tried to picture our headlong flight along the narrow cobblestoned Königsegggasse. Overnight my familiar world was defamiliarized. Could this be the origin of my fascination with the quotidian— the familiar everyday world?

Looking back, I see the unannounced arrival in our apartment of the two SA men as the decisive break with my familiar (predictable) world. I see them vividly: two impassive men in gray overcoats, one wearing the bright red swastika armband, as they spoke to my mother in low, unthreatening voices, now and then almost covertly glancing at me. I couldn't determine if something was amiss until they had left with a polite "Auf Wiedersehen" and my mother calmly explained that we had less than an hour to pack a few belongings—I believe it was one suitcase each—and leave. I was permitted a maximum of two small toys. Two? How to decide? My grandmother in near panic kept running back and forth, while my mother, cool, unflurried, made quick decisions, since there wasn't sufficient time to summon my father. On the way out, clutching a tiny suitcase and two cherished toys, I passed the kitchen and caught a glimpse of the *Pischkotentorte,* that triumph of Viennese pastries, itself an article of faith, prepared that morning (it must have been a Friday), on the otherwise empty large kitchen table. An hour after we'd been told to vacate the apartment, my mother returned to retrieve something valuable she had forgotten, almost running into one of the SA on his way up to seal our apartment door. In my mind, toying with disaster, I kept seeing over and over again how my mother, leaving the apartment minutes after it had been sealed, might have had to face the wrath of the Gestapo . . .

I have only the vaguest recollection of staying with neighbors until, several weeks later, we were permitted to return—our eviction then as mystifying as our unexpected return. What I find Kafkaesque is the preciseness of certain details—the number of suitcases we were permitted, the exact time by which we were to leave the apartment—while the overall purpose of our ejection was not spelled out.

Soon after, the streets of Vienna took on the appearance of a staged spectacle—one of those beloved operettas that skirt reality—for the frenzied, flag-waving Viennese did not merely proclaim their solidarity with Germany and embrace their Austrian-born Hitler; rather, they embraced the Anschluss, seizing the opportunity to display those tantalizing new emblems, the paraphernalia of Nazism, and in a state of exuberance perform a celebratory dance. A heady performance. How invigorating to be able to dress up! That's what it took to become a Nazi. A breathless encounter, as the Viennese—whose dialect, after all, is replete with double meanings—absorbed with a shudder of ecstasy the aesthetics of the swastika. Vienna—dying and fading Vienna—temporarily invigorated.

The sepia photo of the three of us, my parents and me, was taken shortly before we left Vienna. On the back of the photo is a farewell inscription to my grandmother: "Unseren lieben Omama zum Andenken an ihre Kinder, Adolph, Friedl und Walter—Wien, 12 September 1938." My mother in a dark brown tailored costume on my left, my father on my right, both inclining their heads ever so slightly toward me at the center. All three faces smooth, surprisingly composed. When this photo was taken, my father was far younger than I am now, but despite his youth, despite the dreamy faraway look, by his bearing he imparted utter probity, responsibility, and prosperity. My mother's lovely open smile, a beguiling smile, does not in any way diminish the keen intelligence of her eyes. Perhaps it is the way her dark hair is parted that gives her the Spanish look in this photo. And I, my ears extended like two radar dishes, my dark brown hair neatly trimmed, in a natty tweed suit, checked shirt, and a dark blue and white necktie I remember fondly to this day, stare straight ahead, a reluctant smile on my face. Years later, in Shanghai, the strict Australian headmistress of my school complained that I had an annoying habit of staring at her. No doubt if I stared at her it was due to my incomprehension. I cannot think of any other reason. She, however, found my gaze disconcerting. My mother promptly went home to look up the word "disconcerting" in our German-English/English-German dictionary. "I'd like you to explain why you keep staring at your teacher."

The gold watch chain dangling from the buttonhole of my father's suit jacket is visible in the photo. How well I know the chain and the Doxa pocket watch attached to it! Both are stowed away in a safe-deposit box. Safe for what? My mother has a distinctly Rubin face, oval with a long slender neck. My father's face is square, with a short neck I have inherited.

In September of 1938, when this photograph was taken, they were closely studying their Knauer Weltatlas for an escape route. They had not, as yet, hit upon Shanghai, China. China? That was yet to come.

What has gone unsaid concerns my uncle Oskar, the gentle, meek accountant, the bachelor, who stayed behind. Where and under what circumstances was he killed? In his last communication, a postcard with a stamped swastika mailed in 1941, Oskar sadly informed my father that their father, my grandfather, had died. What puzzles me most is that my father's mother, his sisters, Adele and Rita, and Oskar himself were killed without this matter ever being fully discussed in our household. Of my father's family, only Adele's destination, Maly Trastinec, and date of her departure, June 2, 1942, are known. On the orders of SD Reinhard Heydrich, most of the 15,000 Austrian and German Jews sent there were killed upon their arrival. Stripped of their belongings, they were taken to a pinewood several kilometers from a former collective farm outside of the village of Trastinec and shot.

THE WRITER

New York, Traveling to Germany

E ver since the publication of *How German Is It* in 1980, a
number of friends and acquaintances have gone out of their
way to introduce me to Germans—be they visitors to the U.S. or
Germans residing here. On this occasion John and MarieRose
Logan had wanted me to meet a German executive, a friend of
theirs. When I entered the Helmsley Palace Hotel, where we were
to meet, I saw the man I took to be Werner, monklike in a volu-
minous forest-green loden coat, pacing the empty lobby. He
came toward me hesitantly, the fixed smile on his sharp-featured
face like an unaccustomed adornment. Then, still clutching my
hand, he shook his head dubiously. "I didn't expect you to look
quite the way you do," he admitted, his remark weighed down by
a scrupulous, if burdensome, need to be forthright. When we
stepped outside to wait for John Logan, who was to drive us to
his home in Westchester, Werner, apparently still dissatisfied with
his initial appraisal, continued to size me up—endeavoring, it
seemed to me, to relate my novel, which he had just read, with
my person. By the time John arrived, Werner, an executive for a
major German chemical company, unable to contain his exasperation, had burst out that my novel had infuriated him. "Alone, the
incorrectly spelled German words!" he maintained indignantly.

"They'll be corrected in the next edition," I assured him.

"Granted that you appear never to have visited Germany," he grumbled, "still, the errors make the content seem less and less reliable."

At dinner, our conversation stayed focused on present-day Germany, a Germany I hadn't as yet visited. Werner, clearly proud of his Prussian roots, spoke at some length of his family history, not failing, almost pedantically, to note that the German educational system still emphasized the revered cultural icons: Goethe, Heine, Hölderlin. About the latter, whose poetry he had been reading on his flight to New York, Werner, remarked that both he and the renowned poet came from the same area in Germany and shared a similar upper-middle-class background and an education in which tradition, history, and culture were esteemed. To my ear, Werner began to sound more and more like a character seeking inclusion in my novel. Is that why John and MarieRose Logan wanted us to meet? He explained that when traveling abroad, as soon as German fellow travelers discovered his fluency in Portuguese and Spanish, they'd invariably elect him as their interpreter. Bare-chested, sunburnt, he participated in the carnival parade in Rio. While beaming at me, he slightly, ever so slightly, twisted his torso to suggest a dancing motion—"No one, absolutely no one, would ever suspect me of being German," he affirmed with undisguised pride. "The moment I arrive in Rio, I distance myself from the Germans."

What especially troubled him, Werner admitted, was the novel's provocative, if equivocal, ending. "Why does the narrator raise his hand in Nazi salute?" What point was I trying to make? I explained that at the end, by raising his arm, the narrator was responding to a routine test by means of which a hypnotist determines his subject's susceptibility to hypnotism. Admittedly, given the context, the gesture took on a double meaning; it was also a Nazi salute. "Exactly," Werner said, not concealing his distrust. "What are you suggesting?" I explained that I intended *How German Is It* to elicit a multiple, if indeterminate, response. I was inviting the reader to bring his or her accumulated German material, his or her particular version of Germany, to the text, for is there anyone outside of Germany who doesn't hold a decided view of Germanness? Rejecting my explanation, Werner returned to his past: he was nine at the end of the war and could recall each day being asked to raise his right hand in a salute—the hand raised to a level so that he could see the dirt under the fingernails. For him, as a child, it was a perfunctory task. Having embarked on his past, he then informed me that his grandparents in Hamburg were Anglophiles, while his parents were Nazis. His father served in the Wehrmacht, but unlike his mother, who to the bitter end stubbornly clung to her convictions, he soon became disenchanted with Hitler. On the drive back to the city, in what may have been a further attempt at unburdening himself, Werner inquired if I had lost any members of my family. "Lost?" I said. "Yes, half my family." However, I didn't take the trouble to inform him that the family I had lost, to use his euphemism, had remained virtually invisible to me, so that their loss was somehow evanescent. I didn't press him for personal details. I didn't inquire if he had lost any members of *his* family, for my question might balance in his mind our respective losses. He repeated his earlier question: "Why did you write that book?" In essence, all his questions were an attempt to extract from me a plausible—to him—explanation to confirm his conclusion that the novel was written out of a perhaps justifiable, even spiteful anger at Germany. He was put out not to receive that explanation. He acted as if I were willfully withholding the truth, for he had come to accept that truth—to anticipate it?

Barbara Ungeheuer's request for an interview was one of the first of several from German reporters. She was trim, impeccably dressed, not a blond hair out of place, and had a somewhat glacial charm. I could not resist inquiring about her family. To my surprise, she mentioned that her father, briefly rector at the university in Freiburg, was succeeded by Heidegger. When I inquired, she reluctantly gave his name, Wilhelm von Möllendorf. It was months before I grasped the significance of the name.* During

* Möllendorf, a neighbor of Heidegger's and a Social Democrat, was elected rector at the University of Freiburg in December 1932. Two weeks after taking office in April the following year, the rector was dismissed by the minister of culture for having forbidden the display on campus of an anti-Jewish poster. According to Heidegger, Möllendorf then approached him, urging him to accept the position.

the lengthy interview in her apartment she kept prodding me gently, the way you would a backward child, clearly dissatisfied with my remark "We tend to apply straightforward explanations in order to explain away what is contradictory or difficult to reconcile." Smiling encouragingly, she kept trying to extract a motive.

The following week she rang up with a dinner invitation. On the phone, with a sharp, edgy laugh she revealed that a friend of hers regarded *How German Is It* as the Jew's revenge. Dumbfounded by her remark, and what it seemed to reveal about her, I couldn't come up with an appropriate response, especially since Barbara Ungeheuer's self-conscious laugh led me to conclude that it might be she, not some nameless friend, who held that view. She did, however, succeed in implanting the provocative word "revenge" in my mind—a word that heretofore simply hadn't occurred to me.

I took Barbara's statement to intimate that underlying *How German Is It* was an emotional component I wasn't prepared to acknowledge. Several times during the interview she singled out my reference to black leather coats in the novel as proof—if proof were needed—of my intent to stereotype the Germans. Impatient with this pedantic nitpicking, I mentioned her comments to a friend who, trying to be helpful to my annoyance, pointed out that the SS wore green, not black, leather coats.

At the Ungeheuer dinner, the other guests were Jerzy Kosinski and his wife, Kiki, and the historian Otto Friedrich, whose *Kingdom of Auschwitz* had just then appeared in abbreviated form in the *Atlantic Monthly.* Also present was Friedl, Barbara's husband, a reporter and evidently a passionate admirer of Kosinski. It was impossible not to like Jerzy. Hugely entertaining, he monopolized the dinner: at one moment impersonating a Soviet NKVD agent intimidating a Russian tourist couple on a Swiss ski lift, the next, in quest for material for his novel-in-progress, pretending to be a sheriff as he relentlessly questioned a madam about the operation of her luxurious Upper East Side brothel. Still, there was something a little frantic and unsettling to Jerzy's role—as if we, the audience, had imposed this onerous task upon him. Why he should wish to substantiate each of these hilarious anecdotes by pulling out his wallet to show us the sheriff's badge and other IDs was a mystery. Everything in Jerzy's masterful performance was sleight-of-hand. He commanded the center stage out of a need to control everything that pertained to him. Was it to avoid the unexpected? To circumvent or delay the lamentable events of soon afterward, when he, the master conjurer, whose foibles were the paradoxical pillars of his strength, was accused by several reporters of not having personally experienced the ordeal he described in his autobiographical work? I left the dinner concluding that whatever Barbara had hoped to bring about simply hadn't transpired.

Barbara Ungeheuer surprised me with another dinner invitation. This time the guests were Rabbi Arthur Hertzberg, the noted lecturer, and his wife. Rabbi Hertzberg sat next to me, out of his depth, a little perplexed, as if unclear of his role. Since both he and his wife were strictly kosher, they politely declined to eat anything but salad and rolls. I felt as if Barbara, still dissatisfied with my response, had brought us together with the hope of eliciting some hitherto withheld gem, some little nugget of information. This time, in fact, she was surprisingly outspoken. On the subject of Germany, she maintained that we, the Americans, were occupying Germany. Her sister kept her informed of the American army's rank misbehavior. "They shoplift, they rape . . . No one is safe." She stared at me, gauging my response: "I assure you," I said, "they're totally impartial in that regard. I don't detect anything specifically anti-German in the behavior you describe." The irony was lost on her. As if to offset her indignant remarks, her husband, Friedl, spoke wistfully of his youthful love for America, of his discovery of American literature and films. Several times, with notable deference, Friedl referred to the elevated status of Barbara's family—as if to indicate that she, by contrast, was somehow a more estimable and nobler reflection of Germany. When I inquired whether she had completed her article on *How German Is It,* Barbara didn't conceal her irritation: "No. Because

I don't believe what you say. Because I suspect that deep inside your gut you harbor altogether different thoughts and emotions." Oddly enough, by her opposition, by her "nationalist" indignation, she succeeded in adding substance to the double-edged picture I was forming of Germany.

Das Rheingold is being shown on Channel 13.
    "What glows over there?"
    "Have you never heard of the Rheingold?"
    "The world's wealth and limitless power await him who makes a ring from the Rheingold."

I wrote "The English Garden" shortly after I had seen Uwe Brandner's movie *Ich liebe dich, ich töte dich* in 1975. In turn, the short story led me to write what became the novel *How German Is It*. I relied on old Baedekers, not the least convinced that the many castles depicted in the ancient guidebooks still survived . . . Without much success I tried to glimpse present-day Germany in Wim Wenders's and Fassbinder's movies. My intention in writing *How German Is It* was to present an equivocal yet neutral text to which the reader would convey his own emotional Germany . . . I succeeded only too well. Many readers seemed to exclude the familial and sexual conflicts altogether as they read it with an eye only for the consequence of past tribulations.

At a party, in conversation with Robert Lifton, I spoke about my forthcoming German book tour. He had spent seven months in Germany, interviewing former concentration camp doctors for his book *The Nazi Doctors*. Since he too was a doctor, most of them, he said, felt at ease in his company. As "colleagues" they could converse unashamedly. As one put it in all seriousness, "I tried not to think of the place I was in. I tried to make believe it was, for instance, a garbage disposal plant." On ascertaining that Robert Lifton was Jewish, something he hadn't concealed, another doctor remarked: "I realize there was a great misunderstanding between your people and mine—but it's time our two peoples joined forces to fight the common enemy."

"Communism?" Robert Lifton inquired, not following his drift.

"No—the Moslems!"

Call from Bavarian Radio. They're planning to air an interview with me and would love to include a reading from *How German Is It*. The lady at the other end spoke with a hoarse voice I had difficulty understanding. It couldn't be a secretary, I decided, as I explained in my best German that I'd mull it over. Did they have any particular section in mind? "Pages 136 to 139? The discovery of the mass grave in the town center?" Why wasn't I surprised? I said no when they called back. By itself, the section would provide a one-dimensional impression of *How German Is It*.

Call from the director at the Deutsches Haus. He explained that he wasn't trying to be indirect when he twice, instead of calling me himself, had Joel Agee ring up to inquire if I'd agree to participate in a panel discussion of how the Jewish or German-Jewish writer regarded Germany. Jacov Lind was to be one of the participants. I explained that despite my great respect for the participating panelists, the reason I declined was that we're always going over what by now had become routine and formulaic. Someone like Walter Laqueur, I suggested, might provide new impetus. I wrote *How German Is It* not to rationalize Germany. The director, not terribly sympathetic, promised: "We'll have you on another occasion for a reading."

What was it about Germany? Why am I so prepared to identify self-discipline, stoicism, law-abiding people, even a decided lack of humor and a certain insensitivity, as overwhelmingly German? We proceed by stereotyping. How else? What is it that we love about the Italians, the French, the English? We define ourselves and others. An eternal struggle between a particularism and universality?

When I ran into Jacov Lind, exuberant as ever, near the Chelsea Hotel, he invited me up to his huge, uncluttered studio apartment overlooking Twenty-third Street. I mentioned that I would be leaving on a book tour for Germany shortly and inquired about his experiences in war-ravaged Germany, which in 1943 was teeming with foreigners. Passing himself off as a Dutchman, he worked on a barge until it was sunk by RAF fighters. Throughout the war, he avoided capture and certain death by one skillful gambit or another. He spoke of the past with that fondness one reserved for one's near-misadventures. Throughout, he seemed to have had countless sexual opportunities—though one, to his dismay, resulted in a minor medical problem which required the immediate attention of a doctor: no easy matter in Nazi Germany, given that any doctor would at once detect that he was circumcised. Before I left, Jacov almost jovially described his lone return to his former Viennese neighborhood in '45, treating the event as a lark. His former neighbors didn't conceal their astonishment to see him alive. They gawked: "Look at him!" Genially, some referred to the trickle of returning Viennese Jews as *Gasofen Tachinierer*—gas oven shirkers—something Jacov neglected to cite as an example of that inimitable Viennese humor in his revealing autobiographical writings.

When I questioned several friends and acquaintances who had visited Germany about what I might encounter there, their stories were far more revealing of their own dispositions than of German society.

At a dinner when I mentioned that I was leaving for Germany, one of the guests, a prominent American artist, described his reactions when his wife, a modern dancer, was invited to attend a dance event organized by the noted German choreographer Kurt Jooss. She rang him in Paris with the good news, and after some cajoling persuaded him to join her in Germany. It didn't help matters, he explained, that the dance group was being lodged in an imposing hotel that, he was informed, had been the prewar residence of the Krupps. On their first day, getting out of bed after his wife had left for her dance class, he neglected to wash or even shave. Donning a raincoat over his striped pajamas, as if it were the most natural thing to do, he took the elevator down to the lobby. By then it was ten, and he was one of the last to be served breakfast in the near-empty dining hall. Unconcerned that by his outlandish appearance he was calling attention to himself, he then left the hotel intending to explore the downtown area. Randomly following a pair of stylishly dressed ladies into a fashionable cafe, he picked a table next to theirs, deriving pleasure from their evident distress as he gorged himself noisily on twice as many of the identical pastries they had ordered. Aglow with the satisfaction of having vanquished an enemy, he headed for the railroad station, all the time acutely aware of anyone old enough to have served in the army during the war. The next day was a virtual repeat of the previous one. Following breakfast, unshaven, again attired only in a raincoat over his pajamas, he grimly set out for the railroad station with renewed combat in mind. This time, emboldened, he deliberately sought out older men. Within the labyrinthine station, he succeeded in pursuing a well-dressed man carrying a briefcase into what he by then knew to be a cul-de-sac. Finally, confronting the cornered man, he spread open his raincoat, and to the latter's total mystification gleefully exposed his striped pajamas. "Didn't anyone try to stop you or report you to the police?" "No. Not once." By the third day, his wife, nearly out of her mind, threatened to summon a doctor unless he agreed to leave immediately. An hour later he was bundled into a Paris-bound express train. The moment it crossed the border into France he felt overwhelming relief. He was himself again.

At a PEN function I chatted with the wife of a writer who had been a fighter pilot in World War II. I remember asking him what it was like to fly over Germany in the last months of the war. "Oh, we ruled the sky," he declared exuberantly. "We'd blast anything that moved out of existence. Cars, trucks, trains. Boom, boom, boom!" When I repeated his remarks to her, she looked astounded, then, emphatically shaking her head, stated: "He never flew fighters. He never fired a single shot. He flew transports only, shuttling supplies and troops." She didn't seem to care that she was contradicting the images he had so painstakingly planted in my mind.

At Kennedy I was the last to board the 747, minutes before take-off. The distinguished-looking, middle-aged, gray-haired lady in the seat next to me pulled out a book, on the cover of which, in large letters, was printed Klaus Mann's name. I inquired whether it was a book by or about Klaus Mann. She said it was a recently published biography and then, almost by the way, added that Klaus Mann was her brother. If anything, Elisabeth Mann's presence served to validate and enhance my trip. An oceanographer living in Halifax, she was on her way to a conference in London. She explained that she rarely, if ever, visited Germany. Though strongly tempted to, I felt it would be impolite to discuss her father—instead, we spoke about contemporary literature. Though, I must admit, the only time she showed any emotion was when she spoke of the dogs she was raising.

I'm obliged to Cornelia Foss for a revealing anecdote about Thomas Mann. Lukas Foss was told the story by Golo Mann. Apparently, at the age of five, in a recurring nightmare, Golo was visited by a diminutive man dressed in black. Each time, he'd wake up in a sweat, quivering with fear. When their governess informed his mother of Golo's nightmares, she turned to Thomas Mann for help. A time was set aside for his visit to the nursery on the second floor—a room he rarely entered. Approaching Golo's bed, Thomas Mann asked his son to recount the dream. Having listened to the detailed description, he said emphatically: "The next time this tiny man in black approaches, look him in the face and calmly say: 'Papa said for you to go away.' " Golo followed the instructions and was never again visited by the mystifying figure in black.

Amsterdam

Each time I peered through the Pentax viewfinder an intolerably familiar picture postcard presented itself. Captivating as Amsterdam might be, it served as the mirror of my impatience. Tired of interviews, I'm consuming too much coffee . . . too many pastries. Even my hunger is a measure of my impatience. My editor Mai and his colleague laughingly refer to their hangovers. They're almost competitive about it. Both prefer woodsy places, whereas I find the staid bars they derisively call bourgeois more inviting. There, distance is not diminished. One can sit back and observe others.

What prompted me to enter the antique store . . . and then, after aimlessly looking around, point to the dozen or so gray-green tin soldiers neatly lined up in a dusty glass vitrine in the window and ask if they were German, knowing perfectly well that they were? Yes, replied the mournful-looking owner—whom I took to be Jewish. He then made a mild comment in English about the distinction and ability of the German army and the excellent craftsmanship of their toy soldiers, adding that he wished that from now on the Germans would restrict themselves to the production of *toy* soldiers. Throughout, I was aware that there was something disagreeably compulsive about my action. I behaved as if these dusty World War II tin soldiers in the window still held a forbidding drawing power. Chabrol's film *Les Cousins,* in which toy soldiers play a symbolic role, comes to mind. Taboos exercise a curious appeal. Had I bought them, would I have displayed them on a shelf as an incitement, hoping that they'd enable me to locate Germany more precisely?

Masterpieces in the museums. The days race by. This cannot be right, I said to myself, as I responded to some question from an interviewer. After a few days I think of the appointments that lie ahead as so many challenges.

When Willem, the book reviewer writing an article on *How German Is It,* established that I'd never set foot in Germany, he offered to drive me there for the day. Two days later we set out— my first foray into Germany.

As we sped along the flat landscape, I kept asking myself, What do I feel? Relaxed in the comfortable front seat, I felt only a pleasurable anticipation. "Once we're in Germany," Willem assured me, "there's no speed limit, and we'll really pick up speed." As we neared the border, Willem stated that I could request the border guard to stamp my passport.

"Is that the procedure?"

"No."

"Then why do it?"

He looked at me closely—as if he might have misjudged me. "Don't you want a memento?"

The German border guard barely glanced at us. I was surprised by his unkempt appearance—his long, disheveled blond hair and poorly cut uniform. Now I was wide awake, intently staring out of the window. Eagerly almost, I snapped photos of the rows of unprepossessing houses, so orderly, so clean, so characteristically German, as we sped through Wuppertal. On closer scrutiny, however, they weren't all that neat and orderly. Clearly, I was bringing my expectations to everything I identified as German, exhilarated whenever I found something that matched my anticipation. Neat German houses straight out of *How German Is It*—could anything be better?

Willem, steering the Saab with one hand, a camera in the other, kept snapping my photo with a zeal that challenged mine. Running out of film, he borrowed my Pentax. By now we had reached Cologne. He took the last two shots of me with the gigantic cathedral as background. To my dismay, when he handed me the Pentax, I wasn't able to rewind the film. To rectify the problem, we headed for a small camera store conveniently nearby. It was my first opportunity to practice my German. I watched as the saleslady inserted the Pentax into a light-proof bag to open it without ruining the film. With a comical look she reported, "Aber da ist doch kein film drin"—But there isn't any film in it. Somehow, it seems appropriate that I'd been nailing my first impressions of Germany with an empty camera.

Standing in the massive cathedral entrance, a red-robed church attendant, hands folded over a protruding paunch, was chatting amiably with a tourist in a broad dialect that was incomprehensible to me. There was something decidedly pleasurable in seeing, unless my eyes deceived me, what a filmmaker might present as an essence of Germanness.

As we traveled along the Rhine, everything on view seemed slightly exaggerated . . . almost staged—like a reproduction of the original . . . There wasn't much river traffic, mostly small commercial boats peacefully chugging along and now and then a tour boat, with the amplified sharp voice of a tour guide cutting into the loud oompah band music. I kept staring at the mundane scenery as if the boats, the quaint villages, even the river would enable me to view the peaceful present day in a different context. If, as many Germans seem to claim, the Hitler years were only a tiny element in the lengthy and rich history of Germany, what significance is there to be drawn from those events?

At what stage in the reconstruction of Germany, at what point in this tremendous effort will the turbulent past fade, enabling the visitor to Germany to once again view the society with that credulous gaze of a nineteenth-century traveler?

Willem, the authority on Germany, was traveling over familiar ground. With the significant dates at his fingertips, he obligingly kept pointing out the buildings of architectural or historical significance. It was too much for me to digest. Crossing the river on a slow-moving ferryboat, the junked metal and rusting beached hulks in discolored oil slicks near the pier—mementos of the war?—reminded me of Grass's *Cat and Mouse*. Willem vividly recounted how the final days of the war affected the surrounding area. It was bedlam, people everywhere fleeing in terror. Even the ferryboats were strafed.

How German is it? I asked myself as we drove through a nondescript landscape. With few exceptions the house windows in the small impoverished towns along the river were identically square, tilting inward—almost Magritte-like in their otherness. Willem, who had a few more treats in store for me, didn't conceal his impatience to gauge my reactions.

Indeed, I felt as if I had traveled through these villages and seen the craggy, forbidding castles overlooking the Rhine on a prior occasion. The inn where we stopped to eat, a dark, woodsy, low-ceilinged interior replete with stuffed birds on the walls, seemed to authenticate an idyllic picture of the past. Hesitantly, I practiced my German, searching for the right words, deriving pleasure whenever I was able to construct a coherent sentence. We were kept waiting an overly long time for our *Jägerschnitzel* and rump steak. Our amiable waiter, Johannes Klein, apologized: "Sie müssen entschuldigen, aber der Koch hat den Zettel weggeworfen." He must have liked our company, for he kept finding excuses to return to our table, until, toward the end, prattling nonstop about life in Koblenz, he seemed more like an actor performing a parody of the German waiter.

As we drove along the Rhine, then the Mosel, I glimpsed the railroad tracks beneath the tranquil vineyards on the steep terraced slopes overlooking the river . . . Though I may have set off with expectations of a clean, orderly Germany, to a degree the trip really reflected Willem's obsession. Willem was driven, not I . . . He was seeking something far more elusive—dare I say, a Wagnerian Germany? I sensed that I was disappointing him. Did he expect a more emotional, a far grimmer response? He kept asking: "Have you really never been to Germany before?"— somehow doubting my answer.

Toward sunset, the only indication that the villages we were passing through were not entirely deserted was the occasional weather-beaten VW Beetle parked on a sloping, winding road and, here and there, an unexpected encounter with a solitary leather-jacketed young man wedded to his motorbike, a contemporary knight errant, who, when not impassively awaiting the unforeseen, would attempt to shatter the sound barrier as he sped past on a matter of critical gravity. I also spotted a fierce-looking Doberman. Was I especially alert to "Germanic" archetypes, for anything that to my mind would spell out a familiar element? Wasn't this so-called Germanness chimerical? Yet who can deny national distinctions? How else do people, be they French, Italian, Spanish, German, define themselves and others?

Willem led the way up a steep stony trail that culminated in a small clearing where, from a conveniently placed bench, one had an unimpeded view of the tranquil countryside, with vine-yards spread out below, while, in the far distance, three lofty peaks dominated a terrain that hadn't divested itself of its rich ancient history. It was his favorite site, Willem declared. Not only was I being shown his private and personal Germany; my response or lack of was duly noted. Here and there, as we drove through the small villages, in stony niches in stone walls or at the side of old houses, a sprinkling of wildflowers were positioned beneath a cross. Is there any reason why I should question a people's capacity for devotion? "They grow wine here," Willem observed earnestly.

At night, the castles, disappointingly small in the distance, were brightly illuminated. By the time we decided to head back to Amsterdam it was dark, and Willem, who'd been driving non-stop, appeared to have depleted that intense energy that kept him going all these many hours in quest of I don't know what. I kept talking to keep him awake, since at the speed we were traveling the slightest misjudgment would be fatal. When I inquired where his parents had been during the war, I anticipated the customary response—namely, that they'd survived in some small Dutch town—only to have Willem, after a short pause, declare that his parents had spent the final two years of the war in Germany. I concluded that they were slave laborers in a factory or, worse yet, in detention—taken aback when Willem, after a brief hesitation, explained that his grandfather was a prominent member of the Dutch Nazi Party. Not concealing his anger, he mentioned that his grandfather was clubbed to death by the Dutch at the end of the war. His parents, who had fled to Germany in 1943, returned in '46. His father, a former schoolteacher, was promptly put on trial and sentenced to six months in jail. As if discerning what I was thinking, Willem went out of his way to assure me that there had been no Jews in the small town in which his parents had lived. It was beginning to dawn on me why some readers were responding to *How German Is It* as if it were a Rorschach test.

Was Willem's passionate interest in Germany almost a condi-tioned reaction to what happened to his parents and grandfather? Unable to find employment as a schoolteacher, his father moved the family into his grandfather's house. In order to survive they were compelled to sell their remaining possessions, one by one, until his father landed a job teaching German to American soldiers. Subsequently, he became an economic adviser for a large company. Unless I was mistaken, I sensed a grievance, a feeling of victimization, in his recitation. Whom did Willem blame? The Dutch, the Germans, or might it somehow be their adversaries?

Summing up our trip at Willem's apartment a few days later, I could feel that a fatigue had set in. There were just so many questions he could ask. I noticed on a wall of books two narrow shelves in the white formica bookcases reserved for his 35mm slides, neatly marked "rejects." On the mantelpiece was a photo of Willem scaling a steep cliff. Willem still maintained, despite my protestations to the contrary, that I must have visited Germany before . . . Though he readily admitted to feeling affection for Germany, which he visited frequently, to my question of what he especially liked about Germany, his textbook response—"They're reliable, they're disciplined, they're not sloppy in their thinking, they're trustworthy, and they're honest"—didn't approximate the yearning for Germany I detected in him. Was he describing German virtues or simply a resoluteness he felt was absent in Holland?

I prolonged my stay in Amsterdam by several days. Gra, a writer who had interviewed me in New York, invited me to use his tiny flat, a fourth-floor walkup, overlooking one of the lesser canals that had houseboats moored to it. Mai gave me a copy of Willem's lengthy review. It was positive, with no mention of our trip to Germany.

Nice

One might say that we were just another family on vacation in Italy. Just another family: Papa, Mutti, and their little Walter, traveling abroad in December of 1938. Our possessions, including the furniture, down to the worthless little knickknacks in the glassed vitrine, all the things that had come to represent the normal, everyday fabric of our lives, were crated to be sent by train to Copenhagen, from where they were to be forwarded by ship to China. Instead, the crates vanished, as if into a black hole from which there was no possible return.

This, my first trip abroad, differed from previous train journeys in that it was less leisurely. We had considerably more luggage. As always, I was preoccupied with my immediate needs. When and where would we eat? Had my parents forgotten my birthday? Our travel plans were alarmingly vague. Nothing was spelled out. The terse exchanges between my parents seemed to be in a language I did not speak. I soon turned a deaf ear to their conversation. I was not interested in following our route on a map. What were we doing in Genoa? One long train ride followed another. With lassitude I watched the landscape. Where exactly was Italy? Where precisely was France? Maps did not spell out pleasure but, to my mind, a list of future impediments. With glazed eyes I sat in a myriad of hotel lobbies taking note of an ever fluctuating world. Still, now and then a few agreeable hours. I perked up as soon as I received a toy train in Milan. Sitting on the floor of our hotel room, I contentedly watched it go round and round. Returning to play with the train was like returning to a reassuringly familiar world. Though it was strictly against hotel regulations, my mother, in an attempt to save money, prepared our meals on a hot plate in the room. As far as I can recall, no explanation for our present itinerant existence was ever offered to me. Presumably it was deemed unnecessary. Our danger must have been self-evident, even to a child of seven. After a brief stay in Milan, we moved to Monte Carlo, where my father and I traipsed up to the picturesque castle on top of what then to me appeared to be a huge hill. Since I was on my father's passport I was able to accompany him legally into France, whereas my mother for reasons that were not altogether clear had to pay someone to smuggle her into France. It was simple, she said: since there was a fiesta being held on both sides of the French/Italian border in Ventimiglia, my mother, following instructions, carrying flowers and a few things she had purchased at the fiesta, sauntered from stall to stall, crossing the border into France unhindered. She then boarded a bus bound for Nice to be reunited with us.

We were fleeing the Germans, but in Nice, where I was enrolled in school, given the strong anti-German sentiment, I became "the Bosch"—a derogatory word to designate a German.

Was I being prepared for life abroad? For the life of a writer?

While in Nice, I watched my father buy a small bag of black olives which he ate with evident relish. I was flabbergasted. My father, who never revealed a desire for anything, was fond of olives. I kept looking at my father as if to reassess him. Unconcerned, he calmly ate all the olives in the paper bag without offering any to me. I kept wondering if my mother knew of my father's predilection for olives.

The prewar photo of my father on St. Mark's Square in Venice, a cigar in one hand, laughing, as pigeons squat on his arm and shoulders, is a father I don't really recognize. More than once I heard my mother complain to friends when the subject was brought up that my father never took her along on his trips abroad. I try to picture my father, the man who rarely spoke about himself, who never revealed what he truly enjoyed, on these trips to Czechoslovakia, Hungary, France, and Italy. The dedicated, focused businessman. For the one who, already as a young man, was made responsible for the well-being of his parents, sisters, and brother, there may have been little room for pleasure. On one occasion—I was sixteen at the time—carried away by Plato's *The Death of Socrates,* I remember asking him snootily: "And what is your philosophy?" Seemingly unaware of the challenge in my voice, my father straightaway replied: "My philosophy? Why, it's to protect and take care of Mutti and you." He then laughed, as if that should have been self-evident. I was taken aback by his instantaneous response—if anything, it highlighted the insincerity of my question, not to mention my dismissive tone.

One morning I was awakened by loud snores. To my amazement there was an unshaven man fast asleep on the floor beside the bed. How had he come there? I remember racking my brain, trying to come up with an explanation of why someone resembling an outcast should be stretched out on the floor in my room. I kept staring at the face of the exhausted-looking man without recognizing Frank. After what seemed an eternity, my mother entered the room and explained. Twice caught crossing the border into France and sent back to Italy, Frank succeeded the third time, traversing the mountains without a guide . . . What did I make of this? I don't know if it registered.

On a walk with my mother along the Promenade des Anglais we stopped to watch a group of men and women, resplendent in white, from a raised enclosure almost gaily shooting at pigeons that were released from small wire cages. They were practiced shots and quickly dispatched all the pigeons heading out to sea. While I admired the ease and the nonchalant bearing with which the members of the gun club raised their rifles and, hardly taking aim, effortlessly blasted the hapless birds out of the azure Mediterranean sky, I kept desperately hoping that they miss at least once. As we stood watching, riveted by the spectacle, one of the shooters, a young woman, did just that, at least partially, evoking polite laughter from inside the enclosure as the injured bird, in response to my prayer, flopped down a short distance from where my mother and I were standing. As we stared in disbelief at the bird desperately thrashing about at our feet, a uniformed attendant came running to pick it up. Seeing my look of concern, he assured me as he cradled the injured bird in his hand, "It's all right, We'll take good care of it." I gravely accepted his explanation, although by the age of seven I had come to understand that the care would at best be transitory, that when healed the bird would be released in order to become a target once again.

On another occasion we were approached by an acquaintance, a bald-headed gentleman walking his huge Labrador on the promenade. After some small talk he turned to his giant dog, Prinz, and with a fatuous grin directed it to "kiss the lady." The well-trained Prinz obediently rose on his hind legs and, sticking out an immense pink tongue, made a sincere attempt to oblige his master. I was as surprised as he when my mother furiously slapped the dog's muzzle, and then, in an even voice that brooked no argument, said: "If you ever dare to repeat this, I will smack your face." The man bowed and apologized before withdrawing with a subdued Prinz. The last time I saw him was on the SS *Felix Roussel* after we had unexpectedly docked in Bombay. Due to his not having the necessary documents, there was talk of returning him to France. I watched him, head buried in his hands, sitting in his tiny cabin on the bunk bed, shaking with uncontrollable sobs. I don't know if he was sent back to what was a certain death or not. The Labrador, however, given his impeccable breeding, was doubtlessly assured a long life.

A visit to Molinard in Grasse, where after an extensive tour of the factory I was presented with the largest toy truck I had ever seen. But the outsized gift couldn't compensate for my reaction to the many heady fragrances in the perfume assembly line, where rows of white-garmented women were filling tiny bottles: I was sick to the point of vomiting on our return trip to Nice. A few weeks later my father was incarcerated in Les Milles as an enemy alien.

My uncle Phoebus, in the meantime, had arrived in Shanghai. Not wasting any time, according to his letters, he had gone into the import-export business with a Chinese partner. He wrote that he had purchased a house in which we were most welcome to stay as long as we liked. Being Phoebus, he couldn't resist a few choice descriptions of Shanghai: the crippling poverty, the vast number of thieves and prostitutes, rats everywhere on the street, people dying of starvation, disease, not to mention corruption . . . How he must have relished writing those letters! I recall my mother reading one of them, the tears coursing down her cheeks, though she must have remembered his passion for drama, his exaggerations, his delight in teasing others. How gratified Phoebus would have been to see what his letters accomplished: his favorite younger sister in tears!

As always, my mother accompanied me to the barbershop. This time, without consulting me, she requested the barber to cut my hair to resemble my father's. Did she think of it after being informed that my father would be incarcerated in Les Milles as an enemy alien? Facing myself in the mirror, I said nothing. Did I have no opinion, or was I in a state of shock? Did my mother really wish me to resemble my father? Though the French barber valiantly tried to follow my mother's instructions, my hair resisted all his efforts. It was no use. The part on my left stayed in. She shrugged, accepting defeat. And he, released from this onerous task, set to cutting my hair.

School in Nice was a harrowing experience. I learned French in a state of panic. Studying in that openly hostile environment was hardly the issue: day-to-day survival was. I sat way in the rear and tried to be inconspicuous. I don't believe I could ever provide the correct answer to any question I was asked. Grimly, as if my very existence depended on it, I tried to glean some meaning from the thick, ink-stained, much-used textbooks I had been given. I still recall the line drawing of a ruined medieval castle on a page we were expected to study, and then, a day or two later, making a field trip to a ruined castle. We trudged up a soggy hill in a light rain and then, on reaching the ruin on the summit, listened to the teacher's long-winded description in which the *gloire* of France was emphasized. I felt as if my days would never end. I remember being overcome by an acute feeling of "foreignness," as if made aware that the historic site, which the teacher was describing with evident relish, was beyond the reach of my imagination. My one escape from the daily vicissitudes was a small, beautifully proportioned red convertible with detachable tires. To complicate my life, the toy automobile came with an additional chassis, that of a black sedan. At no time could I have both at once.

Each day on my way to and from school I'd pause in front of the jewelry store window in our neighborhood to gaze with wonder and a certain admiration at the tiny figure of Hitler in silver, a triumph of miniaturization, dangling from a miniature gallows, also in silver. People spoke of the *Sitzkrieg*—a seeming contradiction I could not grasp. But nothing could shake our conviction that the impregnable Maginot Line would deter a German assault—a belief invigorated by the endless newsreels we were shown of the multileveled underground fortifications, the enormous cannons, and the state of preparedness of the fighting men.

With inexplicable zeal I kept digging holes in the wall at the side of my bed, a miniature Maginot Line, concealing evidence of my nightly excavations with loose plaster and putty. When my mother discovered the holes, she was perplexed. "Are you trying to dig yourself into the bathroom?" I couldn't provide an explanation. She tried to understand my motive. "What are you up to?" I didn't know. She looked at me nonplused, shaking her head.

I do not recall any books in our apartment in France other than the French-German/German-French dictionary, the Knauer Weltatlas, and the book of perfume with chemical formulas, my father's bible. My mother, an avid reader, was never without a novel, which she'd discard after reading.

A French business associate of my father's, upon hearing me express a wish for a simple protractor for school, took me to a department store and, despite the protestations of my father, bought me a professional drafting set, which, if anything, sparked my interest in architecture.

Did my parents realize that our lives were dangling by a thread? After my father was interned as an enemy alien in Les Milles, my mother and I moved to a cheaper apartment; actually, it was a share. The occupants included Frank and an Austrian Jewish couple, a withdrawn, gloomy writer and his wife, who, I fear, may not have survived the German occupation. With undisguised envy at Frank's independence, I watched him prepare his evening meal at the refectory table in the vast kitchen that along one white-tiled wall contained four or five tiny alcoves, each equipped with a small two-burner gas cooker, one per unit. Neatly arranged in front of Frank was everything I was forbidden: onions, salami, herring, olives, beets, pickles, spicy sausages . . .

When my mother and I visited my father in Les Milles, he looked fit. As always, he seemed to have an inexhaustible supply of cigars and, if only out of politeness, showed himself to be in the best of spirits. "There's nothing to worry about. I'll be out of here in no time," he assured my mother. At a small open-air stand he bought me a meat sandwich. Fascinated, I watched the inmate who ran the stand carve a slice from a huge side of beef and place it on a thick chunk of dark bread. Apparently there was an active black market, with local farmers supplying produce to those who could afford it. In marked contrast to my father, most of the inmates milling about aimlessly in the open were shirtless, unshaven, and unkempt. My father maintained that the outdoor life was a pleasant change. "What do you do all day?" I asked him. "Oh, we go to the woods," he replied vaguely, "and chop down trees. The guards provide us with little extras, for which they are well rewarded. No one works very hard," he assured my mother. She, however, was far from convinced.

Only recently have I acquired a more detailed knowledge of Les Milles, a former tile and brick factory. The incarcerated included a number of well-known scientists, the writers Lion Feuchtwanger and Golo Mann, the painters Max Ernst and Hans Bellmer (both of whom painted large murals there), as well as Walter Hasenclever, who committed suicide in Les Milles. (In her book *The Holocaust, the French and the Jews,* Susan Zuccotti accuses the camp commander of stealing work from the already famous Max Ernst to sell in Paris.) Sixty-four percent of the men at Les Milles were forty or older; a sizable number were teachers, lawyers, musicians, writers. There were a sufficient number of musicians in Les Milles to form a small orchestra. A huge kiln was converted into a cabaret called the Katacombs. Apparently bribe money was needed to obtain exit visas and transit visas through Spain and Portugal. Golo Mann was one of several refugees who succeeded in making the difficult trek across the Pyrenees into Spain.

Only one inmate, according to the records, departed for Shanghai, China—none other than my father.

My resourceful mother, attractive, able to speak French, managed with the assistance of Molinard to free my father. Oddly enough, my incarcerated father was the one least apprehensive about the future. Nothing to worry about, he beamed at my mother. He was beginning to adjust himself to life in Les Milles. In 1984 Alinea published a special edition, *Les Camps en Provence: Exil, internement, déportation, 1933–1942,* about Les Milles and its subordinate camps, from which thousands were ultimately sent to their death in Auschwitz. In a large grainy photo which I suspect may include my father, inmates are shown outdoors, seated on rough benches at their meal. I recognize the location. It's where my mother and I spent a few hours on our visit in autumn of 1939.

We left on the SS *Felix Roussel* for China. The ships of the Messagerie Maritime line traveled fortnightly from Marseille via Djibuti, Colombo, Singapore, and Suez to Shanghai in approximately thirty days. We sailed from Marseille only days before the Germans invaded France. Our passenger ship was one of the last to leave Marseille for China. By late 1942 and throughout most of 1943, thousands were being sent to their death from Les Milles, which had become a staging area. Then, in September of 1943, after Mussolini was toppled and the Badaglio government signed an armistice with the Allies, the Italians pulled out of Nice. The German special SS forces under the command of Alois Brunner organized a particularly ferocious hunt for the approximately twenty-five thousand Jews who'd taken shelter in Nice and its immediate surroundings. In no time there was an economic incentive for the French to turn in Jews.

The first Chinese man I ever saw stood next to the gangway chatting with a sailor as we boarded the SS *Felix Roussel.* I was struck by his oddly deformed face, a face that bore a strong resemblance, I was later to discover, to those of the wizened eunuchs Cartier Bresson had photographed in Peking in 1947. I remember wondering as we boarded the ship if that's what all the Chinese looked like.

How easily one slipped into the organized everyday life . . .

My mother's red-leather-covered alarm clock had been the official timekeeper ever since we had left Vienna. It recorded time that stretched back to our apartment at Königsegggasse 2. My mother carefully considered what she would wear for each meal. As always, I was asked to approve her choice of dress, her scarf, her hat, as she inspected herself in the full-length mirror.

What was I being prepared for?

My father didn't conceal his hope, once there was peace, that I would become a perfumer. He said as much, but he said it wistfully, as if aware that it was not likely. He would have wanted me to receive my training at Molinard in Grasse. By then we were living out of suitcases. Not the most expensive or the most luxurious: simply well-crafted middle-class suitcases. The news of Germany's invasion of France prompted a constant lookout for U-boats and, from that night on, total blackout on board. A few days later there was a moment of panic when, after a muffled sound, our ship listed to one side. My mother was standing next to a passenger who, she said, turned pale. He then explained that in World War I he had been torpedoed. For a moment he had feared a repeat of what had happened to him. Next day we were informed that a blade on one of the propellers had snapped off. As a result we proceeded at reduced speed for Bombay, where it would be replaced. It prolonged our journey by about seven days. While in dry dock my father, the bearer of an Austrian passport, was once again detained with all the other Austrian and German

Jewish men. My mother and I remained on board. My playmates were all French. I wished the voyage would go on for ever and ever.

I was startled to read in Joachim Fest's biography of Hitler that the May 1940 offensive against France was to have taken place as early as November 1939. For one reason or another, according to Fest, it was postponed twenty-nine times. Had it not been delayed, we'd have doubtlessly remained in France and, more likely than not, with the active if not ebullient participation of the French police, been shipped to the death camps in Poland.

Cologne

At the railway station the lady in the information bureau made a telephone call to reserve a room for me at Hotel Central, two blocks from the cathedral. Not seeing any Germans in the lobby, I inquired, "Sie haben nur Auslander?" of the middle-aged desk clerk, who after a quick glance at the register said: "Na ja, am Wochenende bleiben die Deutschen lieber zuhaus." Unlike in Amsterdam, everything somehow appeared more pronounced but decidedly less lively, less colorful. Near the hotel several boisterous drunks weaved back and forth.

Sunday morning. The young, severe-looking clerk at the desk, whom I mistook for a German, was from Ann Arbor. Trying to be helpful, he informed me: "The Germans like it if you say *bitte* and *danke*." Predictably, bookstores were closed. But I spotted a number of the boxed special editions of Fontane, Rilke, Goethe, and Heine on the shelves in the shiny metal newspaper kiosks on the main street, in case of a sudden demand for the classics on Sunday.

At the Wallraf-Richartz Museum, the repeated playing of "God Bless America" as part of a huge Ed Kienholz installation drowned out the conversation in the nearby cafeteria.

While waiting for the U-Bahn, a couple sitting next to me in the station were intently listening to a tape recording of what appeared to be a long-winded political speech. She, in her twenties, nodded in apparent agreement as her elderly companion observed approvingly: "Das europaische Denken . . ."—which to my mind had a fatuous, self-congratulatory ring to it.

From my window seat, even the occasional tall building didn't break the bleak monotony of the outlying districts.

The half-timbered houses I passed on my way to the hotel resembled components of a stage set for a performance of *Faust*. Looking through a multicolored windowpane in a reconstructed medieval-looking tavern, I saw students in preposterous Burschenschaft uniforms holding up huge steins of beer. Was it their cheerfulness or the all-too-evident nationalist self-definition I found so unsettling?

The elderly night clerk on duty was glued to the black-and-white TV, watching a documentary on Hungarian and Romanian participation in World War II. I couldn't resist the familiar lure and sank into an overstuffed armchair. It was no different from the documentaries I'd seen countless times. The destruction of the Romanian Plotzi oil fields and the rounding up and extermination of Hungarian Jews were interspersed with stills of Hitler, Goebbels, and the Romanian chief of staff. A somber TV voice presented the details in German. An hour later I dragged myself away, bidding the night clerk "Gute Nacht," to which he responded with an equally polite "Nacht."

A friend of mine, a prominent scientist born in Hungary, in an unguarded moment let slip that he and his family in 1944 at their arrival in Auschwitz faced Dr. Mengele, often named "the Angel of Death," on the selection ramp. My friend mentioned that in order to appear stronger he had stood erect while puffing out his chest, fully aware of the life-or-death consequence of Mengele's decision. With a wave of his hand Mengele motioned him in one direction and his entire family to instant death in the other. Despite his intense grief at seeing his parents and young sister walk away, he revealed that he couldn't restrain an almost involuntary feeling of relief at having survived the initial selection ordeal.

At the Kölnischer Kunstverein an exhibition entitled "Wiederstand und Verfolgung." A pamphlet that I picked up at the hotel stated that visits to the former Gestapo headquarters, with its twelve basement cells containing drawings by the prisoners, could be arranged.

Now and then I'd spot someone with a cane, limping badly, or a grim-faced individual missing an arm or a leg. In this particularly austere setting, this vestige of the war is like a marker to a barely overcome emotional privation.

When I first saw the vast assortment of trinkets, many of which appeared to be refurbished, in a jewelry-store window on a quiet cobblestoned side street, the not entirely illogical thought occurred to me that a number of the pieces on display might once have belonged to Jews. To my astonishment, as soon as I focused my camera at the window, a disinguished-looking elderly lady whom I took to be the owner stepped out of the store and in German politely inquired, "Was machen Sie?" In my best German I offered a plausible explanation: "I'm a visitor to the city and just taking pictures of whatever happens to catch my eye." I was totally unprepared for her next query: "Are you Jewish?" I hesitated, as if, given the context, my brain needed a brief moment to consider the question; then, as soon as I said "Yes," she invited me into the store, where she explained that she had survived Treblinka, and that her husband, a concentration camp inmate as well, died shortly after the war. To inquire how she could continue to live in Germany under the circumstances seemed indelicate. She spoke unconstrained by the presence of her young German assistant, who was self-consciously busying herself with some task. Our conversation was briefly interrupted by a telephone call from a friend in Berlin. As she made plans to attend a concert in the Scharoun Hall in Berlin, normalcy prevailed—

listening to her speak, I was struck by her composure and confidence. By now, she'd been purged of all fears she once might have had of the Germans. There was nothing they could do to her that she hadn't faced.

Every such encounter offered details that verged on the painful. It was like removing a Band-Aid: one was forced to yank it off to lessen the painful sensation . . .

Frankfurt

Met by my editor Gunther Maschke. He's tall, overweight, ungainly, the large, owlish face a little childish as he came toward me smiling broadly. He explained that he had reserved a room in a conveniently nearby hotel. It turned out to be one of those vast business establishments I customarily shun. Moreover, to my dismay, it was outrageously expensive. Since it was abundantly clear that I couldn't expect Maschke to foot my bill, I said that I preferred to find a room elsewhere. The desk clerk, gazing stonily at Maschke, informed him that a cancellation fee would have to be paid. Maschke looked at me inquiringly, "Nun, was wollen Sie machen?" I had barely arrived and already was confronted with a decidedly unpleasant choice: "I have no intention of paying a cancellation fee," I said. "However, you're free to do whatever you wish." Seeing how matters stood, the clerk dropped the request. "Well, there are other hotels in Frankfurt," sighed Maschke.

Maschke, a ceaseless talker, garrulously recounted his life in Cuba—he spoke of it almost fondly—as we proceeded by taxi to a smaller hotel in the Westend. To my surprise, on our arrival, Maschke, who by now had become engrossed in a heated political discussion with the driver, chose to remain in the taxi.

In the evening when I met him and his companion, Jahne, for dinner at a neighborhood Italian restaurant, he was wearing a suit. When he discovered a few stains on the lapel, he petulantly complained: "Jahne made me wear a suit for the American."

"I made you wear it for me," she responded.

Between courses, Maschke extracted the jacket design for *How German Is It* from a large manila envelope. With a placating smile he handed it to me. It showed a mannequin in a fur coat leaning over the railing of a small rustic-looking wooden bridge. "It's not so bad," Jahne said consolingly, anticipating my reaction. I was stupefied. "It's grotesque! It distorts the book!" I could tell from Maschke's equivocal response when I exhorted him to have the cover redone that it was beyond his control. By the time the two Hungarian translators, friends of Maschke's, and the theater editor for Suhrkamp arrived, I was ready to head back to the hotel. Instead, for another two hours we were treated to Maschke's ponderous assessment of present-day nationalism and Germany's realpolitik. Maschke seemed inordinately pleased with his conclusions: "One cannot expect anything of significance to occur in a society if its people aren't prepared and willing to shed blood for its survival." Blood! Please . . . And he delighted in farcical statements such as: "The Thousand-Year Reich still exists. It's twelve years of action and 988 years of commentary."

Engaged by the Deutscher Ärtzte-Verlag to run their publishing venture, Maschke conducted his business from a tiny office located in his book-crammed fifth-floor walkup apartment. His list of publications under the imprint Edition Maschke was undeniably provocative: it included works by right-wing Pierre Drieu La Rochelle (*Der bolivianische Traum,* a virtually unknown novel set in Latin America); the conservative historian Bern Willms; the ever provocative Mircea Eliade; and the political theorist Carl Schmitt—as well as, to my surprise, the complete Darwin. I hadn't as yet read Schmitt's *The Concept of the Political.* The noted conservative political constitutional theorist, a brilliant juggler, was now attempting to strike out the many former anti-Semitic entries, some arbitrarily inserted into his prewar books as an overture to the Nazi government.

Markus Wiener, who has known Maschke since his own student years in Frankfurt in the sixties, claims that Maschke still retained a certain credibility with the political left—after all, he had been an activist who participated in the antigovernment actions of '68—which may explain why he wasn't being attacked by them. Knowing the political left inside out, Maschke now relished assailing their contradictions and weaknesses in the articles he published in the right-wing press.

Friday. The book party Maschke organized could have been lifted intact from a Fassbinder movie. The large, pleasant apartment with lots of art belonged to an acquaintance of Maschke's, a designer, who throughout the evening hardly said a word. Maschke introduced me to Alfred von Ruhm, a tall, gray-haired, dignified-looking scholar, and his regal-looking wife, as well as to Diana, a young woman managing a boutique. We were joined by Edel, an actor whose intense flashing eyes and raised voice proclaimed a demand for attention.

Was it for my benefit that Diana, who had grown up in Israel, in fluent (albeit slightly accented) German set out to provoke Edel, remarking somewhat spitefully: "I never go out with Jews anymore. It always ends in the coffeehouse." Her nonsensical comment did provoke Edel, who, in what amounted to a retaliatory strike, with the look of someone relishing every word, gleefully called her a pariah, a greasy, black-haired *Ost jüdin,* a Gypsy, cruelly depicting her skin as swarthy, her lips as thick and unappetizing. Finally, having depleted his demeaning portrayal of her, Edel proceeded to cast aspersions on the Eastern Jews now residing in Frankfurt's Westend, the subject of Fassbinder's outrageous play *The Garbage, the City and Death.* Undeterred by Edel's gratuitous assault, she chimed in, as if eager to stoke his performance: "The moment you enter a synagogue on New Year's, someone will press a card into your hand requesting a donation." When Edel, grinning broadly at her complicity, leaned forward and impishly pinched her, she crudely inquired: "Soll ich dir jetzt auch dein Arsch kneiffen?"—a deliberate vulgarism that further incited Edel, who was enjoying his role as a buffoon, for it enabled him to articulate what was otherwise a taboo. His petulant voice rising, Edel asked rhetorically: "Must we still feel guilt? Hasn't the time come when we are able to speak our minds?"

Jahne, Maschke's companion, concurred grimly, only in her case revealing a disconcertingly genuine anger: "I think it's time we liberated ourselves and spoke up . . ." She wore a colorful headdress, a quasi-turban—in solidarity, she explained, with the former *Trümmerfrauen*—rubble women, as they were called—who in the forties, wearing identical headdresses, stacked the bricks they salvaged from the bombed and gutted buildings.

I mocked Edel's exaggerated performance. His compulsive drivel about *Hochhauserjuden*, skyscraper Jews, and *Teppichjuden*, carpet Jews, I said, marked him as a third-rate talent. Stung by the "third-rate," he lashed out: "You are intellectually divorced from what I've been saying. Besides, I'm not German. I'm from Bavaria, where people are lethargic and disinclined to work. We understand the Jewish temperament. We too are outsiders. In fact we admire the Jews—especially their cunning, their anti-authoritarianism. The Prussians here know only to obey."

When the man Ruhm had referred to as the gambler ambled over to join us, Ruhm, with a tentative smile, declared, "I've seen you on TV." The gambler, whose specialty was roulette, happy to have an admirer, promptly rattled off a list of TV shows he'd been on. He then complained, "I'm recognized wherever I go. It's tiresome being a celebrity."

With an eye to bonding with the new arrival, Edel mentioned Jewish-American writers. Both he and the gambler had read Philip Roth. They chortled as they recalled Roth's hilarious descriptions of the Jewish mother—it's as if, in providing a Jewish source for it, they could approach a subject that otherwise was off-limits to their ridicule.

In an attempt to change the subject, Ruhm spoke warmly, if condescendingly, of his stay in the U.S. He admitted to being puzzled by "all that nonsensical waiting to be seated each time one enters a restaurant." However, he was far too polite to concur with Edel's intemperate "The U.S. is culturally a primitive society." The actor, who had had too much to drink, stood at the

buffet clumsily piling food on a plate while loudly informing
Ruhm about his recent visit to a brothel in a *Hubschrauber.*

"What's a *Hubschrauber?*" I asked.

"A helicopter."

"Must have been tricky landing it in one of those winding
cobblestoned streets."

"Oh, no. The best bordellos are located outside the city. But
the most erotic one is on Tucholsky Street . . ." Edel obligingly
provided the number. "One is made to check one's clothes and
most men walk around naked . . . The older ones are offered a little cotton wrap. The madam insists on introducing the guests to
each other . . . she provides them fictitious names and bestows
flattering titles and doctorates on them. In turn, the guests make
a great show of being gentlemanly, by bowing to the ladies and to
each other. As you might expect, crudity is frowned upon. Conversation is genteel, though by their speech the men instantly
reveal their social status or lack thereof."

"Tucholsky Street," said Ruhm lightheartedly. "I must make
a note of that."

As I left, I wondered how much of the evening was the result
of Maschke's stage management. Did he want me to write a
sequel to *How German Is It?* Though anti-Semitic rhetoric has
become stagnant from mindless reuse, to employ it, however
playfully, was to invigorate it.

The following day I met Hans-Ulrich Müller-Schweffe at
Suhrkamp. They're about to publish the translation of *How
German Is It* in paper. He informed me that several officials at
the Heidegger Society, livid at my treatment of the renowned
philosopher, requested that Suhrkamp not publish the paper-
back. The adjacent building, presently a bank, had been the
Gestapo headquarters. In the basement the drawings on the wall
by prisoners had been preserved, Müller-Schweffe said, with that
by now familiar wisp of a smile I've noted on faces whenever a
ticklish subject is brought up.

Würzburg

By ten in the morning the tour buses began to arrive with their full load of tourists. In 1982, they were still predominantly women—waxen-faced, bony ladies with watery eyes and large, clumsy hands that seemed to be in perpetual search of a new occupation, something to unravel perhaps, as they obediently listened to the stentorian voices of the guides, men in their late fifties, accustomed to obedience. But by then Würzburg had reestablished a firm grip on the day-to-day and no one any longer paid any attention to the busloads of women in their shapeless dresses.

The magnificently restored palace, on which a number of architects, including the famous Balthazar Neumann, lavished their attention, enabled the prince-bishops to shed their armor and leave their heavily fortified Festung Marienberg overlooking the city in 1744. Pacing the new gardens, they could now in utter tranquillity redefine their princely objectives. Everything except for a yet-to-be-restored wing was now open to the public. However, what was on view—the spacious palatial waiting rooms, the ornate double flight of stairs, the reception chambers, and the White hall, the Imperial hall, the Venetian room, the lacquered Green room—offered little in the way of information; they merely signified the former presence of aloof courtiers. In truth, it could have been any palace interior. The taste ran to gold and blue draperies and an assortment of uninspiring palace furniture on shaky legs. Discomfort, one was made to feel, was rigorously enforced. It was home to many, though undoubtedly no one was made to feel at home.

In the vestibule of the Residenz, to the right of the grand staircase, a row of framed black-and-white photographs showed Würzburg after its destruction, with the palace, or rather what was left of it, at dead center. Every imploded building provided ample evidence of the intent of the Allies to reduce accident as a factor of survival. In view of the total destruction, Würzburg's rejuvenation, its near-perfect reconstruction, seemed an achievement that paralleled the construction of the Great Pyramids.

Though I've been reminded repeatedly of the fierce determination, dedication, and perseverance that went into the reconstruction, it provided one bonus: escape from pondering the Nazi past.

Later that afternoon, as I was strolling in the inner city, map in hand, a young blond man with an amiable smile approached to offer his assistance. One look at his short haircut and *völkisch* uniform—*Kniehosen,* heavy kneesocks, and thick-soled hiking boots—elicited my instantaneous "Danke, nein!"

"I saw you consulting a map," he good-naturedly explained, "and concluded you might need assistance."

Did my repeated "Danke, nein!" reveal consternation?

Nonplused, he walked away.

Toward sunset, seeing me meander into the Hofpark, camera at the ready, the handful of withdrawn, solitary individuals meditatively absorbing the sweetness of life must have regarded me as an intruder. They were here to take in a moment of true perfection, as the copper-domed roof of the baroque palace retained the sunset's reddish glow moments after the sun was no longer visible, and a large variety of birds, agitatedly hopping from branch to branch in the shaped trees and concealed in the clipped hedges, as if to accentuate this transition from late afternoon to evening, suddenly, frantically inspired, burst into song—their combined mad twitter and chirping leaving one with the impression that this almost artificial-sounding din could only have been manufactured by some ludicrous musical device, perhaps a hand-cranked contrivance such as the one devised by the Swiss painter Klee to imitate a *Vogelgesang*—a birdsong . . . as yet another edenic day, tranquil, uneventful, seamlessly slipped into darkness. *Ein innerlicher Frieden!*

On weekends, it's less than thirty minutes by car to the countryside of vine-covered hills. One can visit medieval villages where people still speak the local dialect. One can sit back lazily in the tiny, sheltered garden of one of the restaurants and drink several glasses of the excellent local white wine, surrounded by a changeless world.

I was startled to read in Pierre Ayçoberry's informative *The Social History of the Third Reich* that in Würzburg denunciations to the Gestapo of "guilty relations between Aryans and Jews" continued long after the Jews had been deported to the concentration camps.

THE WRITER-TO-BE

Shanghai

My exuberant uncle Phoebus came to meet us when we docked in Shanghai a few days after our enforced week's stay in a dry dock in Bombay. As we drove down Avenue Joffre to his house on Avenue Roi Albert in the French Concession, I kept looking in vain for the abject poverty and the rats he described roaming the streets. "How lovely it is to be reunited!" Phoebus remarked, later proposing to my father: "You and I should go into business together. You have the experience, the perfume oils . . . I'll dig up the capital."

I thrived on Phoebus's audacity, his impulsiveness, even his recklessness. In my eyes he could do no wrong. Even his dubious integrity in business matters excited in me a sympathetic response—for wasn't Phoebus confirming my picture of him as the black sheep, who finally, as Phoebus did, moved to Sydney, Australia? How could I ever measure up to Phoebus or his son, George? Was it their impulsiveness and recklessness that made them impervious to fear?

Yet, how was I to explain my uncle's behavior during our brief stay in his house? After an especially heavy downpour, the ground-floor apartment in which we were staying was under a foot of water—a not uncommon event in Shanghai for that time of year. I vividly recall waking early and from my cot watchfully following the progress of my father's slippers as they floated from under his bed across the room. I didn't speak up. I simply waited for my father to make the discovery himself. Phoebus's apologetic explanation that Wally, his second wife, didn't wish to share the upstairs bathroom or kitchen with us was the breaking point. "You'll see, in a day or two the water will subside." My mother looked at him in disbelief. "Wally doesn't want to share the upstairs bathroom and kitchen while we're under a foot of water?" We moved out a day or two later. Phoebus, revealing an unexpected timidity, apologized again: "I hope you won't allow this unfortunate incident to come between us."

I was enrolled in Peter Pan, a private school, where the headmistress, a tall, intimidating lady from Canberra, Australia, tackled my atrocious pronunciation head-on, having me endlessly repeat the article "the" in the class, until she declared herself satisfied. It was a small, nonthreatening environment, with classes of not more than ten students. I promptly fell head over heels in love with Katherine. I was deliriously happy just to be in her proximity. One afternoon, she and a friend invited me up to his apartment, his parents being conveniently out. When Katherine playfully suggested that we write each other notes, I happily complied, not anticipating that she'd next suggest that we read each other's scribbling or that the notes, really a double message, she so casually handed me to read would contain the most astounding endearments in addition to communicating her preference for the other nine-year-old.

Infatuated with England and anything even remotely pertaining to England, I recall a jamboree at the English embassy as the high point of my Cub Scout days. As serious-faced adults looked on, we marched past to the lively music played by a brass band. The event, egg races and all, was straight out of one of those irresistibly cheery Englishy movies I had come to love.

Occasionally I'd be taken to play with Erika, like myself an only child. Erika's father packed a small revolver in a leather holster on his belt. Though I assumed it was for his protection, it served as an indication of their elevated status and success. Depending on the weather, tea was served indoors or in the garden. I remember Erika as having pigtails, a vast assortment of toys, and as far as I could tell, like myself, few friends. Our final visit to the grand villa is the only one I vividly recall. It began ominously, for the moment my mother and I entered the vestibule, I found myself confronted by a girl my age in a pleated tartan skirt who, standing in the doorway to the living room, gravely examined me. Completely unprepared for another visitor, I was still mentally girding myself for this unanticipated encounter when she was joined by another, then, to my horror, yet another girl, all in identical tartan skirts. By the time the fifth girl with the same creamy olive complexion and what can only be described as an identical disconcertingly probing look of curiosity appeared, I panicked and, breaking away from my astonished mother, bolted out of the house, running for dear life down the street to duck around the nearest corner. Once I had recovered from that initial shock, though my heart was still pounding, I couldn't resist peeking round the corner to see the entire group—the five sisters, my friend Erika, and our mothers—standing on the villa's front doorsteps, as if assembled for a group portrait. Their combined look of astonishment at my odd behavior sufficed to launch me, as if pursued by demons, in the direction of home without stopping along the way. When I next met Erika and her parents in Hongkew, several years later, they had moved into a modest apartment not unlike ours. Her father, having been incarcerated briefly for some financial double dealing, looked haggard. The pistol I so admired was conspicuously absent—a sure sign of their precipitous economic decline. My mother cheerfully spoke of our getting together. Though Hongkew was a small community, I don't recall seeing them again.

Wide-eyed, I watched from across the deserted tree-lined street as a Chinese policeman lined up four Chinese delinquents, nailed for trespassing or some minor infraction, if that. Perhaps they had stepped on one of the pristine lawns of the French Concession villas in the vicinity of Peter Pan. Complying with what must have been his sergeant's caprice, but showing an unquestioning alacrity as he did so, the Chinese policeman lined them up according to size—the tallest to the left—then, as if preparing for some gymnastic exercise, made them bend low, hands on their knees for support. A few more trifling adjustments were made, all unhurried, for there was all the time in the world, until the sergeant, a White Russian, who with hands on his hips was keenly following the proceedings, declared himself satisfied. With the Chinese policeman impassively looking on, the sergeant took a few steps back and then, like a goalie about to dispatch a football far into the opposite side of the field, delivered a massive kick to the first boy's rump, stopping briefly to calculate the result, as any athlete might, before switching his attention to the next boy in line. Predictably, the smallest, with a loud shriek, sailed forward the farthest; for a split second he was airborne, bringing a smile of gratification to the otherwise stern sergeant's face. I watched, memorizing every detail of this designed cruelty, a punishment out of all proportion to anything the boys may have done, storing it away for the future. After all, that's what writers do.

From our second-floor window I saw a barefoot rickshaw coolie step on a broken piece of glass and with a piteous howl sink to the ground next to the rickshaw, clutching his bleeding foot. His anguished look of despair commingled with incomprehension is still etched in this Chinese picture album I carry in my mind. I was stricken by an emotional melding of empathy and a heightened awareness of my own inability to assist the profusely bleeding man: realizing that this incident might well spell out his death, for how would he recover? It was beyond our ability to help. I called my mother to the window. She brought him something to eat—more to ease our own distress. I watched him hobble away, sorrowfully pulling his rickshaw, and leaving a trail of blood.

Walking down our lane, I stopped to watch in fascination as the young woman, our neighbor, tapped her fingers gently on the windowpane of her second-floor apartment, doubtless in order to hasten the drying of her freshly painted fingernails. From where I stood I could only see the captivating white hands and the bright red fingernails, tapping, tapping, as if to attract my attention with their message. This memory of the disembodied hands that seemed to have a power all their own, like some Freudian detail, merges uneasily in my mind with a number of Duchampian art objects: the dangling gloves . . .

My uncle Phoebus had invited my parents and his Chinese partners and their wives to a festive dinner at a Chinese restaurant. Then, following the "banquet," characteristically not consulting anyone, and disregarding the outright look of alarm on the faces of his Chinese partners, Phoebus declared that he was taking them to the Shanghai Race Club for drinks. My mother was quick to murmur to Phoebus that Chinese were not permitted into the race course, but Phoebus pointedly ignored her warning, so confident was he at the time of his own influence. Even the limousine chauffeur seemed to understand that this trip would end in a grave loss of face. The Chinese partners tried ineffectually to change Phoebus's mind, but he remained adamant— as adamant as the Sikh guard at the entrance: "Sorry, sir, but Chinese are not permitted into this area." Phoebus would not accept the refusal: "They are my guests," he declared grandly, and then, in the face of the guard's steadfast refusal, demanded to speak to someone in authority. To everyone's embarrassment, Phoebus continued to argue long after it was apparent to all that he wasn't going to succeed. "It was horrible," my mother said.

I no longer recall what precisely I told my uncle Phoebus to provoke him to decimate my entire army of toy soldiers. I know I challenged him. In a fit of anger I may even have called him *Schwein*. But how to explain this sudden reversal? This emotional turnabout? Was it because he, my favorite uncle, having at long last broken with the despicable Wally and moved into our building to share an apartment with Omi, his mother, now, only six months later, was prepared to return to his second wife—a move that, to my mind, reflected his indecisiveness and weakness?

More likely, my anger was directed at Phoebus's overbearing, proprietary manner at the table, his self-assured, matter-of-fact displacement of my father. Quite possibly he had triggered my anger by helping himself to the last slice of dessert I regarded rightfully mine. Certainly, his gargantuan appetite dominated the table . . . My uncle had upset a delicate balance of power. At any rate, I can still recall the fixed smile on his face as he stood up from the table and walked to my room, where, having located my toy army, which stood on parade, he knelt on the floor and, without losing his smile, proceeded calmly to snap off the head of each soldier, solicitously returning each decapitated soldier to its rightful place on the parade ground of my floor. I remained in the doorway, paralyzed, incapable of speech after a first entreaty, a strangled plea. The devastation was rapid. Heads came off. My parents, who couldn't have anticipated Phoebus's retribution, did not intervene. They disassociated themselves from the destruction of my army. I was on my own. Once in a while my uncle would look up to ascertain that he had my total attention. If I didn't howl, if I didn't have a tantrum, it was because I recognized that this unpredictable individual, this unpredictable agent of destruction, might be provoked to even further havoc. I was dazed and defenseless in the face of this gratuitous, disproportionate assault on my dearest possessions. Wasn't he exceeding his authority? Who else but Phoebus could have understood that? It was retribution time. To snap off the gray-helmeted heads of my soldiers and to replace each one on the parade floor required a special understanding of me. Of my family only my mother could have been said to share this insight. Only she was in a position to fully apprehend my uncle's gesture. Both she and my uncle must have understood that in order to reach me they would have to resort to extreme measures. One look at my smug face . . . at my sealed face . . . one look at my unwavering hostile glance informed them of what was needed to breach my recalcitrance.

I still possess Phoebus's diary. In what way do I possibly resemble him? Do I share his unpredictability? His gloom? The first two words in the diary, "Kummervolle Tage"—sorrowful days—

announce the somber color of his entries and his bleak vision. It is a brief diary, only a dozen or so entries over a period of almost thirty years. Each event a self-contained drama, a stage setting in which Phoebus—having placed such an inordinate emphasis on details, on the actual place and time—remains, despite his passionate language, a distanced observer of himself. The diary resembles a sketchbook in which are illustrated a series of tableaus. The scenes are carefully framed. There is almost a painterly concern with the presentation of the event. Some of the entries were made long after the event.

> Sorrowful days. At three in the afternoon on June 24, 1916, my dearest brother Fritz died on the field of honor. He was only 23. Struck by shrapnel on the right side of his neck, blood flowing from a pierced artery, he sank to the ground without a murmur. Two of his friends buried him in Kielce, Ostraowice, Denkow, past the wood on the road to Ruda Koscielna, near a brook at the side of a mill. We have his diary. He spent six months in the field with the Forty-first Infantry Regiment. He will remain forever etched in my mind.

Then, less than five weeks later, on the occasion of his father's death:

> I wildly raced up the stairs and threw myself on my father, embracing and kissing him, beseeching him to speak, to say something. His eyes, when I raised his eyelids, stared blankly at me. I placed my ear to his chest, desperate to hear a heartbeat. I spent the night vigilantly at his side. On the afternoon of the following day the undertakers arrived. They carried my father's corpse down to the street and, having unceremoniously slid the coffin into the horse-drawn covered carriage, drove off at a clip. My mother and I followed on foot for a short distance, until she broke down. The funeral took place the following day, a Monday, July 13th, at the Centralfried-

hof. We had arrived at nine. By ten we were permitted into the mortuary and invited to view my father. By then his face was yellow and in parts even black. My mother keeled over. She fainted more than once that morning. For days she spoke of taking her life.

I still have in my possession a dozen or so photographs of Phoebus, our black sheep. Phoebus in a gym's boxing ring, wearing boxing gloves, looking confident as he posed with a sparring partner and their trainer, who has his arms around both men's shoulders. My favorites of Phoebus are the ones of him in the company of beautiful women: playing volleyball—both Phoebus and the tall, statuesque woman in the swimsuit at his side have their heads raised expectantly as they await the return volley from across the net—or on a beach reclining next to a voluptuous-looking blonde who resembled his first wife, Nelly. Wearing sunglasses, he had raised himself slightly and with a thoughtful, inquiring, but not friendly look was staring into the camera.

I have several photos of Phoebus in uniform—two of which show him pale, walking stick in his left hand, while recuperating from a bullet wound. Then there is a photograph I never show anyone of Phoebus in the entrance to his shoe store, Yvette, at Fasangasse 18, for the photograph would diminish, if not nullify, the role of black sheep I have accredited to him. In the photo, his three employees, all with that sorrowful hangdog look of middle-aged shoe salesmen, are standing to his left and right, in a way so as not to obscure the two large store windows, one with men's shoes, the other with women's. I don't know the occasion for this photograph. It may have been a celebratory occasion—though from all appearances my uncle did not seem to evince any particular pride of ownership.

The nomenclature of black sheep I bestowed on him is misleading. Yet so much of Phoebus's personal history lends itself to this appellation. "He has Phoebus on his brain," my mother would say when I begged her for more stories. But she would happily comply. Phoebus was, by far, the most colorful person in our lives.

About his first marriage Phoebus had written in the studied, self-conscious language of someone unaccustomed to putting his thoughts on paper. Phoebus, the amateur boxer, the man who didn't seem to know fear, was in love. I found it difficult to reconcile his often fretful diary entries with my portrayal of an ever assertive, self-confident Phoebus. "She was acquisitive, spoiled and concerned with only herself," Phoebus wrote of Nelly, his first wife. He had been cautioned by a well-intentioned friend that Nelly was not "unblemished" or some such fusty term. But Phoebus couldn't bring himself to believe this. "After we separated she did everything to turn my son George against me." Ironically, shortly after Pearl Harbor, when the European Jews in Shanghai were forced to move to Hongkew, my uncle found himself living only a few houses away from Nelly, her husband, and his son, George, who by then bore his stepfather's name, Fischer. "When I saw them on the street I didn't greet them, for fear that this innocent gesture might be misconstrued," my uncle wrote. So for the next seven years, which included the bombing of Shanghai in 1944 and 1945, they lived in close proximity without ever exchanging a word. On one memorable occasion Phoebus and George found themselves back to back in a crowded tram on Broadway. Predictably, neither one spoke up. George stepped off the tram at the first opportunity. In his diary Phoebus reacts emotionally: "How I would have loved to embrace my son. To live together with him."

In 1945 my cousin George appeared in a high-school production of *Arsenic and Old Lace* in the role of Mortimer, the favorite nephew of the two arsenic-dispensing aunts—an appropriate role for him. He played it well—exuberantly, almost. To my mind, he resembled Phoebus: he too was opinionated, smug, self-confident, even insufferably arrogant. The only time I recall meeting him, just after the war, he was lording it over a group of students on the Kadoorie School grounds. He looked at me closely, then greeted me affably, admitting me to the circle of admirers, though

he couldn't resist saying "Hello, cousin" with an ironic inflection—
his calling card—that reminded me of his father. I stood by
uneasily, hoping I wouldn't be the next target as he twitted one of
the male students, the one least capable of defending himself, the
one who with a worried expression kept looking for an opportunity to escape. Everyone laughed—especially the women, who
found George irresistible.

I didn't make friends as much as I discovered them. I viewed them
with the satisfaction Columbus must have experienced on spotting land on the far horizon. What would this friendship yield?

What was I looking for? What did I hope to extract from this
friendship? Was it the joy my mother and her friends had experienced? After we had moved to rue Prosper Paris in the French
Concession, my first friend was Dwight Irving Gregg, an American
who lived in what I recollect to have been the only tall apartment
building in our vicinity on Avenue Joffre. I remember him as
being blond, thin, and extraordinarily pale. What did we have in
common? Little except that we both had few friends. I shared his
interest in guns and toys. His mother was pleased to see me come
and play with Dwight, who looked as if he suffered from some
mysterious ailment. His stepfather, a doctor, went out of his way
to tussle with Dwight and act fatherly in a manner that struck
me as totally unconvincing. By the age of nine I was becoming
an expert in incompatibility. Though not only Dwight but his
mother as well seemed glad that I came by, some six or seven
visits later, after we had played all his games, I seemed to have
exhausted what the friendship had to offer. I stayed away, for no
particular reason . . . Had I, by then, extracted everything I could
from the relationship? Given the situation, Dwight, when I think
of it, had every reason to be furious. In retrospect, seeing Dwight
on the second-floor balcony, rifle in hand, shouldn't have surprised me as I approached his building. He knew that I daily took
this route from school. If anything, the rifle—a recent gift from
his father—highlighted our difference. No one would ever allow
me a rifle. Though I understood the threat, I stubbornly resisted
crossing to the safety of the other side of the street. As I neared

the building, he aimed the rifle at me. I kept walking at the same deliberate, unhurried pace, without looking up. Dwight fired at the last possible moment, at an extreme downward angle. I felt a sharp, burning sting below the collarbone but kept walking as if nothing had occurred until, out of his sight, I was able to dislodge the pellet.

It seemed that with each day our downstairs neighbors in rue Prosper Paris, the Luongos, became more vociferous in their allegiance to Mussolini. To me, the older son's rifle on the wall in the alcove near the entrance was an attestation to the might of the Axis power. I still played with Tony, the younger son, who now and then could not resist giving the Fascist salute. But my closest friend was John, who lived with his father, an English engineer. In his room, from behind our respective fortifications, lustily singing "Wanting You" (a song popularized by Nelson Eddy and Jeanette MacDonald in *The New Moon*) at the top of our lungs, we would joyfully almost pound each other's fortified toy soldiers with building blocks.

At best I was a reluctant fighter—an inept and unwilling fighter. I had to be shamed into fighting. And shamed I was regularly. I fought with Mark, I fought with Tony. I had to fight to convince them that I wasn't afraid. Rarely, if ever, carried away by anger, I always considered myself at a distinct disadvantage, for if I hurt my opponent badly I'd only succeed in enraging him. In a fight with Mark, a fight from which I could not extricate myself, I inadvertently struck him in the windpipe. To my dismay, he collapsed, lying on the pavement in a fetal position gasping for breath, while the others stared at me accusingly. For a moment I thought I had killed him. My next concern, once he had recovered, was that after this event it would be so much more difficult to fight him.

Though I had a crush on Lily, who was English, I was much too shy to convey this to her. I stubbornly refused to apologize for some insensitive remark that had hurt her feelings. It was clear to everyone that she was avoiding me. Even Mark, who mockingly sang "It's never too late to say I'm sorry," signaled to me to do the one thing I was incapable of—apologize. A week or two later Lily fractured her leg and for what seemed an eternity hobbled everywhere on crutches, her leg in a monstrous cast. Every time I saw her I was reminded of my obtuse behavior—though I'd hesitate to conclude our fight had any bearing whatever on her mishap. "Lily's such a brave girl," my mother would say. Lily's response to my mother's repeated solicitous inquiry "My dear, how are you feeling?" was invariably a stoic, Englishy "Much better, thank you!" that I soon found intolerable. At my mother's request I may have visited Lily once, but I still couldn't bring myself to apologize—even though by now the unresolved event had become a sizable knot in my throat.

Soon after the Japanese attack on Pearl Harbor, when Lily and my English friends proudly disported red armbands with the letter B for "British" in black, I was made acutely aware that I had no such symbolic letter to feel the least bit proud of. Several weeks later, without any advance notice, we were assembled in the large hall at Peter Pan and informed by our disconsolate headmistress—who, with her colleague, was about to be incarcerated for the duration of the war in a Japanese prison camp—that this was our final day of school. I was heartbroken, for it was one of the few times that I enjoyed attending school; yet paradoxically, on walking home with my booty of books from the library and a massive, useless adult cricket bat, I felt quite joyous. I don't think I understood the contradiction—I simply noted it.

In a carefully worded edict the Japanese issued (the words "Jew" and "Jewish" were pointedly omitted), all "aliens" would need to register and move to a designated area in Hongkew, a blighted section that the Japanese, in their initial attempt to gain a foothold in Shanghai, had wrested from the Chinese in the Sino-

Japanese war of 1936.* Heavily shelled during the fighting, it was now being rebuilt by entrepreneurs to accommodate the large influx of Jewish refugees, for by 1942 as many as 18,000 immigrants were residing in Hongkew. The German Jews were dominant, numbering approximately 7,500, while the second-largest group, the Austrians, numbered 4,000. Within this mini European community, yet smaller groups—Romanians, Czechs, Hungarians—formed their own, less visible mini enclaves, inasmuch as this was possible. There were a small hospital, pharmacies, several schools. There were a number of makeshift lending libraries, numerous coffeehouses that doubled as meeting places, and even several bridge clubs. Entertainment was abundant: theater groups put on performances; there were musical recitals as well as a cabaret and a number of newspapers. Soccer—a great uplifter—made life bearable. The highly revered soccer league, consisting of eight teams, fiercely competed for the annual cup. The soccer stars were the local celebs. Law and order didn't break down. Most noteworthy was the fact that the community rigorously upheld what were essentially European values and maintained its hierarchies, with its attendant respect for the Professor, the Lawyer, and the Doctor. The community, by no means self-sufficient, managed to house some 2,600 indigents in what were euphemistically named *Heime,* which in most respects were anything but "homes." David Kranzler, in his invaluable *Japanese, Nazis and Jews,* presents a comprehensive picture of the abysmal living conditions in the *Heime,* which were "protected" by guards who seemed to fulfill a double function: discouraging strangers from entering the premises while keeping an eye on their dispirited occupants.

The house we moved to, on Chusan Road, the main shopping street, was one of a long row of more substantial and more solidly constructed three-story stone buildings, each with a two-story annex overlooking a tiny courtyard at the back. For the most part, the Chusan Road stores were located on the opposite

---

* Russian and Sephardic Jewish residents were exempted, because "the Japanese were exercising extreme care not to alienate the Soviet Union which had remained neutral in the Pacific war." See *Escape to Shanghai* by James R. Ross.

side in what were newly reconstructed and decidedly less sturdy flats. I recall a large bar near the corner in which, during the war years, one could hear the riotous laughter of Japanese officers being entertained by attractive European women. At the time, it was something I could not even bring myself to acknowledge. Directly across the street was a deli. I also recall the Landau pharmacy and an electrical supplies store. Down the street to our left, an open two-story cement structure housed a small but thriving market. From my father's office I had an unobstructed view of the squat-looking watchtower, always manned by an armed guard, at the southernmost corner of the high-walled penitentiary, a city unto itself.

On the ground floor of our building, in what once was the "Belle Etage," the grandest quarters, lived an upper-middle-class German family, who when they moved were replaced by a somewhat jaded Dr. Zimmer. On the second floor, facing the rear, I can only recall a German Jewish tailor improbably named Wang and his wife. An industrious man, in great demand, he skillfully turned my worn blue winter coat inside out. Unfortunately, the reverse fabric revealed a heretofore imperceptible white windowpane pattern that opened me to ridicule at school, so that wearing what looked like a new coat became absolute torment.

It was a familiar life, in that people went about their daily pursuits behaving much as if they were still back in Europe.

After a year at Peter Pan, with its tiny classes and noncompetitive students, I found myself ill prepared for Kadoorie, where the students were not only more competitive but more contentious, keener and tougher, and where, given its size—between thirty and forty in our class, evenly divided between boys and girls—the pecking order was more defined. Among the characters who stand out was the ever amiable Hans Eberstark, who, a year or two my senior, subsequently excelled as a mathematical prodigy in Berlin. My brother-in-law met Eberstark in Munich in the fifties when Eberstark successfully challenged a visiting Indian mathematical genius, claiming that he could do the other man's "tricks" in half the time. There was also Zymbalista, the class bully, who for a brief period made my life sheer hell—being so much tougher than the rest, he remained unopposed.

My father, having located someone to replicate his beloved Molinard perfume and cologne bottles and another company to reproduce the yellow boxes and labels, continued to manufacture a near approximation of the Molinard fragrances—at least his customers, which included WingOn, Sun, and Sincere, the prominent department stores in the former International Settlement, were under that impression.

Informed by a neighbor that I was at the back of the house trading blows with another boy—not an unusual occurrence—my mother came down to inspect for herself. One look sufficed. She was not taken in by our exaggerated squirming or by the grunting and groaning as we staggered back and forth, each gripping the other in a headlock. With a disdainful "You're both faking it," she walked away. Her contempt was unambiguous. We shamefacedly parted, trying to look as if nothing out of the ordinary had taken place.

Once or twice weekly in the afternoon of the summer of '43 I'd accompany my mother to the tranquil, tree-shaded outdoor cafe at the end of the 24 Lane off Ward Road—it faced the tall, ivy-covered rear brick wall of the then feared Japanese gendarmerie. I suspect my function, something not entirely clear to me at the time, was to serve as a quasi-chaperon; my reward, an eclair and iced coffee. My mother would join the group of five or six like-minded regulars at the *Stammtisch,* including Professor Willi Tonn, the Sinologist and founder of the Asian Institute, one of the few who was fluent in Mandarin, and Klaus Peters, an Austrian architect. I, the only child at the table, felt immensely pleased whenever I could, however briefly, hold the attention of the adults, especially Professor Tonn, with what I considered to be my perspicacious observation. Their conversation, in German, was witty and irreverent. Everything around us—the delectable

Austrian pastries, the waiters, the customers—all seemed light-years removed from China. How my mother had come to go there in the first place is a mystery. Be that as it may, the architect, who now earned his living as a restorer of paintings, had immediately won me over with a gift of a wood T-square and a set of triangles. Frequently he'd walk us home, I trailing at their side, half-listening. I liked him; I thought him amusing. Did the cafe's pleasant, relaxed atmosphere, the group, the animated conversations, even the Viennese background music, remind my mother of everything she had once had in Vienna?

My father avoided these afternoon cafe gatherings, especially this chatty, intellectual group, like the plague. He sensed that he wouldn't feel at home. When my parents went out once or twice weekly, the conversation with their acquaintances, generally businessmen and their wives, was altogether different. Everything, it seemed to me, was spelled out, the jokes more rapid and obvious. My father felt at home in that he could withdraw without anyone noticing. He looked as if he was paying attention, but he wasn't. It may not have mattered in their group, since no one was being particularly witty or clever, but in Professor Tonn's group it might have disconcerted the others, for the group needed everyone's participation. Occasionally, even I was invited to join in and eagerly did so to gain approval from one of the several ironic gentlemen paying attention to my mother.

One day my father seemed put out. The look of acute embarrassment, which I could not recall ever seeing on his face before, simply wouldn't lift. What caused it? Had someone commented on my mother's harmless afternoon visits to the cafe? Now—in retrospect—I recognize the look. It's the look of someone who, without advance warning, is being squeezed by an acute discomfort and, possibly, even doubt. Even my father's voice had changed. When addressing my mother he seemed to be appealing to her. For what? Even her name, Friedl, sounded unfamiliar on his lips. In speaking her name, he seemed to be testing it, as if unsure of its pronunciation. All this I sensed only vaguely. My parents stood and moved about in the room as if not knowing what to do with themselves. I became acutely aware of their every motion, their every remark. Yet, not a word was said that might reveal anything unusual. It was the *way* they spoke. My father would flee to his office at the first opportunity. If anything, my mother was even more remote than before.

A month later, when my mother and I ran into Peters, I noticed that he too had been affected by whatever had taken place. Indeed, in his sudden awkwardness he resembled my father. I was struck by the self-consciousness of their conversation. Even his customary politeness now appeared stilted. My mother's face was cool, remote—she had become unreachable. "We miss you at the cafe," the architect said sadly. My mother replied that she had so many things to do that she simply didn't have the time. On that note, they parted. I ventured to say that I liked him—that indeed, he resembled Phoebus. What did my mother reply? Nothing to reveal what she felt.

By the age of twelve and thirteen I borrowed books from no less than three lending libraries. Mostly they were well-thumbed, musty, and stained. Yet, despite my excessive passion for books, I remained a careless and indiscriminate reader. I read Havelock Ellis, the Baroness Orczy, Maupassant, Zane Grey, Mark Twain, and every mystery by E. Phillips Oppenheim I could lay my hands on. Nonetheless, until years later it never occurred to me to write—to make that all-too-plausible transition from an avid reader to someone who entertains the idea of becoming a writer. In school I entered a short-story competition and, to my astonishment, walked off with the first prize. It was my first short story. I didn't win as a result of the quality of the writing, which was excruciatingly bad, but on the strength of the ingenious plot I had brazenly lifted from a collection of short stories in *The Rover Boys Annual*—appropriately, it was about a cheat who, in the guise of friendship, to save his pals the trouble of writing a story for a short-story competition in school, presented each with the identical story.

Yet, I recall feeling, as soon as I began to write down the story in my own words, a resistance, an impediment that wished to obstruct me from carrying out my objective. I wrote page after page with an increasing anger at being tied to this interminable text instead of free to do something more pleasurable.

After being praised in front of the class by Mr. Kleinermann for inventing such an ingenious plot and awarded the first prize, a book, I lived in trepidation for the remainder of the term that our English teacher, unlikely though that might be, would happen across the *Rover Boys Annual* from which I had lifted the story. I was not unaware that in winning by plagiarizing I had added a certain richness to the original plot. The pity was that I had no one with whom to share this.

Late one summer afternoon, after what must have been a neighborhood brawl, a Russian, his left hand gripping his copiously bleeding right hand, strode past our house without a glance in my direction, singing the Russian anthem at the top of his lungs. There was something incongruously affecting about the solitary individual as he marched ecstatically down Chusan Road as if in lockstep with thousands of compatriots of the October Revolution, the trail of blood he left behind evidence of his epic struggle.

As far as I was concerned, the Japanese remained a remote but disquieting presence. They were the ultimate authority—the invincible Oriental power. Numerous stories of the brutalities of the Kempetai, the Japanese military police, in the notorious Bridge House circulated widely in Hongkew. In our area their only visible presence was the armed guard in front of the Japanese gendarmerie at Muirhead and Ward Road—though the invariably short, stocky, bowlegged soldier didn't quite measure up to the reported Japanese military supremacy. In the early forties, when the war was still going well for the Japanese, I'd catch an occasional glimpse of several Japanese officers frolicking with a blond hostess or two behind the frilly white curtains of the Chusan Road bar. At school, there'd be an infrequent visit from

Japanese high officials, none in uniform, who'd be escorted by the principal to several classrooms, where they invariably showed a polite interest in whatever the students were being taught. On at least one occasion they came bearing a gift—I recall one such presentation where the principal made a little speech in which she thanked a beaming official for his gift of a large Oxford English Dictionary for our school library. How had they acquired it? On another occasion, a lazy summer's day, two Japanese officials—one of whom was none other than the feared Ghoya, then the ghetto's chief administrator, a self-ordained king—after observing me play ball with a friend in the 24 Lane to the rear of the gendarmerie, joined in. Ghoya, a maniacal individual whose actions frequently bordered on unbridled lunacy, asked me to toss him the ball. I complied gingerly. He flung it back enthusiastically. It was a brief exchange, lasting not more than a fearful five minutes. Every now and then Ghoya, a slight man, inexperienced in tossing a ball, would look at me to see if I too was enjoying myself. The only other time I saw the Japanese was on my way home from Kadoorie School. I'd briefly stop to peer through the fence of the Japanese school and marvel at the students' disciplined conduct, so unlike ours. Their silence especially struck me as uncanny. It was broken now and then by a deep, near-unanimous resonant grunt, to indicate approval of a thrust or parry by one of the two combatants at the center of the circle of students, who, in their white robes, sitting bolt upright on the ground, gave the appearance that they were attending a religious ceremony, not a martial-arts class.

At Kadoorie School I didn't even make an effort to study Japanese. I understood it to be futile. Zero was what I had come to expect; zero was what I received. I shriveled up whenever Herr Posner—who, to my mind, resembled the chief interrogator of an Oriental secret society, though, for all I knew, he may have been Jewish—as much as glanced in my direction. I tried not to offer him any reason to do so. I also received zero for Chinese. At least the Chinese oral test was simplicity itself. One by one we would be called to the front. When it was my turn, the imperturbable teacher, a weary-looking, elderly Chinese man, contemplated me gravely but without expectation as he said something totally incomprehensible in Chinese. More than likely he could see from my bewildered look that I didn't grasp a single word. At least by his unambiguous question, "Ho u beho?"—which I understood to mean "Good or bad?"—the Chinese teacher was not one to prolong the torture. Everything depended on my response. I had a fifty-fifty chance. "Ho," I conjectured, trying to divine the answer on his lips. "Beho," he said. One final question. I wagered on "Beho" this time. He shook his head and dismissed me with a disdainful wave of his hand. To him I wasn't even a presence. Zero.

Zero for Hebrew, too, until my parents engaged the forlorn-looking teacher to tutor me. Only then, in our house, did he discover my abysmal ignorance of Hebrew. He couldn't fathom this. "What kind of a family are you?" he asked. Evidently, German and Austrian secular Jews remained a mystery to him. All the same, he was more than willing to provide me with the answers to the final exam—a useless offer since, to me, the answers were as incomprehensible as the questions. With a certain prompting, he finally had me copy out the answers, and then proposed that I slip him the prepared paper at the final exam. Though it was cheating with the teacher's connivance, for me it simply presented another grotesque hurdle. It felt as if I once again were being dangled from a pole in a swimming pool. I had no one to confide in. Yet, I reasoned, others managed. Others learned how to swim; others passed the language tests without knowing how to speak Japanese or Chinese or Hebrew. If not for my grades in literature, geometry, and history, I'd have been doomed.

Once, I noiselessly crept up behind my mother as she was opening our apartment door and ever so lightly tapped her on the shoulder. To my dismay she fainted, sinking to the ground without even turning her head to establish who it might be. "It was meant as a joke," I feebly tried to explain to her and my father afterward. "It wasn't anything I had planned. It wasn't deliberate."

Evenings at nine, in what was to become a ritual, we'd sit around the radio and intently wait for the nightly Russian news report. Though our shortwave reception was disconnected (shortwave reception was a punishable offense) and the radio tagged accordingly by the authorities, we were able to receive a nightly Russian news broadcast beamed from a powerful distant station. Toward the end of the broadcast, the announcer in a deep, gravelly voice would utter the magical word *zahvatili*—the one word we had been waiting for. It meant "captured," and was followed by a string of mostly unfamiliar and often to us unpronounceable names of hamlets, towns, and cities, recaptured in the past twenty-four hours by the, to us, invincible Soviet army. Feverishly we'd attempt to locate them in our tiny Knauer Weltatlas. What exhilaration! I had a vivid image of the Russian forces inexorably marching west in the direction of the ultimate evil, Berlin!

Distinguished by an armband, a whistle, a club, and an unmistakably forbidding look of duty, many members of the Pao Chia, the local auxiliary police, consisting of some 3,500 men between the ages of twenty and forty-five, guarded the exits of the approximately forty-square-block area. They also served as air-raid wardens, and like the more sinister and less disciplined guards at the *Heime*, took their duties with a seriousness out of proportion to what they had to do. An extreme case of bullheadedness is the story of Fred Schrantz, a relative of Phoebus's wife, a member of the Pao Chia who, carried away by some inexplicable Germanic zeal, in an altercation with the driver of a Japanese army truck who had dented his bicycle on Chusan Road, insisted on payment for the damage. He kept pointing at the stripes on his arm, indicating his senior rank in the Pao Chia. Last seen, before his body was fished out of the Whangpoo the following day, he and the bicycle were on the back of the truck, being driven away. (There are numerous versions of the above account, but James R. Ross's in his well-researched *Escape to Shanghai* is by far the most convincing.)

Compared to the round-the-clock carpet bombing of Germany or of the Japanese mainland, bombarding Shanghai late in the war must have been small potatoes, a mere sideshow for the Allies. We were a secondary target, never more than a dozen bombers overhead. All along I'd been convinced that we were bombed by B-17's, until recently, checking a copy of *The Army Air Force in World War II (June 1944 to August 1945)* in the library, I established that the planes bombing the Shanghai docks and warehouses, the shipping and airfields, and the railroad marshaling yards in the Hangchow area, as well as mining the confluence of the Whangpoo and the Yangtze, were predominantly Superfortress B-29's. Much as I disliked the bombing, it was the discordant chatter of the antiaircraft batteries located on the roof of the massive Ward Road prison nearby—sometimes firing, it seemed, without pause, whether or not planes were overhead—that I found most unnerving. The sound of their combined fire was deafening—paralyzing. Ironically, the huge prison compound, which housed an air-raid shelter the public was encouraged to use, might soon have become a legitimate target due to the vast quantity of ammunition we later discovered to have been stored there, not to mention its manufacturing enterprises employing cheap prison labor—another tempting target. The most severe bombing occurred on July 17, 1945, an overcast day, when this time twin-engine A-26 bombers missed their target, the Chiangwan Airdrome (an earlier claim that the Japanese radio station was the target is now disputed), striking instead an open-air market in Hongkew. Of the more than 250 fatalities, over 30 were Jewish refugees. At least 500 people at the market or living nearby were wounded and hundreds made homeless.

By now, at the first sound of the alarm, we'd grab a few belongings and, hearts pounding, madly race down the stairs to the dubious sanctuary—deemed the safest place in the building— of Dr. Zimmer's ground-floor office. He'd greet us pleasantly enough, though there was never an attempt at conversation. It was clear what we were there for. As a rule, the air raids from start to finish lasted under an hour. Though my parents never revealed anything the least bit unfavorable about Dr. Zimmer in my presence, I could discern, if not outright disapproval, a lack of that unqualified esteem they were wont to show Dr. Kaufmann, our family doctor, no doubt on account of Dr. Zimmer's patients: those tantalizing ladies who came and went at all times of the day, many of whom I found, arrayed in their heavy makeup, expensive furs, and high heels, exceptionally captivating.

On July 17 there was no early warning: by the time the sirens began to wail, the antiaircraft batteries were already in action. I was drawn to our window by the sound of singing, not the muted everyday sound of prayer or even the exultant chanting that greeted the High Holidays. Looking across the courtyard, I could see the members of the tightly knit community of the Ward Road synagogue, dressed in black, thronging the lower floors, swaying in prayer, their voices pitched high, filling the air with such acute urgency, such passion that for once I, by heart a skeptic, a doubter, felt my resistance fade. Their sustained singing was unlike anything I'd previously heard—it seemed to shape an impenetrable field, albeit one of sound, to fend off destruction. At that unforgettable moment, before tearing myself away from the window to follow my parents to ground-floor safety, it wouldn't have surprised me to see the four-story structure housing this community, which had stuck together through all kinds of vicissitudes, soar skyward in response to their thunderous rhythmic appeals to the Almighty.

It was the heaviest raid to date. In Dr. Zimmer's consultation room my parents were seated on the couch, clasping hands and, as far as I could ascertain, so self-absorbed that not once did they glance in my direction. The other couple from the second floor were sitting further to the rear, while I occupied the chair at Dr. Zimmer's desk, with the chipped and somewhat stained-looking white enamel medicine cupboard containing rows of ominously gleaming surgical instruments to my left and the old-fashioned examination couch with its shiny metal leg supports where the, to me, ever mysterious female ailments, maladies that were never discussed in public, could be diagnosed and presumably treated, to my right. If anything, the couch with its silver stirrups only heightened the distinction of male and female.

Though the sound and vibrations of detonating bombs soon intensified to a crescendo, Dr. Zimmer—who, I later determined, bore a close resemblance to Trevor Howard, who was to become one of my movie heroes—remained immobile in his chair, pensively staring into thin air, in marked contrast to my parents and the other couple, who by then were huddled on the floor, with my father protectively covering my mother with his body. At first, despite the explosions ominously rocking the building, seeing how indecorous my parents looked on the floor, I was determined to follow Dr. Zimmer's example. Nervously clutching the arms of the chair, I kept glancing at Dr. Zimmer—was it to gauge his expression, which appeared as fixed as if set in stone? After another nearby eruption, this time fully expecting the ceiling to cave in, unable to contain my terror, I threw myself headlong, a bundle of fear, to the floor, inhaling the carpet's dusty odor as my nose squashed against the finely worn Turkish fabric that had once graced the doctor's Berlin living-room floor, while my hands pressed down as if to infiltrate myself into the solid, trembling floor. I prayed as I had never prayed before for the detonations to stop. With each successive thud the house shook and the floor after a microsecond's delay shuddered in response. In the occasional lull between detonations, for what seemed an eternity, I studied Dr. Zimmer's trousered legs and his shoes beneath the desk. When the bombing finally subsided, though the antiaircraft continued their maniacal chatter, I glanced up to confirm that he hadn't budged. I tried to make the transition from my ignominious cowering position on the floor back to the chair as inconspicuous as possible, though from Dr. Zimmer's frozen expression he remained oblivious of my movements. We returned to our apartment, too stupefied by the intensity of the bombardment to exchange a single word. The religious community, when I checked, was quiet, and intact.

The following day, a friend and I, as if drawn by a powerful magnet to the area that had sustained the worst damage, managed to slip through the barbed-wire barricades erected to keep out looters. The guards and police paid no attention to our presence.

Scattered here and there were still-smoldering blackened pieces of wood. The acrid smell of burnt wood and charred flesh became more penetrating the farther we went. I recognized nothing. On a deserted square which must have been the site of the open-air market, the many dead and dismembered bodies were still piled high in three or four almost fastidiously neat heaps. Without a word my friend turned to retrace his steps, while I, handkerchief pressed to my nose, grimly forged ahead, crossing the desolate square, having to pass between the heaps of bodies in order to do so. The only exit was a narrow lane that was swept clean except that here and there, randomly scattered, lay a hand, a leg, body parts that the otherwise thorough cleaners appeared to have overlooked. Back home, claiming to have come down with a cold, I went straight to bed, ineffectually trying to blot out the experience.

The war's ending was anticlimactic. It took everyone by surprise. Evidently Shanghai rated so low that when the war ended we still found ourselves under Japanese control until—after what seemed an eternity but actually was two weeks—the tardy American navy finally materialized. The first inkling I had of Japan's defeat was one afternoon when, on leaving our house, I saw a man jubilantly waving his hands, almost skipping, as he announced to one and all that the war had ended. Yet, there was something about his appearance—his decidedly goofy face—that made him a less than reliable messenger. But in no time he, this unlikely emissary, was followed by a more credible individual bearing the identical message: "The war's over!" Forever skeptical, I headed for the Japanese gendarmerie on nearby Muirhead Road, disappointed to see, as always, an armed Japanese guard at the gate facing the deserted square. I tried to decipher the expression on his face, with little success. If Japan had been defeated, why was the Rising Sun still fluttering from the police station's flagpole?

That night, the square was teeming with hundreds of Chinese of all ages hurling invective and, from appearances, clamoring for the death of the lone Japanese sentry—was it the same short, stocky soldier who had been on duty that afternoon? Though the crowd easily could have overwhelmed him, they kept a safe distance. Now and then, a more venturesome Chinese youth darted forward, doing a little Oriental dance to taunt the soldier, only to retreat the moment the soldier lifted his unwieldy-looking rifle, to which an immense bayonet was attached. Sometimes as many as three and four young men, exhorted by a ringleader, advanced to act out in pantomime their loathing, wildly leaping, their hands cutting the air to convey humiliation upon the recipient— the short peasant soldier—who appeared unresponsive to what was a performance more suited to the stage, until they came a little too close. However, the instant he raised his rifle, they quickly retreated. The war was over, but not quite yet. As I watched from the safety of the outer edge of the crowd, all the lights were out in the gendarmerie windows. After waiting fruitlessly for something to happen, I left.

A protracted void followed. To me it appeared endless. Just as before there had always been rumors about the war, there now were rumors of riots and vandalism. The victors failed to materialize. The despised but still intimidating Japanese army remained in control, albeit less visible than before. Still, no one was prepared to challenge them—that is, until the Americans arrived. For the time being, the vast city of Shanghai lay there, submissive, patiently waiting to be occupied, waiting to place its bottomless resources, its harbor, its hotels, its bars and whorehouses at the feet of the victors. Shanghai waited the way a courtesan, having just rid herself of a former lover, might timorously await the arrival of the next, still uncertain as to his taste, his experience, his desire for love, determined, however, at all costs, to overcome any doubts she may have had about her fading beauty. All she needed was to be desired and she'd blossom once again. But until the victor's arrival there was a lassitude, a sense of fatigue. Everything was suspended and motionless. However, along certain streets there was a sudden inexplicable burst of activity: Chinese workers were constructing bars, while the stores and warehouses along Broadway were feverishly restocking the lacquered junk, the carved figurines, the crafted teak coffee tables, the trays and ornamental screens, everything the jubilant

Americans, Australians, and Brits would want to take home as mementos of the Orient. As for the women—those incredibly eroticized wide-cheeked Chinese, Eurasian, and White Russian women—were those small-breasted, slim, quick-moving women rehearsing their act? Perfecting their stories of past tribulations and survival? Readying themselves for the day the Allies finally made their appearances?

Then, one day, without any warning, without any fanfare, they arrived. No celebratory fireworks, no twenty-one-gun salute—not even a tugboat's hoot of welcome. Seeing the white-helmeted MPs and shore patrol at the harbor facilities on Broadway looking so unruffled as they cursorily checked IDs and waved cars through, I felt let down by the absence of hoopla—by the everyday appearance of it all. Surely the end of the Second World War deserved something more jubilant. In a sense, the ensuing four years of America's presence were already concentrated into those first days of their arrival. Everything there was to know about the Americans was to be absorbed in those first twenty-four hours. Everything!

The Seventh Fleet might have been tardy, but once having arrived and promptly occupied every possible space on the docks along the length of Yangtzepoo Road, the fleet more than made up for the delay with an avalanche of commodities. One had the impression that the sailors, whooping it up on the streets, were packing the newly opened bars before the ships had adequately docked. Not to be outdone, the Chinese merchants responded in kind with a lavish display of their wares—those familiar lustrous Oriental icons: Chinese dragons engraved on silver cigarette cases and emblazoned on the back of garish silk shirts—while on Nanking Road one could see marvelous Chinese women in their tantalizing qui pao or cheongsams, the tight-fitting dresses slit to reveal the upper leg, their impassive, masklike faces conveying a purposeful sexual attitude as they strode rapidly on some assignation as deliriously scripted as Robbe-Grillet's *La Maison de rendez-vous.* The gleaming destroyers and cruisers remained at anchor in midriver amidst the chaotic traffic of sampans and junks, in full view of the Bund, while the drab workhorses of the navy—the

LSTs and LCDs, the cargo vessels, ships lacking glamour—tied up at the Whangpoo docks next to PT boats and an occasional submarine. Officers in starched whites, with a virginal look of satisfaction, as if they had just received priestly absolution for all past shortcomings, were striding along Nanking Road. The Seventh Fleet was a veritable food emporium, much of it destined for the sidewalks of Broadway, where the stacked American supplies, the cumulative packaging feat of the midcentury, everything advertised in those glossy magazines *Time* and *Life,* went on display in its original wrappers and boxes only days after the fleet had docked. How could Germany or Japan ever have contemplated defeating the U.S.? One need only buy a pack of Wrigley's or Camels or the *Saturday Evening Post* to acquire one of the icons of this powerful nation. Unlike Europe's, America's history was far more agreeable, for it accommodated Walt Disney and Donald Duck . . . Even the LSTs and Liberty ships presented an enticing invitation.

Overnight, the Japanese seemed to have vanished, though the moment the vast armada, the conquering fleet, some of it already rusting and ready for the scrap heap, made its presence felt, a number of the more brawny Germans and Austrians in our community, seeking redress, somehow ferreted out several of our former Japanese captors, including Ghoya, whose unpredictable conduct as the official in charge of issuing passes out of the ghetto made him by far the most feared and detested official. Anything—it might be the most innocuous response to one of Ghoya's unexpected queries, or the composed bearing and dignified appearance of an applicant—could trigger Ghoya's rage. A short, stocky man, Ghoya displayed a particular animus to tall men—on occasion, working himself into a lather, he'd step onto his chair in order to more easily reach the applicant's face, which he'd slap repeatedly. There was no end of stories circulating of Ghoya's oddities. An amateur violinist, he was known to visit refugee musicians and play chamber music with them.

There exists a photo of Ghoya just after he had been roughed up by an avenging group of young Jews. As if to gainsay the black-and-blue marks on his face, evidence of the pummeling he has received, Ghoya tries to smile as he stands stiffly at attention, holding his hand in a pathetic salute. There's something utterly incongruous about the photo. Divested of power, the erratic former "King of the Jews" seemed to have shrunk, much to the disappointment of his pursuers, into the insignificant petty bureaucrat he'd once been. One of the participants in the beating, an amateur boxer, later disclosed to me almost sadly: "He didn't try to flee or put up any resistance . . . He just stood while we bashed him about."

In those first exuberant days, it was not unusual to see several American sailors goading each other—how to explain this first startling impression?—as each one gripped a rickshaw's handlebars and blithely raced down Broadway with a flustered-looking coolie uneasily occupying the passenger seat. Could these nineteen-year-olds be the victors? It seemed so improbable. Those first few days were memorable as the city, after taking its measure of the "invading" Americans, with the ease of an accomplished courtesan took note of their wants and their so-called menu: Coke, hamburgers, ketchup, and beer. We can handle this, Shanghai seemed to say. After the lengthy Japanese occupation, this was a breeze.

The Chinese laughter conjoined discomfiture and mockery as they observed these overly large yet childlike creatures who seemed to lack an essential Oriental ingredient of manhood—namely, dignity. The word "shame" simply did not appear to exist in the American lexicon. In turn, the city wasn't at all coy; it didn't pretend to be a former crown colony. The guides didn't lead the new arrivals to monuments, estates, or museums; having quickly mastered the essential lexicon, "young girls" and "fucky, fucky," they promptly steered them to a myriad of whorehouses and bars. If no one alluded to China's former greatness, it may have been because Shanghai's rich past was the history of foreign domination—of opium trade and inordinate European opportunism.

By now the Japanese had faded from memory. How quickly they had become yesterday's news! Overnight, the American presence expunged everything I had experienced. With one magic stroke our "European" past had been erased. No loss to me! For the time being, my brain accommodated only American products. What now mattered was the new convertible Buicks, the latest songs on the hit parade, and a series of intoxicating movies—*The Purple Heart, The Ox-Bow Incident, The Shanghai Gesture.* Everything America produced was irresistible, down to the minipacks of four Chesterfield cigarettes or the canned rice pudding with small chunks of pineapple. Yet America itself remained elusive, too vague for me to grasp. I began to devour the best-sellers with a passion. Friends would come over to listen to the songs of the hit parade and programs such as *Duffy's Tavern* on XMHA. Now that all—or at any rate most—restrictions had been lifted, I acquired a lethal knife my mother made me return, a silver cigarette case with an engraved dragon, and a massive silver ring. In my loafers, colorful Hawaiian shirt, and aviator sunglasses, smoking Camels, I was indistinguishable from the multitude of young men who hung out at the Shanghai Race Course . . .

I expended a great amount of energy sneaking past MPs and SPs at the harbor facilities; but then, having achieved my goal of boarding a ship, be it the hospital ship USS *Repose* or an LST or even a lowly PT boat, I was at a loss of what to do next. To me the sailors, mostly good-natured if somewhat bored, still possessed the attractive shine of all things American. What I do recall is their total lack of curiosity. They had no idea of who my friends and I might be and what in the world we might be doing in Shanghai of all places.

In what was to be a final glimpse of the Japanese in 1945, I saw about a dozen of the previously feared soldiers in loincloths only, crouching in that inimitable Asian fashion, as they waited to board a nearby anchored converted LST that was to transport them back to Japan. It was hard to imagine they'd ever been a component of a powerful army.

I wonder if the two Chinese policemen I passed on my way to school, laughingly kicking a bulky package—actually a dead infant neatly wrapped in newspaper and tied with cord—back and forth across the street, were simply passing the time by imitating the behavior of their European superiors, or was this mindless cruelty a grotesque antidote for their sense of powerlessness? No. Of course not. They were simply kicking the package—the content was insignificant—as they might a ball, for recreation, unthinkingly. I still recall the whoosh the package made as it slid over the hot pavement. The ubiquitous package, which was how dead or unwanted infants were disposed of, lent itself to kicking, and they needed a pastime—nothing more, nothing less. I tend to theorize, to speculate too much about motives. Sometimes, motives are simply an afterthought.

Shortly after the war, when I saw Lily once again, I briefly spoke to her parents while she stood some ten feet away by herself. I could not bring myself to walk over to her, and she, watching me talk to her parents, was evidently unwilling to come over. Why did they not call her over? I also met John. He was leaving for England the following day. We spoke a great deal to hide our mutual awkwardness. We spoke of everything but the war years. No mention of his incarceration or our stay in Hongkew. It was as if the war hadn't taken place.

With a group of high-school students on a day trip to Lungwa, several hours by boat from Shanghai, we visited a Chinese pagoda in a dusty Chinese village, then finally settled down for the picnic on a grassy slope overlooking the water. No one seemed put off when a boy I particularly detested, to self-conscious laughter at the prank, obscenely slipped a condom on the large salami, the centerpiece of the picnic. By the time we returned on the small boat, which noisily, and with much shaking and vibration, plowed through the Whangpoo River, it was dark. Leaving the boisterous group on deck, I took shelter next to a girl on a bench inside the overheated, dark cabin. Hesitantly I placed my arm around her. Not encountering any resistance, I slowly, heart pounding, unbuttoned her blouse and then, after further wriggling maneuvers, succeeded in placing my hand on her breast. Not a word was exchanged.

A group of us, all a little tipsy, went in search of Mom's Place, near the racecourse. Having finally located the small building, we boisterously pounded on the front door, calling for "Mom," our voices revealing both our age and inexperience. Finally, in response to our commotion, a young woman opened an upper window and, looking down on us, in a throaty, inviting voice said: "Sorry, boys, there are just the two of us." For a long time, thrilled by her voice and by her acceptance of us as adults, I kept thinking of the woman in the window saying "Sorry, boys"— words that had sent an electric charge through me.

It was around that time that I happened by chance upon a mazelike building in which Chinese jugglers, puppeteers, actors, magicians, singsong girls, and storytellers in long gowns and carrying folding fans entertained the audience, which sauntered from one chamber to the next. Losing all sense of direction, I walked down long corridors, circled a courtyard, then another, now stopping to buy something to eat, now watching a puppet performance, then a man on stilts, then a peacock chained to a table . . . all the while aware that I was the only non-Chinese in the crowd. When I described my experience, my friends showed a complete lack of curiosity. In retrospect this doesn't come as a surprise, for China and all things Chinese were not only excluded from our textbooks at school but also from our minds. I vividly recall drawing the maps of Africa and Australia in class but not once the map of China. I can recall being made to memorize a long list of Israelite kings following the split under King Rehoboam into the northern kingdom of Israel and the southern kingdom of Judea, but not once did I hear mention of a Chinese emperor. After all, why study China? The thinking went that one could look out of the window and pretty much absorb all there was to see of China. It seemed as if everyone was quite prepared to overlook China's vast history, its astounding culture, accepting the Spenglerian premise that a society unable to repel invaders was somehow lacking a crucial will and purpose—an inner strength—as a result of which it deserved its fate.

When a friend and I stopped in the entrance to stare into the large, gaudy-looking Chinese dance hall, two men at a table beckoned us to join them. As a lark, I waved back. When they kept on beckoning, we joined them at their table. Speaking a broken English, both pretended to know us. At first I thought it fun to go along with the charade, but the effort at small talk soon became taxing. When the band struck up, my friend and I, along with dozens of young Chinese men, headed for the long line of dancing girls in slit dresses daintily perched on tiny three-legged bamboo stools. The young woman I approached didn't have a single word of English. It was a relief not to talk. Dancing on the crowded floor with the doll-like Chinese woman became an ordeal as well, once it dawned on me that payment was required, since I had no idea of how or where to obtain the necessary tickets. After thanking the dancer, I made my way back to the table. I couldn't tell which was the more arduous, dancing or the contrived conversation. At the deafening sound of the orchestra we dutifully set off for one of the two gigantic dance floors. When I chose the same expressionless doll-like girl with too much rouge on her cheeks, she looked resigned. Back at the table I said that we had to be leaving. Our quasi-host promptly said that they would be leaving as well. The evening was not over, since we all took the same tram. Our polite exchange sounded like an English lesson for beginners: "How old are you?" "Do your parents live in Shanghai?" "Do you speak French?"

Several years after the war my father discovered that Phoebus, his full-time sales representative, was also working for one or two of his competitors. "Do you intend to let him get away with it?" stormed my mother. When my subdued-looking uncle arrived for what was to be their last business meeting, he was not invited into our place for coffee. For over an hour he and my father remained closeted in the office down the hall. I didn't see Phoebus again until his departure for Australia. At my mother's suggestion, we met at a nearby street corner, although it would have been so much more convenient to say goodbye in one of the neighborhood cafes. But my mother would not, under any circumstance, sit down with Wally. We shook hands, with my uncle, my unpredictable uncle, somewhat anxiously gazing at my mother, not knowing if she'd permit him to kiss her goodbye. But then, once they were apart, once there was not the slightest chance of their ever getting together again, they entered into a lively correspondence. "My fondest greetings to your husband and son," wrote Phoebus somewhat formally. Had he forgotten my name? I referred to him as the black sheep because to my mind it conferred on us a special status. Knowing Phoebus, he would have been amused. Perhaps that is what he had in mind all along. "Is it true," I asked my father, "that Phoebus was less than upright with respect to the business?" My father, while he did not deny it outright, simply laughed in response—to my ears, an embarrassed laugh.

Among the many photographs I have of my family, there is one of my mother in a dressing gown, one arm affectionately placed around my father's shoulder; the other, partially resting on the railing of our balcony on rue Prosper Paris, gently pressed against his lower chest. He—his short-sleeved shirt buttoned to the top but without his customary necktie—looks faintly embarrassed. Where was I when this photograph was taken? Who took it? It invalidates so much of what I have described. Did they feel a need to keep their affectionate relationship a secret from me? But why? Or is my vision of them so hatefully distorted?

I no longer recall how I came to find myself in the somewhat shady company of a small group of gamblers . . . One was a jazz musician; another, with the build of a prizefighter, had just had a run-in with an American sailor, who in a fight over a woman (what else?) broke his nose with one solid punch. They played poker, while I, delighted to be in their company, intently listened to their laconic conversation. Uncritically, I soaked in their experiences, their black humor, their inventive curse words, their sardonic descriptions, absorbing their toughness . . .

"I warn you," my mother said, seething with anger after she discovered a condom in my pocket, "if you come down with a venereal disease, it's off to the hospital with you. You won't stay another night under our roof."

There were no less than three movie theaters, the Broadway Cinema on Wayside and the Wayside on Broadway along with a third just off Ward Road, a few blocks from our house, the name of which I don't recall. Remnants of another age, they were run-down and, except for Sundays, poorly attended. I'd select a seat in an empty row light-years from the proximity of others. As the house lights dimmed, we stood up for the Chinese national anthem, which I can hum to this day. Sitting through a double feature of *The Purple Heart* and *Blood on the Sun*, I wondered if under similar challenging circumstances I'd measure up? In the gilded theater lobby, on display neatly arranged under glass, were the Hershey bars, O'Henry bars, and Rocky Roads. In addition to the local fizzy orangeade there were Coke and 7-Up. And always, filling in the background, neutral, noncommittal, non-threatening faces as inscrutable as wallpaper. I'd enter the movie emporiums in the full glare of a Chinese afternoon to emerge after dark, always mildly unsettled by the transition. Walking home, still dazed by the exploits I'd watched on the screen, I felt like a space traveler returning from another dimension, not completely reabsorbed into the drab world surrounding me. Mentally, I braced myself for the reality awaiting me at home.

In all my reading at sixteen I had not yet come across the line: "Je est un autre"—I am another—a line by Rimbaud that was to strike me with the force of a sledgehammer. At sixteen, I was nonplused when a kid I hardly knew, revealing his hatred, angrily accosted Betty, the only girl I knew with a sexual history—in my presence, no less: "I don't care who you go to bed with, as long as you don't sleep with *him*. If you do, I'll break every bone in your body." I couldn't begin to understand why he threatened her and not me! What was he to her? She to him? If I avoided her hence-forth, it was not so much out of fear but out of embarrassment: I hardly know him but he hates my guts.

My farewell to Shanghai . . . timorously ringing the doorbell of an imposing town house on Soochow Creek, diagonally across from the post office—a former merchant's residence. Who had given me the address? I persuaded a friend to accompany me. At sixteen it was not the kind of journey one undertakes by oneself.

To my relief, having passed scrutiny, in itself a kind of test, we were admitted into the large drawing room, which was cluttered with bric-a-brac, underscoring not only refinement and wealth but a kind of decorum. Weren't the tapestries, paintings, tall statuettes, all of dubious origin, like so many cherished icons, there to reassure the visitor: a home away from home? The severe-faced White Russian lady who came to greet us eyed us critically. To her right, the curved white marble staircase with its gleaming banisters. Our exchange was limited to a few words. Mercifully they sufficed. A sixteen-year-old was not yet polished in these matters. What time was it? Afternoon, of course. Movie rather than brothel time. The time at which sixteen flourishes. The Chinese servant led us into a long, narrow, bright-red-wallpapered room to the left of the stairs. Four docile, doll-like young women in sleeveless Chinese costumes entered and stood in a line, not moving a muscle, while the madam remained a censorious presence in the doorway. To my left, reaching to the ceiling, were glass vitrines filled with tiny objets d'art—gifts from appreciative clients? Not wishing to dawdle, I chose blindly. I followed my selection upstairs. At the far end of the corridor a Chinese servant, squatting on his heels next to a portable vacuum cleaner, didn't look up. The bedroom was antiseptically clean. Nothing in it encouraged lewdness. By comparison with the parlor below it was almost chilling. I took note of the electric shaver, to me another potent American emblem, next to a hairbrush on a pristine glass shelf in the immaculate bathroom, to which the door was wide open. I was reflected in a number of large mirrors. The woman, not wasting time, lay down, taking extreme care not to muss her elaborate hairdo. She pulled up her beautiful robe, exposing her slim legs and waist. She wore nothing underneath. With a petulant expression she listened to me nervously ramble on about myself—the way one does in a dentist's chair in order to postpone the treatment. The elongated tilted mirror facing the bed depicted a partially undressed, slim Chinese woman. I glanced at the mirror, at her slender, smooth, ivory body, overwhelmed by a feeling of unreality and, worse yet, a sudden, decided lack of desire . . . The only sound the woman made was a cricketlike *tsk-tsk* of impatience. Afterward, I comforted myself with the thought that it was the visit, itself an accomplishment, to this luxurious bordello that mattered. Not that I had gone there for the interior, for the museum effect, for the history. When I finally walked down the carpeted steps, the madam stared pointedly at her watch, to indicate disapproval, while my friend, with a puzzled smile, misconstruing my lateness, asked: "Whatever took you so long?"

Everyone was leaving—everyone anticipated the stormy conclusion. Soon, any day, Mao's army would materialize. This time, however, the Chinese forces wouldn't resemble the long, ragged, undisciplined army columns I'd observed shuffling into the city in 1945.

A week or two prior to our departure a friend and I stopped at a sidewalk shooting booth on Wayside Road. It was noon; the sun was out. People, mostly Chinese, unhurriedly walked past as I took aim with a pellet gun at one of the colorful targets in the ramshackle booth. I had no reason to fear an attack from anyone. When I was grabbed by the throat from behind, I let out a yell and furiously jabbed the person behind me, convinced that my assailant was someone I knew—finding it inconceivable that a group of young Chinese would, without provocation, attack me so close to the heart of the European quarter. All my prior clashes with Chinese boys had been peculiarly stylized. On the one or two occasions I had been attacked on my way to school, the Chinese boys would invariably advance, screaming "Tang, tang!" one open hand rigidly extended, challenging us to respond in kind, while we, my school friends and I, after gaping uncomprehendingly at what to us might as well have been a ritualized dance, ignorant of the appropriate response, settled the matter energetically with a few effective punches . . . Now, while being assaulted in a decidedly untraditional Chinese manner, I saw my friend glancing over his shoulder as he scooted away for dear life . . . Presumably, with the imminent arrival of Mao's army, my attackers considered my aiming a rifle an act of sheer provocation. After trading punches, I managed to extricate myself, only to be pursued up Wayside Road, all the while conscious of the incongruity of being chased like a thief caught picking someone's pocket. Near Chusan Road I made a dash for a middle-aged European couple standing in the entrance to their house. Letting myself into their small front garden, I approached them with my not unreasonable request. Didn't they resemble my family? Out of breath, I explained my predicament, while my pursuers, their hatred polished to a fine gleam on their faces, stood expectantly at the garden gate, awaiting the outcome. I was not yet accustomed to such a reversal of roles. To the rear of the couple, in their hallways, I could see the stacked wooden crates with their names and destination stenciled on them, indication of their impending departure. In the genteel, cultivated voice of a lady from Berlin or Vienna, a voice that still resonates in my ears to this day, the woman not only asked me to leave ("Sie können nicht hier bleiben!") but at the same time seemed to reproach me for placing her in such an awkward predicament. "Five minutes is all I need," I pleaded. "They'll soon be gone." Emphatically she shook her head. "Sie müssen weggehen!"—a statement meekly echoed by her husband as he retreated into the house. "These men wish to beat me up," I said plaintively as she followed him inside, shutting the door in my face. All this while people were passing by, a few casting curious glances in my direction. But no one lingered, no one offered to intervene.

Having withdrawn with the dexterity of conjurers, the European couple left me no option but to exit as well. As soon I swung open the low metal garden gate, I was once again enveloped in the warmth of the three men's angry embrace—I could taste their rage on my lips. After another exchange of blows—in that close proximity, each of my frantic punches landed on target—I broke free, bolting down the road, barely conscious of the retaliating hits, racing toward Chusan Road, the center of our shrinking enclave, where my pursuers finally gave up their pursuit. I was so cowed by the incident that I didn't leave the proximity of our house for days. I couldn't even bring myself to mention the assault to anyone—suddenly, to discover myself to be the enemy!

A friend showed me a photo of his cousin lounging on the beach in Tel Aviv, a Sten gun in his hand. It was the weapon that held my attention, not the houses in the background or the scruffy-looking beach. At sixteen I was inordinately captivated by weapons. I may not have had an idea of what Israel looked like, but to me the photo of the young man casually holding a Sten provided an essential and promising piece of information. It seemed as if we were traveling to a country where it was essential to carry a weapon . . .

I was a few days short of seventeen when we left Shanghai. The Chinese on the street were already wearing their padded winter garments. The city we were leaving still retained a foreign presence. However, the number of large ships in the harbor had dwindled. There were still the few naval rejects, LSTs and Liberty ships, along with a number of rusty merchant ships, at anchor in the vast harbor. All the Japanese POWs had been repatriated, and the gleaming white hospital ship, the USS *Repose,* was long gone on some distant goodwill mission. Despite propaganda to the contrary, the Chinese Red Army was inexorably drawing closer. There was markedly less activity on the Bund—fewer lines of chanting coolies loading and unloading the barges. Still, the city presented an appearance of normality. Everything still seemed to function: businesses were open, and so were the banks and government offices. Foreigners were still to be seen—looking introspective, as if on some demanding personal mission. The ending—an outcome one could only dread—was drawing near. Defeat was in the air—it coexisted with a denial that anything had changed. Yet, as everyone awaited the Red Army, one could reason: But there are still the movies, the trams are running, there's food, there's electric power . . . Even the Kuomintang officers were still to be seen, though in their tailored uniforms with the exaggerated wide epaulets out of a Viennese operetta, they didn't inspire confidence. It was common knowledge that the Kuomintang, perennially short of cash, was selling its U.S.-made weapons to Mao. As for the wealthy and the Chinese ruling class, they did what the affluent and powerful customarily do in any crisis: namely, flee pell-mell, in this instance to Formosa, soon to be renamed Taiwan. We'd still stand when the Kuomintang national anthem was played in the movie houses, but no one was deceived. Think of it—a peasant army under Mao that had never been to a city this size would soon arrive, to gawk at the colorful displays in the windows of WingOn and Sincere, the two largest department stores. This time there was no attempt, as there was prior to the arrival of the Americans, to spruce up the bars, the dance halls, the brothels. In our immediate area the money changers, more brazen than ever, were openly trading on Chusan Road. The price of the U.S. dollar kept rising by the hour. Trying to beat inflation, I invested all of my capital and acquired $3.35.

At the time we left China, the then still unknown French photographer Cartier-Bresson was framing the retreat of the undisciplined Kuomintang forces in his Rollei's viewfinder, photographing Chinese officials coolly, imperturbably practicing tai chi on the grounds of the Imperial Palace days before Nanking, then still the capital, fell to Mao's advancing and now unstoppable army. Only a year before, impelled by a deep dissatisfaction with my life, I sought out the *Life* magazine photographer in Broadway Mansions, hoping to persuade him to take me along as his assistant on his trip to the interior. What would I have done if he had agreed? Along Nanking Road one could still see the occasional tall, blond, leggy wives and companions of American officers entering and leaving the Palace Hotel. By then the Little Club was closed. It wasn't just the winter of inflation, of successive defeats of Chiang's army; it was the rout of America, which despite its overwhelming power could not sustain Chiang in power—could not sustain the level of corruption.

Late in December 1948, my parents and my grandmother and I boarded a converted Liberty ship with an Italian crew, bound for Israel. To avoid passing through the Suez Canal we circumnavigated Africa. On the final stretch, from Italy to Haifa, we transferred to two smallish freighters. For several days we endured a rough crossing, made worse by the lack of food. The young kibbutznik in charge of the passengers tried to describe Israel to me. Whenever I passed his cabin door, hearing from within snatches of Hebrew folk music being played again and again on a portable record player—the music, if nothing else, filled me with a longing for a similar dedication, a similar purpose, a similar unshakable sense of identity.

THE WRITER

Vienna

I walk along Mariahilferstrasse
looking for Mariahilferstrasse
I'm on Mariahilferstrasse
and I can't find it.

THOMAS BERNHARD

For a longish stretch that afternoon there were just the three of us in the dining car of the train from Würzburg to Vienna. Intermittently a train, speeding in the opposite direction, would pass with that singular pulsating high-pitched sound, offering a glimpse of someone, not unlike myself, seated by himself at a table in a snug identical dining car with the tiny shaded lamps on each table incongruously aglow in the daylight. There was something oddly reassuring and tranquil about these lights. A touch of home? Our dining car steward had retired to a distant corner, where he was dolefully gazing out at the landscape we were whizzing past—the late-afternoon sun casting a reddish tint on the pastoral setting that stood out, rich with meaning, like some transcendent picture from the remote German past. How familiar is it? I kept asking myself as we headed for the Austrian border, trying to imprint on my mind the particular shapes and clusters of rustic farm buildings along the way, the better to identify the distinct differences, if any, between rural Germany and its neighbor, Austria. Somehow these differences mattered.

I was returning to Vienna, I kept reminding myself, a city I hadn't seen since I left it as a child in 1938, and now, after ten hectic days of traversing Germany, I was on the lookout for anything that might enable me to elicit a memory, or at least an affective response—if only in order to view myself in a different light, in an Austrian context.

The conversation of my fellow travelers, which I at first listened to with only half an ear, sparked a memory of sorts. It seemed to be the kind of genial exchange that can only take place between strangers who will in all likelihood never set eyes on each other again. Soon, intrigued by the exceedingly personal account of the storyteller (whom from his speech I took to be Viennese), I gave up all pretense of reading Thomas Bernhard's *Beton,* a book I had picked up in Frankfurt. In fact, this large, rather sloppily dressed man, with his verbal excess, his self-deprecating humor, might just have stepped out of one of Bernhard's later novels. The other man, really a study in contrast, was less forthcoming; but then his role was that of a listener. Everything about him— his somber gray suit, his briefcase, his polished shoes—attested to a businessman. The metal-frame glasses lent his elongated face a peculiarly severe look, though now and then, out of an apparent need to encourage the storyteller, he'd smile, a chilly, unsettling smile. From his speech I placed him somewhere in northern Germany—but German or not, how could he resist the verbal flourish and the sheer storytelling inventiveness of his Viennese companion? Ah, it was a fine Viennese performance. Isn't *plaudern*—chatting—something at which the Viennese excel? How the two had arrived at such an intimate exchange is not difficult to surmise, relaxed as they were in the gently swaying dining car, smoking and drinking wine. The storyteller kept returning to a subject that evidently held a great fascination for him—and well it should, for he was talking of nothing less than his daughter's simultaneous affairs with two (as he characterized them) almost interchangeably good-looking and pleasant young

Viennese men, one an architect, the other a musician, though neither, according to the persuasive storyteller, was especially successful or in any way outstanding. Bemused, as if something kept eluding him, he shook his large head in comic bewilderment, unable to stop toying with his daughter's amours. "Alone her organizational ability to keep one lover from discovering the existence of the other is worthy of an Einstein," he said, and then asked rhetorically: "But why does she persevere? Can't she make up her mind?" When the listener interjected to inquire if his daughter was actually sleeping with both men, the storyteller, annoyed to have the flow of his story interrupted, nodded brusquely to indicate yes and then, in that inimitable ironic and bantering tone, resumed where he had left off. He was able to hold the businessman's undivided attention as he was holding mine, because he had the Viennese gift of gab, the rich, pliant Viennese language enabling him to shift back and forth from irony to seeming candor, from self-deprecation to ridicule, until the "hypnotized" listener simply confined himself to an intermittent, agreeable "ja" in order not to obstruct this limitlessly diverting flow of words. How and why this event was familiar I cannot say, but it was. It was light-years removed from anything I had experienced in my two weeks in Germany. I knew I was approaching Vienna, a city of misleading intimacy, a Vienna that is vividly imprinted in my imagination. I didn't know what to expect.

We arrived late. At that hour the cavernous station I had last seen as a child accompanying my parents as we left Vienna in December 1938 was empty and desolate. The taxi driver, a man in his sixties, who drove me hell bent down deserted, totally unrecognizable, dimly lit streets to my hotel, perhaps alerted by the Viennese traces in my German, inquired: "Ihr erster Besuch?"— Your first visit? If I didn't answer truthfully, it was because I had no wish for a prolonged exchange—you might say, a familiar exchange.

In a sense, from the moment I arrived in Vienna, the city of my early childhood, the question How familiar is it? was continuously on my mind. Given my exceptional alertness to every sound, to every vibration, everything I encountered, from the impersonal desk clerk at the hotel, who had handed me a message from my friend the Swiss writer Jürg Laederach, who was waiting for me at a nearby bar, to the chummy group I found seated at the table with Jürg in the bar's Art Nouveau interior, evoked a pleasant sense of the familiar. I expect it was, above all, the inviting language, the melodious Viennese, that triggered my response. By its very softness, by its inviting lilt, it is a double language, in which most of what is being said cannot—must not!—be taken for granted. Vienna is the very antithesis to Germany, for everything in Vienna retains an odd mix of humor and understatement. Even a slight—I emphasize "slight"—Schadenfreude cannot be ruled out. I admit I felt excited, as if at any moment I'd stumble across some vital piece of information, an essential truth to which my recurring sense of the "familiar" was key. So, from the moment I joined Jürg Laederach, who was deep in conversation with his friends, a gallery owner and an interior designer (they were discussing—"dissecting" would be a more accurate term—a friend's disastrous love affair), I felt as if I was resuming a conversation I'd left off some time before. One could almost say I felt at home.

A day later, I sauntered, as if unaware of my destination, from the Kärtnerring near where I was staying toward what had at one time been the center of my awareness, the location where—for me—everything of significance had originated. Unhurriedly I passed Zollergasse, where my father's business had been located. Sitting at one of the round marble-topped tables at the nearby Cafe Aida—had it always been in that very site?—I observed a matronly-looking lady who minutes earlier had arrived by taxi and now, with motions of practiced refinement, was fastidiously consuming two Viennese specialties: first a generous portion of *Apfelstrudel*, followed by an elaborate concoction of chocolate smothered in whipped cream. A familiar world? How could it not be? Even her tiny felt hat, worn at an angle, a small rectitudinous fortification intended to discourage all advances, marked her Viennese respectability and virtue. I ordered another *grosser Brauner.* A familiar world? One could slip into it so easily. An unruffled and calm, if not serene, world. One could easily spend hours in the cafes. The city was full of agreeable, out-of-the-way retreats that offered Gemütlichkeit. Comfort was uppermost in the minds of the Viennese.

I proceeded up Mariahilferstrasse, stopping to examine the contents of a shop window or gaze at a church I vaguely remembered—all time-delaying tactics to postpone my arrival at the house at Königsegggasse 2. To my dismay, the houses and stores lining Mariahilferstrasse—even the large department store Gerngross, once the pride of the area—looked worn and neglected, the gray, dusty facades covered by a historical fallout of ages. Had the street always been so run-down? Hadn't they spruced it up a bit for Hitler's exuberant entry into Vienna—for Hitler had traveled the length of Mariahilferstrasse on his way to the frenzied reception awaiting him at the Hofburg and Heldenplatz, to the heart, *das Herz,* of Vienna? With the aid of a large foldout map I finally reached Esterhazygasse. Moments later I found myself staring critically at the building on the corner of Königsegggasse. Though the house in all respects resembled the house in which I had spent the first years of my life, it also, in some indefinable way, failed to do so. Examining it carefully, I searched my memories, if only to extract from my past some detail to illuminate this long-delayed return. At length, mildly unsettled, unable to activate any strong emotional response, I walked away—only to return for another look. Finally, almost dutifully, I photographed it from several angles. If anything, I experienced a satisfaction at feeling so indifferent. It was just another house! As my eyes scanned the row of windows on the third floor, I located the windows of my former room, from which, unless I am greatly mistaken, I had followed with hypnotic attention the careful motions of a man across the street who, like a trapeze artist, precariously balanced on the narrow window ledge, one hand clutching the window frame, risking his life to suspend from between two windows the celebratory banner that reached all the way down to the first floor: the black swastika, that already ominous emblem, tiny by comparison with the enormous red-white-red banner prominently occupying the center of the elongated white area. Is there in that house, where the tenant on the fourth floor had overcome such hurdles to hang out the banner, still some trace of that event? A memory of his zeal? Of his exuberance? A recollection of that day, shortly after the Anschluss, when the gaily fluttering banners up and down the street signified for Austria—above all, for this unique city— an exhilarating moment in history, an unprecedented moment of joy? Everyone seemed caught up in the fever. The annexation by Germany may well have been viewed as an opportunity to finally shed some of that Austrian ambivalence with respect to pleasure and convert the Austrian skepsis, the elaborate courtesy, the nuanced exchanges, the bureaucratic indirection, the slight deviousness, into a reenergizing of the society.

The house in which I spent my early childhood isn't all that far from one of the huge reinforced concrete flak towers that to this day loom menacingly over the immediate neighborhood, the few remaining scars on the tower's exterior providing the only evidence of a period of intense antiaircraft activity, with the converging Russian, French, English, and American aircraft crews posing, among other things, a linguistic threat to the viability of the German language. The incongruously large, gray, slablike flak tower on the edge of Esterhazy Park, where I used to play as a child, reminded me of the early Magritte that had hung in the living room of my former publisher J. Laughlin—it showed a hilltop village in the midst of which ominously opaque cubes, spheres, and pyramidal shapes towered over the tiny, naively painted red-roofed houses and church spires, their alien geometric presence defamiliarizing the quaint village. This Viennese flak tower, which also served as a bomb shelter, 150,000 cubic meters of hardest reinforced concrete, was too massive to be demolished without endangering the houses in the surrounding area. Hitler had planned, after a final victory, to face the colossal structure with black marble, transforming it into a war monument. A sign

on one wall—"This object is being administered by the Bundes-
baudirektion Wien, Telephone 92 39 92"—conveys a bureaucratic preciseness. What else to call it but an object? Presently,
plans are under way to transform the edifice into a luxury hotel.

At dinner with Jürg and several Viennese writers in the small
neighborhood restaurant with the improbable name of Oswald
und Kalb—popular for its *Knödel, Beuschel, Schinkenflekerln,*
even the *Aprikot-* or *Powidl-Palatschinken* and *Kaiserschmarn* I'm
so fond of—I found myself seated beside Dorothea Zeeman,
who, in her just then published autobiography, *Die Jungfrau und
der Reptil,* went to inordinate length to detail her affair with the
late Heimito von Doderer, a prominent Austrian writer whose
intricately plotted two-volume novel *The Demons* I had read
when it first appeared in English in 1960. Doderer's colorful past
included two years during World War I as a POW in Russia, a
doctorate in medieval history, and an early membership in the
Austrian Nazi Party until he resigned in 1938, that is, until the
Anschluss. In *The Demons,* set in the Vienna of 1926, the long-
winded narrator, a retired civil servant, maintains a journal to
which a group of his congenial Viennese friends, are recruited to
make their own contributions. What had struck me then as
familiar were the indolence, the slow-moving passage of time, the
occasional grotesqueries, the whiff of seduction, and, throughout,
the seemingly overriding need for bodily comfort.

In Dorothea's autobiography, the mildly grotesque, the teas-
ingly revealed intimate details resemble Doderer's own writerly
approach. Would he, her mentor, her lover, have approved? After
sleeping with Doderer, she recounted the celebratory occasion in
her apartment, where she showed him off to her friends, mostly
fellow artists, writers, along with a former lover or two. Given
Doderer's conservative politics, the outcome shouldn't have come
as a surprise. Doderer, a spectral figure from another world, was
outraged by her seeming duplicity. He accused her of bringing
him face-to-face with his sworn enemies. Was all of this Viennese
sleight-of-hand? Now that Doderer was dead, she couldn't resist

twitting her former lover, the "master" who seemingly was a captive of his own overwrought baroque imagination, by disclosing how Doderer, magisterial in his long dark silken robe, tied her hands to the bedpost, proceeded to whip her with a silk whip that inflicted no pain whatever, and, more to the point, left no imprint.

In vain I kept looking at Dorothea Zeeman, who combined the flirtatious with a matronly dignity, for traces of that particular past. Somehow, our wide-ranging conversation never once touched on Doderer. Instead, inferring my fondness for Thomas Bernhard, who is the antithesis to Doderer, she spoke a little dismissively of Bernhard's *Lebensmensch,* life's companion, a woman some thirty years his senior. Like most Viennese I've met, she also spoke a little derisively of Bernhard—as if being Viennese entitled her to this point of view. For the Viennese believe they see through him and his ever-complaining, peevish, self-justifying, self-immersed "I," which dominates his every book, be it novel or autobiography. Bernhard doesn't fool them one bit. Dorothea implied that Bernhard wrote with the intent to shock, though she conceded: "People are fond of him since he's got *eine gute Goschen*"—such a fine mouthpiece.

Woken by street noise at seven, I shut the huge double windows and, my head awash with things I intended to do, unsuccessfully tried to go back to sleep. I hadn't even begun my search for my cousin George. In all, there were seven Georg Fischers listed in the Vienna phone book. After eliminating a carpenter and a plumber, I was left with five possible telephone numbers to call—hardly an onerous task. But now—when it was so simple, just a matter of a few calls—I delayed it. How odd.

The Stefansturm bells were pealing endlessly when I passed. The cathedral was packed. To the sound of organ music and a youthful choir, wafting incense, a somber-faced procession solemnly proceeded up the center aisle toward the brightly lit altar with a magnificently red-robed bishop holding a miter in the lead. How different could this be from the pageantry that preceded it for hundreds of years? The choir sang:

Auf Zion hoch gegründet steht Gottes heilge Stadt,
Daß sie der Welt verkündet was Gott gesprochen hat.
Herr, wir rühmen Dich, wir bekennen Dich; denn Du
Hast uns bestellt zu Zeugen in der Welt.

(On Zion built on high stands God's holy city
To proclaim to the world what God has spoken.
O Lord, we exalt you, we avow you; for you
Have summoned us to witness in the world.)

The varnished, age-old wood floors in the Kunsthistorisches-museum creaked at every step. Holbeins, Breughels, Cranachs, Dürers, and Tintorettos competed for one's attention. I was reminded of Bernhard's novel *Alte Meister* (Old Masters), in which the fractious first-person narrator, Bernhard's alter ego, recounts the daily visits by an elderly musicologist to the Kunst-historischesmuseum, where for hours on end he sits in seclusion gazing at Tintoretto's *White-Bearded Man.* In essence, the novel offers Bernhard yet another opportunity to evaluate taste and once again, not unexpectedly, to disgorge his bilious views of Austria as a truncated pygmy state and its citizens as living a lie. When it came to Vienna, Bernhard was incalculable. In *Beton,* for instance, Bernhard asserted that, unlike other cities, Vienna failed to reciprocate the affection it received. Yet, didn't Bernhard (admittedly in an earlier novel) write: "For me there isn't a nicer place than Vienna and the melancholy I feel and have always felt in the city . . ." Was it the presentiment that he might drown in its melancholic "sweetness," its nostalgia, its supreme comforts, that compelled Bernard to resist Vienna by every means possible?

On the spur of the moment, using a wide-angle lens, I photo-graphed several buildings in the vicinity of the Graben, manag-ing to include in the photo two young men perched on the curved ledge of a fountain at the center of which, gracefully ensconced on the vertically grooved pedestal, was Cleopatra, with one fetching breast exposed—ah, alluring Vienna!—to the asp encircling her right hand, while she, as if oblivious to the danger, serenely gazed at the emperor's former residence. In a playfully ironic voice, a voice quite alien to Germany, one of the sixteen-year-olds inquired why I would wish to photograph those monstrous buildings across the street. "Deswegen," I replied. That's why. And the young man, discerning in my fatuous response a challenge, instantly remarked, condescendingly using the familiar *du* to establish a false intimacy: "Du liebst das Schirche, net wahr?" You love the cruddy, isn't that true?

After a visit to Shakespeare, the English bookstore on Sterngasse, I sauntered through the deserted former Jewish ghetto, one of the oldest sections of the inner city. Predictably, there was a Judengasse and a Judenplatz, where in 1491 Jews were slaughtered en masse. It doesn't require much imagination to re-create in one's mind the sounds that must have emanated as a result of this carnage. The nearby Gestapo HQ, another source of acute pain, has long ago been demolished. Seeing a policeman armed with an Uzi in front of a building as neglected and shabby as its neighbors, I crossed over for a closer look at what turned out to be a synagogue. Just then a young woman stepped out of a side entrance. To my inquiry if the synagogue was open to the public, she replied, "Not since the recent bombing." At her suggestion I pressed the buzzer for further information, taken aback by the overtly suspicious, thickly accented voice of—was it a guard?—who, in response to my question, brusquely stated that the synagogue was open Saturdays only. An abrupt click terminated any further exchange. Around the corner another policeman, identically outfitted with bulletproof vest and Uzi, showed a like indifference to my presence. Given the historical context, the large sign advertising Levi's over a clothing store near the Judenplatz appeared mildly incongruous. In this setting, that once often maligned name, Levi, now evokes a pleasing image of blue jeans and hip clothing instead of that ever potent caricature the Jew.

Dr. Franz Richard Reiter at the Rundfunk after an interview spoke candidly about the then popular Austrian chancellor, Bruno Kreisky, a political juggler and picture of contradictions. "He represents a kind of Jewish mania. He used to be a friend of

Wiesenthal; presently he courts the friendship of Arafat and Khadafi." Though Kreisky had lost relatives in the concentration camps, he had few compunctions in recruiting former rank-and-file Nazis in his bid for power. He referred to them as the New Democrats. Politically, as leader of the Socialist Party, he created an alliance with the then dominant postwar People's Party. All the same, Kreisky enabled hundreds of thousands of Soviet Jews to pass through Austria on their journey to Israel.

The one true moment of elation came when I set foot in the Belvedere. It was easily more than ten years ago that I had spent the better part of an afternoon in the New York Public Library reading about the garden in the profusely illustrated book by G. A. Jellicoe, an English landscape architect. What was it about the Belvedere that made it so meaningful? Was it the metaphysical intent—the delineation between the upper, formal and the lower and more labyrinthine garden, each level under the domination of its respective palace? Even though I had not come to Vienna primarily to see what Jellicoe referred to as the most perfect examples of baroque gardens in Vienna and perhaps in all of Austria, it was an added inducement—it breathed life into my journey. To be sure, I wouldn't omit Schönbrunn, the Staatsoper, the Stefansturm, all elements, as far as I was concerned, of my *temps retrouvé,* but I expectantly approached the Belvedere (was it really on account of Jellicoe's masterful presentation?) not as a visitor in quest of an idealized past or an admirer seeking a reentry into present-day Vienna, but as someone who was aware that this specific garden might, it just might, provide a mnemonic center of gravity, a kind of black hole, in which an encounter with oneself could not be ruled out.

As I slowly proceeded up the central gravel path, passing the weather-worn sandstone figures of partially draped gods and goddesses set back, almost concealed, in the niches of the tall, wall-like clipped maple hedges—here a goddess holding a sword aloft while keeping one perfectly shaped leg coyly extended, there two mythic figures, the male of the pair holding a rooster—I felt like a participant in a staged event, a timeless occurrence, for everything in Belvedere's exuberant design seemed as vital as the day it was constructed by Hildebrandt and Girard. Everything, from the remoteness to the alluring symmetry, annunciates taste— taste that stands supreme. It is taste rather than the unreliable play of emotion that is playfully threaded into the design, taste that governs the dynamics of the gardens as well as the design of the upper and lower palaces. In essence the high intelligence of the garden provided an elaborate exercise, a diversion for people, randomly walking, sitting, reading, a vivid record of their often capricious choices, in which what mattered was not the measured duration of life but how one moved in relation to everything else.

I was reading *Beton* slowly to make it last. I kept it in my jacket pocket along with a notebook that was filled with observations of my recent German trip—really sparse notes, scribbled late at night, when I forced myself to write, or during the day, hastily, out of a sense of duty, because the notes might come in handy at a later date—not because they provided me with the slightest satisfaction. I did not derive any pleasure from writing them and, in fact, could barely bring myself to decipher what I had written so far, though this proved necessary if only to maintain a kind of continuity. Once I crossed the border into Austria I stopped writing altogether. True enough, in my notes I referred to the conversation I overheard in the dining car on the train ride from Munich, but hardly a word about Vienna itself. It wasn't a deliberate omission. Now that I'm here, my childhood memories have become less relevant. My visit to Vienna has reduced their significance.

On my return to the hotel, I found the maid had conspicuously placed on the night table next to the bed a German magazine folded to the page on which advice on how to tip in Vienna was provided for the German travelers visiting that city.

In addition to an interview or two, there was the reading at the Shakespeare bookstore. To my delight, there was a large turnout. On my last night, Hans Haider, the newspaper editor, and I drove to Grinzing, the locale of the Heuriger, where the new wine was celebrated annually. I was fatigued and somewhat downcast after meeting so many people, and Grinzing was the last place on earth I wished to visit.

The first place we drove to was shut, and so was the second, an equally bleak restaurant. Clearly this was the wrong time of year for Grinzing. Haider, however, remained optimistic. He had set his heart on showing me Grinzing. The only restaurant that was open, a huge place, was empty and uninviting. I hardly had time to study the menu when Haider apologetically explained that he had forgotten his wallet in the office. A Viennese comedy? In course of our conversation, I mentioned the paucity of reviews in Austria of my novel. He replied that his colleague had reviewed *How German Is It*. To mollify me, he added: "What we first have to do is introduce you to the Viennese public." He then suggested that I write a short impression of my visit for his newspaper, though, sensing my reluctance, the editor, with a kind of graciousness I have come to associate with Vienna, politely hastened to reassure me: "It needn't be favorable, you know!" During dinner I referred to my meeting with Dorothea and to Heimito von Doderer's novel *Die Strudlhofstiege,* only to be informed that the steps actually existed. Returning from Grinzing, Haider obligingly made a detour to drive me to the Strudlhofstiege. Once there, he led the way past a small fountain set in the wall, the water spurting from a fish's open mouth, the plaque close by bearing Doderer's evocative poem about the ornate steps, and so eager was he to show me the steps that he raced up one side of the decorative double flight of Art Nouveau steps, two steps at a time, waiting briefly in the dim light from the ornate turn-of-the-century street lanterns for me to catch up at each of the three levels and gaze down at the charming view below, a view marred only by the car he had parked aslant in the middle of the tiny cobblestoned square, with its headlights ablaze, its doors incongruously wide open, so that it imparted a somewhat ominous surrealist touch. All the same, the double steps communicated a nostalgia for the past—was it the faded, somewhat musty past Doderer so skillfully evoked? And yet, wasn't there something distasteful in that revival of the past—a necrophilic touch?

Undeniably, there was something about Vienna that, like a soft, inviting bed with an eiderdown blanket, encouraged one to take a brief nap—for just a few hours or a lifetime. By a twist of fate it could happen that one entered a cafe as a young man to reappear, having consumed an innumerable number of pastries and cups of coffee, aged though still unblemished. One need only scan the entertaining but utterly trivial articles on the court life of Maria Theresa or Franz Joseph in *Die Presse,* written as if they were present-day events, to become aware that the terror of history didn't lie heavily on this city—it was merely a convenient frame of reference that enabled me to ponder how I might have spent the next ten, twenty, thirty, or even forty years in a certain house, in a certain district, under the omnipresent shadow of a flak tower, had my parents decided to return to Vienna, something they briefly, ever so briefly, contemplated.

Israel

From the Carmel, the repeated canon salvos in celebration of the 1949 armistice added an unexpected theatrical component to our arrival. Now, at the culmination of our journey, having circumnavigated Africa to get here, most of the passengers standing on deck seemed to have nothing left to say to one another. After hours of idly waiting for permission to enter Haifa harbor, the panoramic beauty of the scenery was lost on us. Frankly, not having received any food other than a can of sardines and one inedible biscuit each, we were starving.

On our arrival, several members of Betar, the rightist youth group, anticipating special attention, declared their membership to the officials inspecting our passports, not realizing the extreme unpopularity of the then disbanded Irgun Z'vai Leumi and anyone associated with the right wing. To their bewilderment, instead of receiving favorable treatment, they were promptly dispatched to an army base. The wounds were still raw. Ben-Gurion's orders to immobilize the SS *Altalena*, the ship carrying 900 immigrants and weapons for the Irgun, was recent history. The stranded vessel could still be seen from the Tel Aviv promenade when I arrived.

When we finally disembarked, Rudy, a classmate who had preceded me to Israel by barely eight months, was the first on

hand to greet me. In a startling transformation, the once recalci-
trant student who sat unnoticed in the back row looked amaz-
ingly fit in his air force uniform, sporting lieutenant's bars on his
shoulders. How does one become a lieutenant in less than eight
months? I wondered. Rudy was exceedingly reticent when it
came to his life in the air force. He took it upon himself to show
me Haifa a week after we had settled in Ra'anana, a small community south of Tel Aviv, introducing me to several pilots, all
volunteers, who now that the fighting was over were making
plans to return to Canada, South Africa, and England. How
could I fail to respond to their camaraderie? I was seventeen,
aglow with adventure.

The first words that greeted us in Ra'anana were in Yiddish:
"Es geht regnen!" My mother, doing her utmost not to be discouraged, sought to draw a positive conclusion from every sighting: "Look, cows. Look, a factory"—as if, given these essentials,
life couldn't be all that dismal.

I saw no reason to doubt the Israeli captain who, having
come to Ra'anana to photograph the new arrivals from Shanghai,
mentioned a vacancy in his unit of the army press corps the
moment I expressed mild interest in becoming a photographer.
Without hesitation, I accepted his offer of a lift to nearby Tel
Aviv and a bed for the night the moment he promised to arrange
a job interview the following day. For me, the encounter only
further substantiated the encouraging impression I was beginning to develop of Israel. Admittedly, in my eagerness to get away
from Ra'anana, I was solely thinking of my own immediate
future. Though the captain's attentiveness as he invited me to
accompany him to a huge press party on Hayarkon Street, then
to a restaurant on Allenby, and finally to a movie seemed a trifle
excessive, it never crossed my mind that someone at least fifteen
years my senior, a former navigator in the RAF, was going out of
his way to please me. When he casually inquired if I had a girlfriend, my "no" was emphatic. Mentally, I was preparing myself
for the job interview. For me, the party he took me to in the press
building I was to visit regularly years later, the dinner in a restaurant I never entered again, and the movie on Allenby Street were

a somewhat strained interlude. I was on my best behavior. Later that night, in his tiny photography studio, I accepted at face value his nonchalant explanation that he only had a double bed. This was Israel. I couldn't help noticing his pistol on a shelf within easy reach above our heads. I wondered if it was loaded. Our conversation was mainly about World War II. I peppered him with questions about his role as navigator on a bomber in the RAF. In bed, having turned the light out, his initial approach was so torturously slow and furtive, inching toward me only to withdraw the instant I edged away, that for what seemed a longish while, as I was trying to fall asleep—partly, I suppose, because I didn't want to believe it—I wasn't entirely convinced if that's what it was. Finally, I crawled out of bed, explaining that the bed was too crowded. In a way, life is uncomplicated for a seventeen-year-old. Looking irate, he produced a folding bed from beneath his double bed. Five minutes later I was fast asleep. The next morning, not having given up on the interview, I was quite prepared to dismiss the incident. It didn't dawn on me until the captain stated that he didn't have any time to see me at his office that there was a stipulation to joining his photography unit.

April 1, 1949. Without a word of my intention to my parents, I took the bus to the army camp near the crossroad to Netanya. Three days later, during which time most of my possessions were pinched, I was transferred to Sarafand, a huge military installation, a city unto itself, with tree-lined avenues, an attractive shopping mall that included a modern two-story swimming pool, and, to my astonishment, several hundred demoralized Arab prisoners from the recent '48 war behind barbed wire, watched over by unkempt and equally dispirited-looking Israelis.

On the first day in boot camp we, the seven "Europeans," were taken aside and bluntly informed by our sergeant not to expect any privileges. At least a third of our unit were recent immigrants from North Africa who were quick to take offense. Unaccustomed to discipline, quick to detect slights, they'd erupt in rage at the slightest provocation. Perhaps the most debilitating condition was the widespread thievery. It was endemic. Mostly trivial items: socks, underwear, shirts, anything that had been washed and hung out to dry. Everyone had to resort to it, if only out of a desperate need to replace a stolen item. Of the Europeans, I was the only Austrian. The German-speaking Swiss was a chemistry student from Zurich; of the two Dutchmen, one was a former lightweight boxing champion, while the other was born in Malaya, where his father, the minister of finance, was executed by the Japanese. The Czech, who was considerably older than the rest of us, was an engineer. The two Hungarians were strikingly dissimilar, one being a moody poet who suffered from recurring nightmares, while the other, Thomas, was a dashing ladies' man, who after his transfer to the tank school was picked by the commanding officer to become his chauffeur.

If I recall my first night on guard duty—two hours on, two hours off—it's only because several boisterous police recruits, in what appeared to be a competitive show of bravado, kept attempting to stab with their bayonets the mice they'd caught and placed in their helmets. Years later, reading in George Painter's biography of Proust a description of Proust's fondness for the "rat hunts" that were organized in the basement of the Hotel Marigny in Paris, I was reminded of the riotous laughter and the squealing of desperate mice that kept me awake until it was time for me to go on guard duty again.

I don't recall the reason for my altercation with several of the North African recruits; all I remember is that my Dutch pal, the boxer, intervened, agreeing to fight them one by one on my behalf. When he failed to show at the appointed time, they hooted derisively: "So, where's that Dutch pal of yours? Is he chicken? He's chicken, claak, claak, claak." When he arrived a few minutes later, having gone to fetch a pair of gloves, his offhand explanation that he disliked getting blood on his knuckles whenever he fought had an instantaneous effect. "Why fight?" they said. "It was just a misunderstanding."

The regimental band struck up a lively Sousa march as we paraded past the visiting British general on what had once been a British army parade ground. Earlier, escorted by our CO and the regimental sergeant major, he had inspected our squad. Briefly, he stopped to speak to me. The CO mentioned that I had grown up in China. When the general asked: "Do you like the food?" the regimental sergeant major glared at me, daring me to complain.

Up to the last moment as we climbed aboard the truck to leave Sarafand I clung to the hope that I was being transferred to the air force. Instead, in the company of some of the very recruits I had kidded that they'd be sitting targets for an array of deadly armor-piercing projectiles, I found myself heading for the tank school in Ramle. It might have been far worse. The so-called rejects were transferred to infantry units in Beersheva.

RA'ANANA

The group of mostly Austrians and Germans from Shanghai, all former city dwellers, were settled in tents until the Swedish pre-fabs could be erected. In this sheltered rural town of chicken farmers, it was the farmers, the small-store owners, the coopera-tive bus drivers who constituted the ruling elite and the Austrians and Germans, such as my parents, who now found themselves to be the impoverished new arrivals. When Erika, one of the German girls, a beautiful eighteen-year-old, fell head over heels in love with a twenty-year-old bus driver who had just been accepted by the Egged bus cooperative, his parents were unalter-ably opposed to the marriage. In those days, an Egged driver was considered a catch. A month later, having sideswiped a truck and demolished his bus—thus ending a promising career—the young man's family was prepared to reconsider their opposition to her. By then, it was too late.

Overlooking the Herzlia beach, less than an hour's walk from Ra'anana, was a deserted high whitewashed enclosure with a minaret inside. What's a mosque doing here? I asked myself. Truly puzzled, I couldn't conceive of an Arab community so close to Herzlia. At the time, the official history of the '48 war was rarely challenged. Now, with the Israeli archives open to scholars, the reexamined history by Israeli historians, such as Benny Morris and Tom Segev, presents a far more plausible, if less elevated, picture of the war.

Much was made of the native-born. People's faces would light up at the mention of the Sabras. Praised for their outstanding fortitude, their inner strength, their lack of selfishness, their stoicism and lack of garrulousness, the Sabras exemplified the shining hope of the society. The Europeans praised the Sabras' stability— their refreshing lack of angst. Even the Sabras' bluntness was regarded as an asset. Clearly, these commendatory descriptions were more revealing of the people who, in an effort to divest themselves of an unpleasant past, derived an incalculable sustenance from them. Frequently one could hear someone assert proudly: "Ani dugri, ani yashar"—I'm straightforward, I'm forthright. In general, discourteous behavior was equated with candor. Politeness, tactfulness were rejected as servile and cosmopolitan— reminders of a disdained European past. Ironically, it was in Germany, in the eighties—the last place in the world that I expected to be reminded of Israel—that I encountered a similar bluntness and lack of tact. Quite possibly for similar reasons: politeness was servile and cosmopolitan!

For a time the black market became a thriving business. Since poultry and eggs were a scarce commodity, Ra'anana, otherwise a nondescript town with one movie house and one pharmacy, became a citadel of lawless poultry activity. All kinds of ruses were employed to bamboozle the inspectors who regularly stopped and inspected all trucks and Tel Aviv–bound traffic. Purveyors of food in Ra'anana would describe the magical storerooms of food the affluent in Tel Aviv had set up in their apartments with the breathless reverence appropriate to a description of the Sistine Chapel. Food was on everyone's mind. When a German Jew invented a passably tasty vegiburger, it made the front page of the *Jerusalem Post*.

RAMLE

The storks perched on one leg next to the main entrance to the army camp added to the unreality. In addition to the tank school, the camp then housed the Seventh Armored Brigade and a small covert air force unit. Each morning a Piper landed on the tiny strip at the rear of the camp. At the entrance gate the guards carried bulky .45's in their holsters. The two World War II Centurions that had played a central role in the '48 war now, like museum pieces on display, occupied a place of honor near the guardhouse. One of the British sergeants who, with his tank crew, defected to the Hagana was promoted to captain. The refitted Shermans, ungainly by comparison to the beautiful silhouettes of the English tanks, were out of sight, housed between tall reinforced concrete walls. The Englishy-looking cottages for the senior officers and their families contained tiny, well-groomed gardens with picket fences. Despite the continuous bustle, the camp—really three separate camps—presented a calm, even reassuring world. Nothing else seemed to exist. There were separate mess halls for officers, NCOs, and privates like myself. Unknown to most, just inside the outer perimeter of the tank school, a local apricot called mishmish grew in abundance.

Bare-chested, bayonets fixed to our Czech-made rifles, standing in two lines of ten men, we faced each other, waiting nervily for the signal to charge, wildly screaming at our opposite number. On this occasion, facing me in the opposing line was a short, stocky man from Turkey. Having the advantage of reach, I deliberately aimed my bayonet at his face, concluding from the way he flinched and dodged that he was afraid. But only three months later, when after some deliberation I turned down an opportunity to join a demolition squad, the short, seemingly timid young Turk accepted and, to my chagrin, became the assistant to the demolition expert I greatly admired.

I was mystified by Ramle. The town was drab, impoverished. In the cafes on the main street sat dispirited-looking, prematurely aged men fingering their beads. Dusty streets . . . now and then, a man leading a mule. I couldn't determine who was Jewish and who was an Arab.

The tank school wasn't prepared for our arrival. Workmen were still installing equipment in the freshly painted classrooms. So, to pass the time as we waited for the instructors to arrive, we were put under the temporary command of a maniacal officer: a captain who, ignorant in matters of tank warfare, drilled us, day in and day out, and—was it for lack of anything better to do?—systematically broke our spirits. In one of our exercises, led by our feverish captain screaming incoherent commands, we invaded the great mosque, originally a twelfth-century Crusaders' church, in the heart of the city, wildly racing around the vast domed interior with fixed bayonets, our frenzied hunt for the "enemy" observed by a lethargic Arab caretaker. It was hardly surprising that by the time the school was finally ready for its first recruits, and Captain Borofsky, a short, feisty, bowlegged, no-nonsense former tank commander in the Russian army, arrived to take charge, our unit, already diminished by several medical discharges, was dissolved. Our former captain disappeared, and most of the men, now considered unfit for tank school, were either trained to become truck drivers or transferred to Upper Galilee to become canteen attendants. Determined to avoid a similar fate, I persuaded the CO of the tank communications unit that I'd be an ideal addition to his unit. By now, having garnered insight into army life, I had no further expectations.

The excitement of a mock war: without exception, the entire tank school participated in the annual maneuvers—the war of the Reds against the Greens. All our armored vehicles, weapons carriers, and jeeps with machine guns mounted in the rear drove out of the camp toward sunset and for several hours, traveling north at a rapid clip, weaved in and out of orange groves and, to the dismay of farmers, occasionally cut across fields of ripe melons. By midnight we slowed down as more and more columns of vehicles linked up with us. Late at night, ordered to halt an approaching column of supply trucks, I gashed my throat on a camouflage pole attached to the side of a tank. Back in the weapons carrier, I felt an inexplicable warm trickle down my chest. At first I didn't realize it was blood. When I did, I wound my scarf tightly around my neck and, hoping that I would not bleed to death, went to sleep.

The column of vehicles came to a halt outside Haifa until daybreak, when we headed for Galilee. A magnificent day. Clear blue sky. Akko in the distance. As far as the eye could see, armored vehicles, trucks, and jeeps. The length of the road, disheveled men in khaki shaving, urinating, gulping down the food in their aluminum mess kits, while a few, prayer shawls and tefillin in place, swaying back and forth as they said their prayers, added to the surrealist picture that spelled out not only a recognizable Israeli essence but also the underlying conviction. It was a maneuver and yet, somehow, it wasn't. As we drove into an Arab village, the Israeli Arabs, long habituated to our military presence, remained outwardly nonchalant as they strolled past our metal toys as if they didn't exist. Had they been informed ahead of time that there would be a maneuver? Or might they assume that the Syrians were about to launch an attack? Several of us were ordered to set up a heavy machine gun in one of the narrow cobblestone streets. The fact that none of us had ever assembled or fired a heavy machine gun wasn't an issue. My one concern was to obtain fresh pita and coffee. Toward midday a driver familiar with the terrain drove us at breakneck speed to a narrow pass in the valley. In the distance I heard rifle and machine-gun fire. This is make-believe, I kept telling myself. Left by the driver at the foot of a steep hill, we couldn't decide in what direction to point the MG. Wishing to dissociate myself from the group, I climbed the hill, exposing myself to rifle fire from our opponents, the Reds. Halfheartedly, I waved to them—and being the fresh recruits they were, they humorlessly responded by blazing away at me with blanks. On our side, no one would have dreamt of returning their fire, for that would entail having to clean one's weapon afterward. More shots. What assholes! I thought. A magnificent view from the top of the hill. To my left the Mediterranean. To my right, the picturesque craggy ruins of Montfort, one of a strategic ring of Crusader castles that protected Akko. Never without a book, I stretched out on the mound and began reading. An hour passed when overhead two lumbering C-16's discharged a file of paratroopers. Despite the mock warfare, the landscape looked so serene. Mesmerized by the spectacle of white chutes nicely silhouetted against the azure sky—were they Greens or Reds?—descending in slow motion, for a moment I didn't realize that the three or four black specks plummeting in a downward curve were paratroopers whose chutes had failed to open. I recall trying to imprint their descent on my mind . . . Two hours later the half-track returned to pick us up. No one I spoke to had witnessed the incident. Once we were dropped off at the village, no one showed the slightest interest in my existence. I had become lost in the shuffle. Walking by myself, I stopped to watch a combined mock infantry and armored assault on an entrenched enemy with several judges, readily identifiable by their red armbands, screaming their heads off as they ran back and forth to tally up the damage inflicted by one side on the other. Without question they were the superstars in this mini drama. Join us, suggested one of a group of soldiers tagged as dead, sprawling on the grass. Several were reading, a few playing cards, all oblivious to the chaos around them. Much too superstitious, I declined and walked on, running into several commandos just back from behind enemy lines. They bragged about how close they'd come to bagging a senior officer—but instead, at gunpoint, they marched back a lowly supply officer, a lieutenant. I ran into someone I knew from Ramle who wistfully said: "If only this was for real." I suppose there was some kind of coherence, some kind of strategy to what to me resembled bedlam.

AHRON

Tall, stooped, exceedingly shy and invariably bellicose, my friend Ahron—resembling a character in one of the more spiteful Evelyn Waugh novels—had come to Israel to join a kibbutz. Ironically, having left England to escape the societal and class restrictions, he became what he had never been before—namely "Habriti," the Englishman.

While we were never close friends, we were allies, and sometimes antagonists observing a temporary truce. For his part, he was censorious of every author I liked. A Francophobe, he considered my favorite Henri Michaux too lightweight, Rimbaud too contrived and decadent, Sartre too Teutonic, and my Spanish find, Lorca, far too colorful and superficial. I revised my opinion after seeing him stop on Allenby Street in Tel Aviv to briefly chat with a street tough who had greeted him like an old friend. Ahron explained that the man, a petty thief, had been his former cellmate in the Jaffa prison. He then divulged his insane attempt to escape from the kibbutz he found intolerable. Not only were the members divisive and unfriendly, but they seemed unified in their dislike of the English newcomer who read Blake at breakfast. Unable to bear it any longer, Ahron, carrying his few possessions, including the volume of Blake, in a small knapsack, slipped out of the kibbutz one morning at the crack of dawn and, having nonchalantly crossed the then lightly guarded border, walked the three kilometers to a nearby Lebanese village. At that time, agitated young Englishmen didn't attract a lot of attention. He caught a local bus to a larger town, where, having exchanged the English pounds he had on him for local currency, he boarded a bus bound for Beirut, unaware that intercity buses were frequently stopped along the way by police on the lookout for dope smugglers. When this occurred, his explanation of why his valid English passport bore an Israeli entry visa was deemed unacceptable, and he was hauled to a nearby police station and accused of spying for Israel. Interrogated for days, until the local police, by then as exhausted as Ahron, dispatched him to Beirut. There, after a further grilling, he was kept in jail until, two months later, the Jewish community was able to make a sizable payment for his release on condition that he report twice daily to the police. Finally, with their assistance, he was smuggled back into Israel, where he was promptly charged with illegally entering a country at war with Israel. He was sentenced to a year; however, after several months behind bars, he was offered a release on condition that he join the army. Given his prior experience as a tractor driver, once he completed boot camp training, he was transferred to the tank school. Having turned down a promotion to lance corporal—I was embarrassed at being seen in Tel Aviv with one stripe—I ended my stint in the army as a private with the duties of a sergeant. As for Ahron, I doubt that he was even offered that much. The army has had long experience in weeding out misanthropes and other recluses.

While I was still in the army, someone gave me the address of a brothel on the Derech Jaffa. I took Ahron along. It was on the top floor of an old industrial building. One entered by a side door and took the stairs, which led directly to what resembled a waiting area with benches at a bus station. The windows along one entire wall gave out on the roof, on the far end of which stood a windowless frame unit with several doors, each leading to an oblong room containing a bed and a dresser. Both of us sat in the waiting area, from which we had an unobscured view of the women, beguiling in their loose, flowing, half-open robes, rapidly walking back and forth from the chambers to what I presumed was a toilet. During their brief absence, as a room was vacated by one man, another would step in. When it was our turn, Ahron stood up, gulping for air, then, with the anguished piercing shriek of an exotic bird, ran for the exit.

One of the women was German. She was slim, elegant, even beautiful. We spoke German. Unsuccessfully, I tried to elicit some information from her. She would just shake her head. I didn't press her. I was quite attracted to her. Once, when I placed my palm, which despite the heat was ice cold, on her breast, she said, "How wonderfully cool," and smiled. To me, this simple comment seemed to demand deciphering.

TEL AVIV

After receiving my longed-for army discharge in 1951, I moved to Tel Aviv, then a city in which people were yet coming to reconcile themselves to the inherent contradictions of, on the one hand, a steadily burgeoning middle class with its concomitant bourgeois values and, on the other, a still upheld and revered left-wing Zionist rhetoric. The Tel Aviv of the fifties existed in a twilight, an uncomplicated period in which the events of the recent past, the 1948 war of liberation and the subsequent independence, functioned as a dividing line between the vatikim, the old-timers, who somewhat defensively glorified the "good old days," and the recent arrivals, outcasts, refugees from North Africa, who, unlike the German Jews, did not even possess an acceptable language. In the ongoing polarization of Sfaradi and Ashkenazi, the taste and sensibilities of an emerging upwardly mobile middle class, then still largely European, was only dimly perceived. The yacht club was still a boat club and the golf club appeared to have been designed solely for the benefit of American tourists.

True, the Tel Aviv I write about is long gone. And the conflict I write about has been superseded by a much harsher discord between the extremist religious groups and the more moderate to liberal secular groups. Zionism (Tzionut), now a hallowed designation, when I served in the army represented bombast and outright blather. Its stated purpose, we'd sardonically maintain, was to obtain needed funds from overseas. The Tel Aviv of the fifties, a raucous, lively, and oddly appealing city I came to regard with affection, had not yet severed its tenuous links to Europe, granted that the European atmosphere that survived in the cafes along Allenby and Ben Yehuda, and in the makeshift concert hall, was that of a prewar Europe. I found its very unsightliness fascinating. The glare of the sun diminished the somewhat raw, combat-zone bunkerlike cement architecture, creating a not unattractive uniformity, transforming it into a city of light and dark, sun and shade. Downtown, many of the protective brick barricades to shield house entrances from sniper fire from Jaffa's minarets were still in place.

My first room, a furnished room, was located in Madame Rothschild's spacious ground-floor apartment on Rehov Hess, a quiet, tree-lined street. I remember her as tiny, sharp-tongued, her French accent somehow adding a precision to what I viewed as her somewhat spiteful, calculating nature. I found her hunch-backed presence unnerving and kept my distance. Somewhere in her distant past a French cavalry officer, a Captain Rothschild, her husband long deceased, in bestowing her his name, provided her with the only link she still retained to that eminent family.

The long, narrow, high-ceilinged room was dominated by a large, ancient bed, a massive chest with three drawers, and a streaked mirror. There were wood shutters on the tall windows that faced the courtyard. Hot water was available three times a week. I expressed my detestation of Madame Rothschild by using her toothbrush to remove the gray hair that clogged the bathtub drain. The narrow dresser with the chipped marble top, on which I heaped my books and on which I occasionally wrote, was set against the window ledge. There was just enough space for a single chair between the foot of the bed and the table. To the left of the chest was a rust-stained washbasin. The room's location, however, was ideal. I was only one short block from the American library, then located in a small villa on Rehov Bialik, where I was an assistant librarian, and a five-minute walk from the Cafe Niza and Rosenheim's antiquarian bookstore across the street from it.

On the white walls of my forbidding room I had hung several large Skira and Abrams reproductions. What was it that made me wish to superimpose on the bleak interior El Greco's austere *View of Toledo* and another, equally exacting painting by Ingres? I had just discovered Mahler's *Kindertotenlieder,* Malaparte's *The Skin,* Sartre's *Nausea,* and the poetry of Lorca and Jacques Prévert:

> *Terrible*
> *Is the sound of a hardboiled egg*
> *cracking on a zinc counter*
> *And terrible is that sound*
> *When it moves in the memory*
> *Of a man who is hungry . . .* *

*"Late Rising," translated by Selden Rodman, in *One Hundred Modern Poems,* selected and with an introduction by Selden Rodman (New York: New American Library, 1949), p. 54.

I scribbled poems into a notebook and tried without much success to keep a journal. I was impatient; I was vastly dissatisfied.
Thomas Bernhard put it succinctly when he stated: "Each person would like to participate and, at the same time, be left in
peace. Since that's not actually possible, one's forever in a state of
conflict."*

Fridays, when the American library closed at noon, I'd return
to my room on Rehov Hess, lie down with a book, and then,
overcome by lassitude, fall asleep, to wake hours later unaware
that it was evening. This happened repeatedly, no matter how
much I tried to stave off sleep. Each Friday, having no memory of
the previous occasion, I'd get out of bed and walk to the window,
still groggy with sleep, swing open the heavy wood shutters to let
in the sunlight, only to discover to my dismay that it was pitch
black outside and that I had lost five or six hours. As I tried to
collect my thoughts, I couldn't even be certain what day of the
week it was. When I finally staggered out into the warm, balmy
night, the streets were deserted and, it being Friday night, most
cafes and restaurants shut. As I walked along Ben Yehuda in
search of a restaurant that was still serving food, I'd glimpse
through open apartment windows families at the dinner table.
Friday evenings drove home my isolation. In the short time I had
lived in Tel Aviv I had made half a dozen friends, mostly older
than myself. Klaus was a violist with the Israel Philharmonic;
Ruth, his girlfriend, was an actress; Bruno, a bank manager;
Max, a graphic artist; Tom, the owner of a music store; Felix
Rosenheim, a book dealer; and Gerhardt, a surveyor. As for Ahron,
my former army buddy, he was driving a tractor somewhere in
the vicinity of Haifa.

My life followed a set routine. Each time the Israel Philharmonic
performed in Tel Aviv, I'd join the dedicated group of music
lovers clustered in a backyard abutting the concert hall and one

---

*Kurt Hoffmann, *Aus Gesprächen mit Thomas Bernhard,* quoted in *Thomas Bern-
hards Häuser,* essay by Wieland Schmied, photography by Erika Schmied (Salzburg
and Vienna: Residenz Verlag, 1995), p. 31.

of the huge wide-open windows that admirably served as a music conduit for the tiny, appreciative, and demanding audience. The accoustics were more than adequate until the intermission, when most of us would loiter near the hall's entrance in the hope of cadging a ticket stub from someone leaving midconcert.

At that time, late at night, if one happened to be in the vicinity of the Tel Aviv zoo, one might hear a lion's roar. I remember walking past some of the newly constructed sterile housing in Zaphon (North) Tel Aviv, the lion's roar still echoing in my ears, feeling as if I were situated in a de Chirico painting. I was reading Dostoyevsky's *Notes from Underground,* swept away by the querulous narrator and the opening lines: "I am a sick man . . . I am a wicked man. I think my liver hurts. However, I don't know a fig about my illness, and am not sure what it is that hurts me." I read omnivorously and indiscriminately, not realizing that what I read in English and German would only heighten my dissatisfactions and doubts. As a writer-to-be, my discontent was boundless.

Two months after our chief librarian, a Miss Davies, was transferred to another USIA library, Miss Anadelle Riley, her replacement, a lanky midwestern American, arrived from Pakistan and methodically eradicated all reminders of the former head librarian. Where the reference library used to be became the periodical room. Where the fiction stacks had been was transformed into the reading area. For several months, during that initiatory purge, I was put in charge of the reorganization. I was her favorite—though that too proved a demanding role. More than once Miss Riley would have me assemble the entire staff in her office simply to determine who might have walked off with her no. 2 pencil. It wasn't a productive inquiry. In marked contrast to the cheerful people at the embassy, Miss Riley defied understanding. Unlike the rest of the victimized staff, I could at least retreat to my periodical kingdom on the second floor. There, far from the conflict downstairs, I presided over a group of budding Israeli scribblers on whom I bestowed unlimited supplies of paper and pencils courtesy of the USIA. One of the regulars, who'd devour the technical journals from cover to cover, had a medical discharge from the air force, where he had built model planes that were tested in a miniature wind tunnel. "I'd spend weeks lovingly constructing a plane to scale," he told me, "only to have it returned days later, smashed beyond recognition, and be told to fix it. I had put all my skill into the plane. One day, I simply refused. I was court-martialed for disobeying an order and sentenced to six months' hard labor. After several weeks of lugging rocks from one pile to another, I had a nervous breakdown and was granted a medical discharge."

I confided my enthusiasm for Salinger's *Catcher in the Rye* to a visiting American professor, who responded patronizingly, "Of course, you're just the age for it." I adopted a dog I found abandoned in the garden of our house, bedding him down on a courier's bag I filched from the library, only to discover that the dog's owner, an elderly lady I had never encountered, lived in the rear of my building.

I lived from day to day with little thought of the future. It was as if my brain couldn't accommodate anything so hazardous. What I most admired in Gerhardt, a former philosophy student, now a surveyor on one of the major highway projects in Upper Galilee, was his virtual disregard of the past and, aside from a meticulous attention to the demanding details of his work as a surveyor, the present and future. I envied Gerhardt's self-sufficiency, his discipline, his intellectual dedication, and, above all, his solitariness.

When the Galilee project was completed, Gerhardt was offered a similar job on the highway project in the Negev. When I asked if he didn't mind being so isolated, he mentioned enjoying the easy camaraderie of the construction crew. On his bimonthly visits to Tel Aviv, he and I would switch in midconversation almost unthinkingly from English to German and back, as if one language were insufficient for discussing the books he had lent me. And yet, though anyone could have instantly determined that we stemmed from Germany and Austria respectively, we never—except on one single occasion—alluded to the past. I don't recall what prompted Gerhardt to mention his getaway from Germany. What I remember is that after his parents had been incarcerated by the Nazis, he was the only one left in the house. Had he been overlooked? He put on his scout's uniform and, having tossed a few essentials into his rucksack, set off on his bicycle from the small town in which they had lived for the Swiss border. It took him four days. Nights he'd camp by himself in a field or in a farmer's barn without arousing the slightest suspicion. The scout's uniform did the trick. When he finally reached the border, he chatted with the German border guards. After a while they ceased to pay any attention to the fourteen-year-old Boy Scout idly cycling back and forth. His opportunity came when they raised the barrier to allow a large lorry bound for Switzerland to pass through. In a burst of speed, pedaling furiously, he raced toward the Swiss side. There he informed the startled Swiss border guards that his family was in a concentration camp and that he wished to join his only remaining relative, an uncle, in Zurich. After waiting for several hours for the Swiss to contact Zurich, where his story was confirmed, he was one of the small number of Jews permitted into Switzerland. He spent the war years in a detention camp high in the Alps. There, for the duration of the war, he first participated in the construction of the camp and then was made the mathematics instructor. After the war he studied philosophy at the Sorbonne. When the Arab armies marched against Israel in '48, he volunteered, seeing action against the Egyptian army in the Negev.

The last time we met, he mentioned that he was considering leaving for Africa. I understood it to be a move into a more intense isolation; clearly, the Negev no longer provided him with the anonymity he seemed to crave. When I first read Kafka's *The Castle,* in which the anonymous K. arrives in a village to claim the job of surveyor he maintains he was offered by the castle, I immediately thought of Gerhardt. I read the book, not sure if it would help clarify the mystery of Gerhardt or if, conversely, Gerhardt's behavior might shed some light on K.'s inexplicable obstinacy.

ALLISON

Is it inevitable that the writer-to-be, variable, inconstant, even disloyal when it comes to obtaining an idea for a story, will view his former friends and lovers as potential material for a future text? After I ceased to be infatuated with Allison, I remained linked to her the way one feels attached to certain fictional characters. At twenty-one, I, the writer-to-be, unable to comprehend the vagaries of Allison's tumultuous existence, divined that her contradictory and impulsive behavior, her very unpredictability, her rich fantasy life augured a promising text-to-be.

After making a sincere though futile effort to locate the book Allison was looking for when she first visited the American library, I asked her out.

At that time she was sharing with two other Englishwomen an untidy third-floor apartment in a ramshackle, war-scarred building facing the then neglected section of the promenade. The second time we went out, I decided to take her to meet Tom, who lived in a huge apartment on Dizengoff.

When Tom mentioned that he was planning a party the following week, it never occurred to me that he had concocted the party on the spur of the moment simply in order to see Allison again.

Later that week, I confided to Ahron, who had come to Tel Aviv for a brief visit, that I was in love, and then, not without a certain misgiving, invited him to Tom's party. To my surprise it was a large, lively event with dozens of Tom's friends. I guess Tom wanted to impress Allison. When I think back, Allison was simply not visible for most of the evening. I saw no trace of her or of Tom. In those difficult, penurious days, Tom must have been a decided catch: alone, the huge apartment, and then there was his music business.

It was past midnight when I walked Allison to her house on the desolate promenade with Jaffa in the far distance. We arranged to get together as soon as she returned from an obligatory stint of air force reserve duty. When Ahron came by to see me in the library, he mentioned in passing that he had decided to prolong his stay in Tel Aviv by a few days.

Each evening, not knowing when precisely Allison would return from her assignment, I'd walk past her house hoping to spot a light in her room. One evening, I ran into Ahron, who I thought had by then returned to Haifa. "What brings you to this particular area?" I asked skeptically. After some prodding, Ahron revealed that he had delayed his return to Haifa because he too was infatuated with Allison. "I realize I don't stand a chance," he admitted. Since I didn't feel I had anything to fear from his rivalry—and, moreover, his infatuation authenticated my own— I suggested that we meet the next evening and then pass her house together.

It wasn't the next night, it may have been the one after, when we finally spotted the longed-for light in her room. While Ahron waited in front of the building, I raced up the stairs, joyfully ringing her doorbell. Her roommate let me in. "Allison's taking a bath," she said. When I announced my presence through the steamed-up bathroom door, Allison asked me to wait downstairs and then, to my mystification, added: "You might run into someone you know."

Ahron and I were standing in the doorway when Tom drove up, dressed to the nines in a pale-gray sharkskin suit, looking incongruously bulky on the small, ancient-looking motorbike he was straddling. Removing his goggles, he stared blankly in our direction, as if at first failing to recognize us. Then, remaining on the motorbike, he stretched out his hand. Neither of us budged. The ten minutes that elapsed were unendurable as the three of us waited in stony silence until Allison, radiant in a white sleeveless dress, swept past with a smile and a perfunctory wave to Ahron and me. Mutely, we watched as she perched herself on the tiny backseat and in a gesture of intimacy, her practiced motions suggesting a familiarity with the motorbike and its owner, wrapped her arms around Tom's bulky waist. Once they were out of sight, once the put-put sounds of his ramshackle motorbike had faded, Ahron and I solemnly shook hands, each going his own way. A conversation about Allison would have been unbearable. We were, after all, still inexperienced in matters of love.

At seven the next morning I was awakened by a vehement pounding on my door. Groggily I opened it to discover Tom, the last person I expected ever to see again, looking fatigued but triumphant, eager to speak to me. Grinning amiably, he announced that he and Allison intended to marry. "Why tell me?" I asked irritably. He explained their immediate need for two witnesses in order to register their planned marriage. "Allison and I couldn't think of anyone but you," he declared. "I believe I have a second witness for you," I replied.

I recall entering Ahron's hotel room and, after peering at his exhausted face, rousing him from a deep sleep. The look on my own face must have resembled the elated expression on Tom's when I explained the reason for my presence.

By the time he and I reached the municipal office on Allenby Street, where Allison and Tom were waiting for us, we were released from our burdensome infatuation. We were freed of any lingering rancor toward Tom, toward Allison. How could we possibly have loved her?

Days later, Ahron came by to visit me at the library. He revealed that he had spent the previous evening with Allison and a group of her friends. She had broken up with Tom, he announced. Before leaving, he casually informed me that Allison had expressed a desire to see me.

Weeks later, when I ran into a business associate of Tom's, he inquired why I never visited Tom anymore.

"After what happened?"

"Oh, you mean Allison? That's long over." He then added matter-of-factly, "She's frigid in bed." Then, earnestly, "Come by. Tom is eager to see you."

"What ever happened between you and Tom?" I couldn't resist asking.

"I was parched . . . ," Allison said, staring at me as if she failed to comprehend the fuss. "I don't see why my asking him for a glass of water as we were making love infuriated him so."

The men I'd see in Allison's company varied greatly. They were young, middle-aged, infatuated innocents or coldly calculating— I'm not certain that she could tell the difference as long as she, the generator of a sexual tension, of a sexual excitement, induced her companion to perform a kind of mating ritual. Yet, nothing endured. The moment the excitement waned, she became impatient. Disenchantment was not only inevitable, it was swift.

My last glimpse of Allison was from a distance: she hailed me from one of the upper floors of the Dan Hotel as I was passing below. Leaning far out of the window, she waved and called my name, yelling, "How are you?" as the face of an American I'd never met but often noticed in the cafes on account of his being wheelchair-bound appeared as if joined to her side, expressionlessly gazing down. Whenever I used to see him, I always had the impression that the small group at his table seemed to be beholden to him. For some unfathomable reason I had formed an antipathy to this man I'd never met. As I waved goodbye to Allison, I had the feeling that my dislike of her companion was reciprocated.

Soon after, on reading Isherwood's *Berlin Stories,* I spotted Allison in the character of Sally Bowles. Years later, reading Capote's *Breakfast at Tiffany's,* I recognized Allison again, this time as the unforgettable Holly Golightly. How could I not have been smitten instantly?

THE GERMANS

If the German Jews have not received their due in contemporary Israeli history, it may be partly their fault. By contrast with the ever expanding, openly striving, garrulously acquisitive upwardly mobile population, the Jekkes* seemed to inhabit a sedate world

*Derived from the German *Jacke,* "Jekke" was a mildly condescending Yiddish term identifying German and Austrian Jews, who despite the humid weather always wore jackets.

so redolent of prewar Europe that it struck many as affected and even artificial. Though Israelis were quick to compliment the Jekkes on their accomplishments and skills, not to mention their integrity, they also inclined to add nastily that in the final analysis little distinguished the German Jews from the Germans.

To some degree that may have been true. Jewish identity was not overly pronounced in the Germanic Dr. Walter Moses, or Dr.-Ing. Ludwig Berlowitz, or Felix Rosenheim, or Rosenkranz—the four men who came to fulfill the role of the authoritative German father I never had, the four who helped shape and color my years in Tel Aviv. Only a few more years and their favorite institutions, their favorite gathering places, their favorite recreations and pastimes would vanish. By and large they were not so much deprecated for their elitism, their so-called arrogance or apartness, as they were caricatured for being inflexible, thick-headed, people who had come to rely unduly on rules and order. They were, perhaps unfairly, considered ponderous, too constrained by formality, rules of conduct, with an excess fondness for "culture," but—as most people were prepared to concede—otherwise trustworthy and dependable in their professional capacity as physicians, dentists, engineers, architects, and businessmen. What they seemed to lack was that undiminished drive, that voracious hunger, that craving for acceptance and eventual success that marked the other new arrivals. Moreover, after surviving the recent '48 war by means of sheer tenacity and single-mindedness, Israelis had come to view the excessive politeness of the Jekkes as a relic of a decadent European world.

FELIX ROSENHEIM

Felix Rosenheim had few pleasures and fewer expectations. On the vitrine in his large, sunlit room, the bust of Goethe overlooked the spartan white interior . . . Next to the narrow cot, which imparted a monklike asceticism, were two bookcases crammed with the books he could not do without. Except for a few papers and his portable typewriter, his desk facing the window was bare. Nearby, on a low cabinet, were the hand-wound gramophone and the ancient 78s, consisting almost entirely of Bach recordings. In order to hone the intellect, personal discomfort seemed mandatory. Whenever I came to visit, we'd listen to the somewhat scratchy recording of Wanda Landowska playing the Goldberg Variations. After each record Rosenheim would get up from his tall stool to solemnly rewind the ancient gramophone and place another disk on the turntable. Sitting on a hard chair in the sparsely furnished apartment, I came to associate my discomfort with a reverence for Bach. I didn't realize that Rosenheim's sternness, his vigilant criticism of my lack of application, my indolence, and what he chose to call my malleable traits represented a fixed and quite possibly by then outdated German ideal.

While working at the American library I'd visit Rosenheim's secondhand bookstore across from the Niza at least three times a week. Generally, I'd spend an hour or two with him after lunch. Speaking German, we never relinquished the formal *Sie*. Once in a while Rosenheim would permit me a glimpse of something he had written; but the poem or typed page of fiction was whisked away before I had a chance to read more than a few lines. His laugh as he removed what I was reading implied that I couldn't possibly understand it. The few poems of his in my possession are composed in the carefully chiseled German of an eighteenth-century writer.

Rosenheim's daily routine didn't vary. In the morning he'd read Goethe; then, after breakfast, weather permitting, he'd walk to his bookstore by way of the promenade. There, uninterrupted except for a few casual browsers and the occasional visitor, Rosenheim would work on his journal and then read one of the newly acquired volumes of Proust. The books in the beautifully bound three-volume Pléiade Edition, small enough to place inside one's jacket pocket, served as my own introduction to Proust. Rosenheim, who from then on was never without one of the volumes, would talk to me about Baron Charlus, Madame Verdurin, and the Duchess de Guermantes as if they were his personal acquaintances.

Now and then he and I would splurge and lunch at the

Cellar, a cozy Austrian restaurant on lower Allenby. While Austria governed the wood-paneled interior with its assortment of stuffed owls, cuckoo clocks, and other kitsch, internationalism prevailed in the shape of tiny English, French, Italian, or Spanish flags on each table. "The Americans no longer come here since they've opened a restaurant at the embassy," one of the waiters declared mournfully to Rosenheim. His green loden jacket and Austrian accent added to the authenticity. It was here that Max Brod, who lived across the street, accompanied by his attractive secretary, frequently lunched. On two occasions Rosenheim had been invited by Brod to read from his writings to a small audience at the latter's apartment. Rosenheim said that Max Brod seemed to react favorably, but he added almost condescendingly that Brod didn't understand his work. As for the audience response, looking decidedly pleased, Rosenheim described them as appearing dazed. "They didn't know what to make of it." Rosenheim also maintained that if he hadn't revealed to Max Brod, Kafka's perhaps only trustworthy friend, his equivocal response to Kafka's writings, Brod might well have helped him find a publisher in Germany. I never questioned Rosenheim's assertions. I knew that to do so would terminate our relationship.

To my disappointment, *Swann's Way* didn't live up to Rosenheim's ardent and evocative description. I found it too dense, too uneventful. Nonetheless, determined to finish reading it, convinced that Proust would illuminate the way, I carried the novel with me as if it were a talisman.

In the fall I took my much-leafed-through *Swann's Way* to the promenade. In the chilly discomfort of the deserted outdoor cafes I had the impression that everything surrounding me, from the empty tables to the dark-skinned North African waiter tending the espresso machine in the back, embodied the melancholic reality awaiting me in the Proust I had yet to read. Each time I happened to mention that I was struggling to read Proust to someone familiar with *Remembrance of Things Past,* they'd smile cryptically, as if recalling a particular memorable and intimate detail—though I couldn't determine if that stimulating detail was set in one of the seven volumes of *Remembrance of Things Past* or had taken place in their own past. A few readers of Proust, for reasons I don't recall, mildly denigrated the author, while others, to my bafflement, claimed to find him amusing. Proust amusing? To me, alas, Proust stayed impenetrable.

One must choose one's influence.

One of the several cafes in the vicinity of Mograbi I frequented, a long, dimly lit establishment, attracted a bedraggled, mostly German clientele who, from their appearance and their working-class dialect, might just have stepped off the stage from a performance of Brecht's *Dreigroschenoper*. What lured me to this cafe? As if to raise the state of unreality, everything in the cafe appeared to take place in dreamy slow motion. To the German-speaking waiters and patrons it must have been crystal clear that I didn't belong—that I was intruding in order to snoop. Ostensibly I went to the cafe to write; but what kind of a story could I hope to elicit from such a profoundly unsettling interior? Not all that far away on Allenby was the Cafe Niza, the seat of bourgeois rectitude, while up the street in the opposite direction was the equally staid Cafe Herlinger, a popular meeting place for journalists until ten a.m., when it was overrun by affluent ladies with time on their hands. I loved those two cafes with a passion, yet it was this shady, run-down cafe with its odd assortment of impoverished, emaciated working-class German Jews, destitution and defeat etched into their lined faces, that unaccountably attracted my interest. As I sat there, writing away in my notebook, absorbing the details, I regarded the cafe and its patrons as the source—my source. No wonder that I came to view the *other* "intruder" in the cafe, a writer like myself, as my rival. I took an unreasonable dislike to his solemn, patronizing air, his ridiculous bow tie, his pedantic English, his steel-rimmed glasses, the perpetual frown on his face, and his outlandish three-piece gray suit. Even the neatly arranged books and notebook on his marble-topped table competed with mine. We must have presented a diverting picture: the two of us sitting in close proximity, writing with a feverish intensity, puffing on our Dunhill pipes, occasionally pensively gazing into the void as we sought inspiration from the unpredictable behavior of the scrawny, often cantankerous patrons—all the while pointedly avoiding each other's presence.

This state of—call it mutual distrust, could have lasted indefinitely had not a mutual acquaintance entered the cafe to speak to my fellow writer, whose name was Bruno, and having spotted me at a nearby table, introduced us. When our introducer left the cafe, our initial exchange—after stealthily observing each other for weeks—was guarded. Neither of us could really provide a satisfactory explanation of why we were habitual patrons in that particular cafe. As if to justify the reason for his business attire, Bruno explained that he came here straight from the bank where he was the manager. Sensing my skepticism, Bruno minimized his job. "It's a small bank," he said dismissively, launching into what interested him—namely, contemporary literature. By the third time we met, in what I took to be an overture of friendship, Bruno revealed that he also worked (if that's the appropriate word) for American intelligence. He didn't go into details except to declare that he was on the best of terms with the head of intelligence, volunteering to put in a good word for me any time I wanted a transfer from the American library to a more challenging job in the consulate. To overcome any lingering doubt I might have, he invited me to visit him at the bank on Rothschild Boulevard. To my surprise, he was indeed the bank manager. Escorting me from office to office, he introduced me to the entire staff, including the youngish bookkeeper, the only one at the bank with a literary inclination. "I've introduced him to Kafka," Bruno declared, whereupon the bookkeeper, grinning bashfully, spoke of the impact reading *The Trial* had made on him. To my stupefaction, not only was Bruno what he claimed to be, he was also, from the little I could see, competent in his job.

From then on we'd meet once or twice weekly for lunch. When I probed him about his intelligence work, he described how he and the head of U.S. intelligence traveled all over Israel to interview newly arrived immigrants from behind the Iron Curtain. Bruno, who was multilingual, would interpret from

Russian, Polish, and Romanian. Though the project was hardly top secret, people in intelligence are customarily not that forthcoming.

After visiting Bruno's orderly and uncluttered office at the bank, I was unprepared for his hotel room, a place far messier and run-down than my own. "I don't have time for a personal life," he stated. "The hotel takes care of my needs—they clean, do my laundry, and take messages. Besides, I spend as little time as possible here."

Soon Bruno's preference for pricey restaurants—usually large, cheerless, and near-empty dining rooms frequented by businessmen and tourists—and his insistence on picking up the tab each time made the encounters burdensome, an obligation. After not seeing him in months, I ran into him not far from the bank where he worked. He looked as if he had just received the worst possible news. "What's the matter?"

"My accountant, the one who reads Kafka, spotted a number of discrepancies in the books," Bruno said with a wry smile. "Someone is embezzling, he informed me, behaving throughout as if he wasn't aware that I was the culprit."

"What did you say?"

"I told him to report it."

"Will the bank inform the police?"

Again the wry smile on Bruno's face. "That's unlikely. I know far too much about their illegal transactions. It's the only way a bank, nowadays, can survive."

"Why embezzle?"

He was surprised by the question. "To entertain my friends. The restaurants, cafes . . . Things add up."

"That's it?"

"I value friendship," Bruno asserted sharply.

Given that Bruno and I frequented the same downtown cafes, the same restaurants, encounters were unavoidable. The next time we ran into each other he appeared to have recovered his former assurance. Looking self-confident, he was strolling down Ben Yehuda with my Shanghai schoolmate Rudy at his side. For a moment I was at a loss for words. My question "How ever did the two of you meet?" must have sounded accusatory. "We met in Aden," Bruno said, explaining that they both had been employed by the Jewish Agency to assist in the migration of Yemenite Jews to Israel.

Over lunch in a small restaurant off Ben Yehuda, from the little Bruno said, I could infer that he had assumed responsibility for finding Rudy a job . . . while footing the latter's expenses. Perhaps it was friendship. On our way out, Bruno admitted that his life was becoming increasingly circumscribed since by now he had to bypass certain streets to avoid the shopkeepers to whom he owed money.

BILHA

Does the writer-to-be view love as the ideal text-to-be?

As a writer-to-be I couldn't have fabricated a more "perfect" affair. After meeting at Klaus's party, Bilha and I ran into each other at the Tachanat Merkazit. She was taking a bus to spend the weekend with her parents, I with mine. By our second encounter at the bus station, I asked if she'd be free one evening during the week. To my delight, she invited me to dinner at her place.

Does the writer-to-be experience as much anticipatory pleasure from the unfolding text as he did at the onset of the affair on which it's based? Bilha's apartment was on the third floor of a brand-new apartment building, the raw-looking exterior of which was as yet unmarked by the weather. If I recall, her apartment had two balconies, one facing identical-looking buildings while the front balcony faced undeveloped land. The huge aquarium of guppies—a gift from her father—standing near a window did little to diminish the overall antiseptic atmosphere. Indeed, everything in the expansive white-walled interior was cool, remote, bordering on the impersonal. A few framed reproductions—an attestation of interest rather than evidence of a strong attachment—provided a certain color. I remember a small watercolor reproduction by Dürer and a painting by van

Gogh near the entrance. The half-empty apartment was an exercise in control—or perhaps I should say "order." In marked contrast, the tight-fitting red slacks she wore stood out as an act of pure bravado. I recall several hours of a somewhat strained conversation in Hebrew. We sat miles apart until after dinner, when we stretched out on the carpet listening to classical music on Kol Israel. Lying next to her on the floor, I was determined to miss the last bus.

Within days of that first visit I moved in, though retaining my room on Rehov Hess. Every morning I timed my departure to the minute so as not to be spotted by any of Bilha's neighbors. The only evidence of my presence in her apartment was a tiny framed snapshot on the aquarium. It was taken by Klaus on his penthouse terrace shortly after I had accompanied Bilha and her class of twenty youngsters on a tour of a nearby bakery. I stopped by to visit Klaus afterward. I recall being deliriously happy.

I introduced Bilha to several of my friends, including Rosenheim. She, in turn, took me to meet Dr.-Ing. Berlowitz, a former associate of her father, who seemed to regard himself as Bilha's guardian. Bilha didn't conceal her affection for the cantankerous engineer, who on our first encounter asserted his authority by reaching for my hand. Gripping it firmly, he turned it to catch the light of a nearby lamp. "You possess a good sense of proportion and a yearning for order," he admitted, while examining it with a dour-faced intensity. "You're flexible, yet, at the same time, immensely stubborn and tenacious. Concerned with abstract concepts, your actions are spontaneous—more likely to be motivated by instinct instead of reason." I tried to extricate my hand, but he wouldn't relinquish his viselike grip. Though almost eighty, he was in good shape, and in the presence of Bilha I had no choice but to endure the lengthy reading. "You're agile and not lacking in stamina." His bushy eyebrows were raised as he waited for my confirmation.

My presence was welcome, if only because there now were four of us to play mah-jongg. I played cautiously, hoping to avoid the "friendly" reprimand, a rap on the knuckles with a wooden ruler, delivered by Dr. Berlowitz with lightning speed.

The fourth player was a pale, somewhat despondent German lady of indeterminate age, who—was it out of a desire to please Dr. Berlowitz?—displayed an almost childlike behavior. In a corner next to the couch, on which his meanspirited dachshund was ensconced, alert to our every move, stood an Art Deco reading lamp with three bulbs, one red, one blue, and one plain. "The colors signal my intentions," Dr. Berlowitz declared in jest. "The plain bulb is for reading and mah-jongg, the blue for relaxation, and the red? Ah, that's for love." The blond lady tittered in appreciation of his humor.

As if to remind me that my place in Bilha's apartment was at best tenuous, any early visitor ringing the doorbell forced me to slip into my clothes and then, as soon as the unexpected friend or relative's attention was diverted, to sneak out of the apartment unnoticed.

At twenty-one, the writer-to-be's ambitious plans didn't rule out love affairs—only marriage.

To all appearances our carefree activities helped obscure our dissimilarity. We concealed our differences. I spoke of everything under the sun except the one thing I considered my priority—namely, writing. In a journal I kept there's evidence that I, fearing a serious entanglement, was trying to extricate myself. How soon was it before I began to stay away—for a day or two, then longer? I hadn't seen Bilha in a week when she rang me at the library and tersely informed me that she was pregnant.

On the first page of a new notebook there's an entry that I'm waiting impatiently for the result of Bilha's visit to her doctor. The fact that I then devote as much space to my futile search for a particular notebook, finally having to settle on the one in which the entry was being made, spoke volumes about my frame of mind.

Days later, presumably after the visit to the doctor, a cryptic two-line entry—"We continue to joke about it. I wonder what she's thinking? I haven't even met her parents yet"—reveals, if not a startling about-face, an abdication to the inevitable that surprises me. By the time Bilha, after a further visit to the doctor, mentioned that she wasn't pregnant, the matter had somehow become moot. I'm struck by how quickly and passively I accepted what only a week before appeared as a quandary—namely, marriage . . . family . . . responsibility . . .

The weekend with Bilha's parents seemed to have made my position irreversible. I fully expected to be grilled by her father. But aside from a few casual questions, I was treated cordially, like any other guest of their children.

I don't know what would have happened had I not lost my job as a result of budgetary cuts. Managing to look grave, the head librarian informed me that the decision had, alas, gone against me. It was decided to keep Edward, the Iraqi library assistant, a relative newcomer, because he was in greater financial need. I didn't believe a word of it. Fortunately, soon after I was offered a part-time job at the USIA.

When I informed Madame Rothschild that I would be leaving the room on Rehov Hess, I could tell that my response to her insistent question "But where have you spent your time?" failed to satisfy her insatiable curiosity. "You're a gambler?"

"No."

"You're a *spion*?" she guessed.

"No."

For some incalculable reason, that explanation satisfied her. She wouldn't give up the idea. The possibility that I might have a girlfriend hadn't occurred to her.

Each day, back in Bilha's apartment, I continue to time my departure in order not to be spotted by any of her neighbors. By the time I reach the Cafe Herlinger at eight-thirty, it's filled with journalists. I take comfort from the familiar interior, heading for "my" table, where I order a three-minute soft-boiled egg, fresh rolls, jam, marmalade, fresh butter, two cups of coffee . . .

Though I'm studying math and Hebrew and attending Technosart to prepare for an architectural career, my heart's not in it. Furtively almost, I write poetry, which I conceal from Bilha. If she were to catch sight of the poems, she'd become even more discouraged. Though we pretend that the growing distance between us doesn't exist, as if by agreement we've ceased to make love, and I no longer ask where she's going when she leaves in the evening. If we have one thing in common, it's an inability to fight. My decision to move to Jaffa takes her by surprise—she even offers to help fix up my new home. It's an offer I decline, at all costs wishing to avoid an encounter between her and Zahava.

JAFFA

Zahava's casual offer to let me move into the then empty Arab house she had purchased for next to nothing in Jaffa's disreputable Shetach Hagadol was providential. It enabled me to disengage myself from Bilha—it would allow me to think things over. Start anew. Write!

After only a brief stay, Zahava, an actress at the Cameri Theater, had become disenchanted with this neglected building she'd bought on an impulse, and with the neighborhood, where by the time she returned after her nightly performance at the theater, the entire quarter was swarming with pimps and unsavory characters cruising for prostitutes or dope.

On the first morning I woke to the sound of bells, startled by their clamor, one bell heavy and deliberate, the others lighter, their resonance out of harmony with the ear-splitting resolution of the heavy bell, its unsettling *boom, boom* digging itself into my brain as I lay gazing at the still-unfamiliar dome-shaped ceiling, struggling to associate the heavy beat with my new surroundings: the empty whitewashed room, the two open windows in the thick walls framing the white expanse of the terrace and, beyond that, the Arab house across the alleyway.

From the roof, surrounded by a profusion of whitewashed terraces and rooftops of buildings, one built perilously on top of another, the only evidence I could see of the harbor's existence was the cement breakwater encircling the fishing fleet, small boats that bobbed up and down each time a boat arrived or left the anchorage. Also visible at the entrance to the port was the cluster of dark rocks, of which, according to legend, the most prominent was where Andromeda was chained—a sacrifice to the Monster of the Sea.

Behind me loomed the massive ochre St. Peter's Monastery, a huge gilded cross glinting above the tower in which the now motionless bells nestled side by side.

My brief and perfunctory inspection of the house—one performed without great curiosity or elation—set a pattern for my future activity. As I stepped into the rooms downstairs, the crypt-like smell of cold clammy walls, decay and putrescence—much like that from dead flowers and decomposing animals, yet more pungent, more penetrating—made me beat a hasty retreat. The odor indicated the presence of something foul beneath all the rubble, layers and layers of it. Having eliminated the ground floor, I similarly excluded the two large rooms adjacent to mine, though in their case it wasn't the result of the clutter: the canvases, books, articles of clothing, the thousand and one items the painter Nissan, the former owner, had left behind—all of which I could have cleaned up were it not for the sudden intolerable itching of my legs. The rooms, I discovered, were a haven for fleas, introduced by the neighborhood cats. Drawing the line at exterminating fleas, I closed the doors of the two rooms, satisfied with the use of the terrace, the roof, the primitive bathroom, and the makeshift kitchen in addition to my room.

Jaffa wasn't a city proper but a vast, unattractive, rubble-filled appendage to Tel Aviv, which I could see in the distance from my roof. All around me, hurriedly evacuated Arab buildings had new tenants. Everywhere I went, dark, inscrutable, uncommunicative, stony-faced people eyed me suspiciously. I couldn't tell the new arrivals and the native Jaffa citizens apart. Unlike in Tel Aviv, everything had an improvisational quality to it. There were hardly any distractions—no movie houses, no bookstores. The few cafes appeared uninviting.

For days I explored the labyrinthine network of narrow, winding streets and circuitous passageways, discovering a short cut to the harbor with its small fleet of fishing vessels by way of the stairs in the house directly across the street, for they were connected to the stairways of the picturesque houses beneath it. From my terrace each morning I'd watch a succession of women—Arabs or Jews?—traipse along the narrow street, a bucket of water, their daily supply, in each hand.

On waking each morning, I'd stare at the ceiling . . . surprised to find myself in the small white dome-shaped room. I've never felt less at home anywhere. Daily I'd spend an hour or two in the cafe on the main square, then drop by to visit the Greek painter whose studio overlooked the harbor. The picturesque surroundings filled me with an unspeakable inertia. Without success I tried to write. Once Rosenheim came to visit. I lied unconvincingly, claiming that I spent my days writing poetry. Every few days I'd escape to Tel Aviv. Only there did I regain a sense of myself.

To my dismay, Zahava rented out the unoccupied space to two Moroccans who maintained they were French and their friend Shosh, a striking Israeli woman. Within a week the trio had disinfected and painted the flea-ridden rooms. Exuding cordiality, and what struck me as an unwarranted optimism, they invited me to dinner. Amitai, the leader, the one who kept the group together, cooked a Moroccan dinner. I marveled at the transformation of the interior. Within a month the three had grown into a community of seven. On weekends there were frequent visitors from as far away as Galilee. Though I was informed that Amitai was madly in love with Shosh, she didn't conceal her interest in women. It was she who informed me that the house was intended for the "homeless." Noticing my look of incomprehension, she repeated the word, smiling as this time she allowed a distinct emphatic pause between "home" and "less." When I hesitated to accept any further invitations, Shosh smiled at me: "Are you afraid we'll corrupt you?"

I kept trying to write, but the interminable bells, the winding streets, my uncommunicative neighbors, the odors . . . served as an impediment. I hadn't anticipated the house in Jaffa, only a twenty-minute bus ride to Allenby Street, to be consistently, almost belligerently unfamiliar.

CAFE NIZA

For years the Cafe Niza, with its Viennese flavor and German-speaking waiters, was my second home. To this day I recall the ingratiating smile of the headwaiter as he sidled forward to greet the regulars: confident, sleek men who displayed their gleaming Ronson lighters on the marble table as if they were IDs of privilege, as they waited with an alert-greyhound look on their lean faces for the arrival of their chic girlfriends—often, married women flashing expensive handbags. Above all, I recall the pleasant Mediterranean lassitude that settled over the cafe once the lunch frenzy was over. In my diary, I recount meeting Bilha at the Niza soon after my move to Jaffa. She remarked that the night before at a dinner party at her uncle's she was presented with a choice between a doctor and a lawyer. She chose the latter. Now that I don't wish to meet Bilha, I noted, I find myself continually running into her.

It was in the Niza, weeks later, that Bilha almost casually confided that she had a lover: the lawyer. When she—usually so reticent, so withdrawn—described her love life in painfully explicit detail, I pretended indifference. It became doubly hard to reveal no emotion since, as we parted, she requested the return of her apartment key. I fumbled for it, then placed my one remaining link to her on the table.

CAMILLA

Ever since Max had acquired the Robot camera and built himself a tiny darkroom, the parties he'd thrown seemed to have taken on a new significance. With the meticulous care Max applied to his graphic designs, he'd orchestrate these events, taking a voyeuristic delight in photographing his guests' uninhibited behavior. The drafting table, the tools of the trade—in fact, anything that suggested work—were swept aside. The lamps were covered, pillows placed strategically on the floor, and a special concoction prepared in a pink punch bowl. Though invited, I didn't attend any of the parties. I only witnessed the preparations and saw a few selected snapshots, the faces of the participants discreetly shielded by Max. In fact, I never knew if Camilla, whom I met at the studio, had been present at one of the events—if, in fact, she might be one of the disrobed women in the snapshots.

I had picked the Kasit to meet Camilla. Unlike the Niza, the Kasit was where the theater-and-art crowd hung out. Concerned that I might not recognize her immediately, I stared intently at every young woman entering the cafe to make sure it wasn't she. I was also preoccupied, trying to unravel the baffling shiny gold band that had hovered in midair in a dream the night before. Whatever the gold band might signify, I intuited that it was connected somehow to Camilla, whom I had met the evening before at Max's studio. The dream continued to puzzle me until, after Camilla's arrival, sitting across from her, I glanced at her hand, detecting on her left ring finger the telltale pale stripe left by a wedding band. I must have caught a glimpse of Camilla slipping off her wedding ring the evening before. "Why didn't you mention it?" I inquired with the innocence of a twenty-one-year-old.

I have a photo of Camilla sitting at my side on Max's couch when the two of us dropped by to see him a week later. Max snapped the picture almost eagerly, using his beloved 35mm Robot camera— a small, bulky, reliable camera which bore a miniature swastika on its silver housing. According to Max, in the German army it was often mounted on machine guns and rigged to snap a photo every ten shots fired. The photo Max snapped of us was something to add to his collection. It's an unflattering shot. He deliberately didn't give Camilla time to prepare herself—to fix her face. We had met only days before, and Camilla was feeling awkward, perhaps even timid, in the face of Max's insistence. At the time, it didn't even occur to me how incriminating the photo might be.

When I introduced Camilla to Felix Rosenheim I dissuaded her from removing her wedding ring. By then the entire theater group knew of her affairs. When she introduced me to the theater's director, he mockingly said "Tidchadshi," a congratulatory word routinely used to compliment the wearer of a new garment.

To Rosenheim's evident amusement, Camilla insisted that I'm *koved*—weighty—the one thing Rosenheim maintains I'm not.

During one of her husband's frequent absences, Camilla accompanied me to Jaffa to stay the night. Next morning I awoke to find her fast asleep in another bed. "You kept tossing wildly," she stated accusingly. Seeing my baffled look, she complained: "You didn't even kiss me."

"Of course I did."

"Not once."

"That's impossible," I protested. "I know I did."

"Not on the mouth!"

For once, I was at a loss for an explanation. I had come so close to disengaging myself from Bilha. We kept on seeing each other for the next few days, but finally, inferring disinterest on my part, Camilla on her way to a rehearsal said that she'd call me. She telephoned to inquire if I wanted to see her. I explained that I was preoccupied looking for new quarters . . .

The Robot camera was not in evidence when I visited Max weeks later. The guests, many sitting on the floor, seemed subdued. And Camilla's impassive husband—the conspicuous other, and perhaps because of it a controlling presence—was sitting by himself on the couch on which Camilla and I had posed for Max. I knew it was he immediately. He was dispassionately surveying the roomful of theater people as if gazing at some alien species. I was drawn to him as one might be toward something that was clearly marked DANGER. I approached and introduced myself. Camilla, I noticed, was seated on the floor, gesticulating and fiercely arguing with a petulant young actor, years younger than she, about the merits of a Chekhov play. Their voices, by far too shrill, sounded as if they were on stage and not just feet away from her seemingly detached husband and myself. He introduced himself, "I'm Camilla's husband," then added: "I'm an engineer." In our conversation, on the couch in the corner of Max's studio, pointedly ignored by everyone present, we discussed the theater as if the topic mattered to us. Yet, since virtually everyone at Max's party was in some way connected to the theater, it wasn't an inappropriate subject. Camilla, still arguing with the pouting young actor, both still tirelessly performing for what seemed to be a disinterested audience, didn't once look in our direction. "Do you know my wife?" the engineer asked, searchingly looking at me. "We've met," I said. It was only when he asked where that I became alert to the danger I was in.

"Here, at Max's." I felt that his suspicion wasn't particularly focused on me but by now was so all-encompassing that no one was excluded. He listened attentively to what I had to say. It was a guarded conversation about nothing. The pipe in his hand had an oddly soothing effect on me. After a debilitating thirty minutes he stood up. He looked at Camilla and her adversary, still going at it unreconcilably. The engineer, eyes slightly narrowed, puffed on his pipe, trying to puzzle out the meaning of it all. Only then did Camilla look up and acknowledge my presence with a curt nod. The engineer extended his hand to me. "I enjoyed our conversation," he said. Seeing that the engineer was about to leave, Max came forward, albeit reluctantly. Camilla stood up and joined us, leaving the sulking young actor behind on the floor.

When the engineer left with Camilla, there was a moment of silence, then laughter—explosive laughter of relief . . . Someone slapped the petulant young actor's back as though he deserved to be congratulated, and he, feeling a need to declare his manhood, smirked while making an obscene gesture that, made as it was defiantly behind the engineer's back, took on an altogether different meaning.

FELIX ROSENHEIM

Felix Rosenheim, a taciturn man, had kept a journal since his arrival in Jaffa in 1936, when he was twenty-four. In essence, it was the journal of a stranger, someone ill equipped to cope with the mental and physical pressures of the climate and the new society. In his journal, the carefully chiseled German prose, the classical German of Goethe and Schiller, conferred upon the content a cool ironic tone. What the irony concealed was the resignation, the lethargy of an aging writer, the eternal European, the uncompromising man of letters, the writer without readers who still hoped, any day now, to be surprised by a long-overdue recognition.

Begun when he first settled in, at a time when Arabs still pastured their camels on the neglected stretch of beach abutting Jaffa's harbor, it was the journal of a man who soon after had picked out his bookstore in the covered entrance to an alleyway on Allenby Street, and nearby, on a quiet tree-shaded Tel Aviv street, his apartment, thereby establishing his boundaries—each day walking from his spartan quarters to his antiquarian bookstore on Allenby and then, in the evening, retracing his steps. His conversation was punctuated by an occasional ironic laugh—a laugh designed to draw attention to the essential incongruities of existence.

Rosenheim never referred to his father—that is, until the latter, without forewarning, arrived in Tel Aviv on a chartered plane from New York, where he had spent many years. Only then did Rosenheim reveal that his father was president of the ultra-Orthodox, non-Zionist Agudath Israel. Unable to get near his father, he watched from afar as thousands of his father's adherents, thronging Lydda airport, greeted their president in an explosion of euphoria: his father, the center of attention for the feverish, shoving, clapping, dancing crowd, their angular, excited Eastern European faces straight out of some fifteenth-century tapestry. After not seeing his father in years, Rosenheim visited him two days later in the commodious house Agudath Israel had made available. He had thought that as president of Agudath Israel his father would wish to reside in Jerusalem; surely Jerusalem would have more to offer him. But for reasons never made clear it was to be Tel Aviv, a city teeming with secular Jews. The party elders had already engaged an architect to design and build a chapel in the garden so that, given his advanced age, Rosenheim's father would be spared a daily walk to the synagogue.

How could Rosenheim hope to escape his father's energy, his father's optimism, his father's success? If he was keeping a daily journal, so was his father. If he was writing a book, his father had published dozens of pedagogical books, critical texts, autobio-graphical books, meditations. Though his name was a dead give-away, there was little chance that he'd ever run into any of his father's numerous adherents and admirers. Nothing would bring any of them to his antiquarian bookstore: not a single German or French title on his shelves would be of interest to these devout followers. Once again, overnight, he was made into something he had struggled to overcome—the outcast. If at their first meeting his father didn't press him with questions, was it not to spare him the embarrassment of acknowledging his lack of success?

DR. WALTER MOSES

Rosenheim encouraged me to see Dr. Moses about the catalogu-ing of the latter's archaeological library, which, along with his col-lection of antiquities, would be housed in a museum the city of Tel Aviv had promised to construct. "Go, see him, he's expect-ing you," Rosenheim said. I obliged him and thus became Rosen-heim's source of information.

Dr. Moses occupied a spacious apartment off Ben Yehuda with a view of the sea. His housekeeper, a gaunt-faced German woman who might have stepped out of one of Dürer's etchings, answered the doorbell. She looked at me with open suspicion as I explained the reason for my visit. As she noiselessly preceded me to the living room, I noticed that she was wearing felt slippers. The huge room, packed to the ceiling with gargantuan stuffed birds in glass cases and colossal pottery from various archaeo-logical digs, was less a living room than a museum to house his eclectic collection. There were shelves of terra-cotta figurines and bronze sculptures. Moses, in his seventies, eyes twinkling, lips drawn back into a smile, stepped forward, hand extended in wel-come. By contrast to the vigilant-looking housekeeper, his wel-come was so warm and cordial that momentarily I had a sinking feeling that he had mistaken me for someone else. Anxious to set me at ease, he invited me to the table set for two. "The perfect servant," Dr. Moses declared with a mischievous smile, as his housekeeper, staggering under the load of an enormous tray, silently entered the room and then, having deposited the tray's contents on the table, exited as quietly.

Dr. Moses poured tea. He had just finished a book by Kazantzákis and urged me to read it. Now and then I caught him looking at me as if studying me. Finally, explaining that several people had expressed interest in cataloguing the library, Dr. Moses took me to see it. One quick glance at the many oversized volumes crowding the metal shelving from floor to ceiling of the large room sufficed to substantiate my apprehension that the scholarly titles in dozens of languages were unlike anything I had previously encountered—certainly beyond my capacity to catalogue. To my relief, the dreaded inquiry into my qualifications was limited to several innocuous questions. Once I stated firmly despite my doubts that I was able to catalogue them, the matter, as far as Dr. Moses was concerned, appeared settled. When I inquired about the salary, Dr. Moses explained that the city of Tel Aviv, which had undertaken to construct the Ha'aretz Museum to house his collection, would also be responsible for the librarian's salary. Then, to allay any apprehension I might have had, he stated, offhand almost: "The job's yours, if you want it."

"I do indeed."

Pleased by my reaction, he indicated that the interview was over. "I'm visiting an archaeological dig in the vicinity of Beersheva tomorrow, and there are so many things I still have to attend to."

The moment I expressed interest in the ongoing excavation of a Chalcolithic settlement by the French prehistorian Jean Perrot, Dr. Moses promptly invited me to accompany him. "Be punctual. We leave on the dot of nine. If you're here at eight, I'll give you breakfast."

Before I left, Dr. Moses led me into his inner sanctum, a small, dark room. Flicking on the lights, he laughed in delight at my expression of astonishment as hundreds of tiny, colorful ancient glass objects crowded on glass shelves were illuminated by tiny spotlights attached to the wall. On closer examination, most, if not all, of the ancient glass revealed explicit sexual motifs: muscular men mounting women . . . Satisfied with my response, Dr. Moses turned the lights off. "Till Saturday," he said, walking me to the door.

I was the first and, as promised, was served breakfast. The others, a middle-aged German gentlemen who was an amateur archaeologist and young Avner, a pimply, bored sixteen-year-old addicted to comics, arrived soon after. On the dot of nine the housekeeper announced that the taxi was waiting for us below. It turned out to be Dr. Moses's exclusive means of transport. I was told to carry Dr Moses's disassembled hunting rifle in a wooden case, the kind more likely to contain a croquet game. Avner, with a look of disdain, lugged two belts of ammunition, while Dr. Moses, a large pair of binoculars suspended from his neck, strode ahead looking very military. We set off, with Dr. Moses in the front seat beside the driver, while the three of us sat in the back, I, the newcomer, squeezed in the center, the gum-chewing Avner to my left and the loquacious archaeologist (who seemed to depend on Moses for sponsorship) on my right.

Every now and then we'd come to a precipitous stop in order to allow Dr. Moses to focus his powerful, weather-worn binoculars on a bird he had spotted. Not comprehending that silence was obligatory, I was rebuked when I continued to speak to the archaeologist at my side. From my brief, cursury introduction to Proust I wasn't as yet able to discern in Dr. Moses the complex and often theatrically erratic character of Baron Charlus.

On a winding secondary road several kilometers south of Beersheva, we halted a few hundred feet from a Bedouin encampment barely visible from the road. The instant the driver honked, a dozen half-naked Bedouin kids came tearing toward us. From the chauffeur's and archaeologist's broad anticipatory smiles I could tell that this wasn't the first occasion. They surrounded our car clamoring for money as Dr. Moses, his face ablaze with excitement, liberally scattered coins, of which he seemed to have a large quantity, out of the window in all directions, intently eyeing the children as they scurried to scoop them up. The archaeologist at my side cravenly followed suit, for to refrain from this harmless frolic might have led Dr. Moses to infer a tacit criticism. Sixteen-year-old Avner merely watched, a grin temporarily displacing his otherwise permanent sneer.

Energized by this Bedouin adventure, Dr. Moses was the first out of the car to shake Perrot's hand when we arrived at our destination, a cluster of prefabs in the middle of an arid, tree-less expanse. After introductions were made, it was decided that before lunch we'd proceed to Bir Abu Matar, the site of the excavations.

"Each Chalcolithic settlement contains traces of several levels of occupation," Perrot explained, as we gazed at the excavated trenches abutting a wadi. "The breaks between one level of occu-pation and the next appear to have been the result of a sudden but temporary abandonment due to years of drought." Then, taking us on a quick inspection of the unearthed settlements, Perrot pointed to an immense round slab that, he explained, had served as a gate, blocking the entrance to one of the settlements. "I'm convinced that when the community left, circa 3500 B.C., they had every intention to return."

At the base camp we were shown several carved bone figu-rines and two finely finished basalt bowls decorated with an incised band of geometric patterns that Perrot explained had been squirreled away when the settlement was abandoned. "From the evidence thus far," he maintained, "the Beersheva cul-ture emerged in the northern Negev quite suddenly, well adapted to its surroundings. Which would prove that it doesn't represent an expansion from the north or its displacement of yet another group."

"And its origin?" inquired Dr. Moses.

"For its origin we have to look outside of Palestine," Perrot said, mentioning similar settlements near Syria.

On our return trip, when the amateur archaeologist at my side made an innocuous comment on the significance of Perrot's excavation, Dr. Moses, turning in his seat to glance sardonically at me, quipped: "I wonder if our nihilistic friend shares your opinion!" When I, at a loss for words, folded my arms across my chest, his condescending smile was supplanted by a look of anger.

Citing the psychologist Georg Groddeck, Dr. Moses complained that by my gesture he could only conclude that I was barricading myself. The archaeologist leaned toward me, whispering irately, "Stop that!"—as if I were an unmanageable adolescent. Even the driver, I noticed, shook his head in disapproval.

I hadn't expected to hear from Dr. Moses again, but apparently he hadn't given up on me entirely, a week later inviting me to accompany him to the opening in Akko of the Municipal Museum, in what was once a Turkish bath built by Ahmed Jezzar Pasha. He intended to leave by ten—breakfast at nine. This time there was no one else present except for Anna, nervously scurrying back and forth between kitchen and balcony. From where I sat I had an unencumbered view of the sea and the promenade, which at that hour was still deserted.

On this occasion Dr, Moses dispensed with the shotgun and binoculars. The chauffeur rushed forward to open the car door for him. As usual, Dr. Moses sat up front. He seemed unusually pensive, not addressing a word to me until we were halfway to Haifa. Then, suddenly animated, half-turning in his seat, he spoke of the Hellenistic influences, describing the mosaics and other Greek decorations, some with pagan themes, that had been found in synagogues.

Throughout the trip he didn't address a word to the driver, though the latter, careful not to express any opinion, seemed to divine Dr. Moses's slightest wish as we sped along the main coastal highway, passing derelict-looking factories, old army installations and refineries, on our way to the city of Akko, jutting into the sea. Once in Akko, the driver seemed to discover his way in the maze of narrow streets without the assistance of a map, letting us off in front of the new museum, where an overflow of guests were blocking the entrance. Several dignitaries hurried forward to greet Dr. Moses. I followed them into the congested museum, past the main hall with its gray marble fountain, staying on his heels as he was escorted from one small whitewashed room to the next. Sunlight filtered through small, round green glass set in the domed ceilings, which on closer inspection proved to be the sawn-off bottoms of beer bottles. Surrounded by the notables of Akko, Dr. Moses was being given the grand tour of the archaeological artifacts, though the displays lining the rooms were all but hidden from view by the crush of guests. Finding my way blocked, I retreated to the main hall, stationing myself next to the fountain to await Dr. Moses's return. It was another half hour before he reappeared and another twenty minutes before he was able to extricate himself.

Leaving the museum, we walked to the large mosque, where, Dr. Moses, after inspecting the many large and small faded rugs on view, spotted one he fancied. In passable Arabic, he inquired if the caretaker was willing to sell it. I couldn't determine if Dr. Moses's ardent interest was feigned or tell from the mosque's care-taker's vacillating response if the latter was indeed hinting at a willingness to sell . . . Deciding not to waste any more time on this shillyshallying, Dr. Moses turned on his heels, heading for the street as if the exchange I witnessed hadn't taken place. We made our way through the souk to the nearby harbor. Seemingly enjoying the commotion in the arcades packed with shoppers jostling one another, Dr. Moses stopped repeatedly to engage in conversation a shopkeeper who had thrust his wares at us. "I come here to practice my Arabic," Dr. Moses explained tendentiously.

The restaurant was within the confines of the ancient harbor. The enormous disintegrating breakwater jutted out from where we sat. At one end stood what remained of a tower, birds nesting on top. Dr. Moses carefully dissected the fish on his plate, chewing each mouthful with a thoughtful expression. The waiter removed our plates, returning with Turkish coffee and baklava.

"Sheer lunacy," remarked Dr. Moses, staring at the breakwater.

"What?"

"When Akko fell, the Moslems slaughtered the Knights Templar to a man. The water over there"—he pointed to the harbor—"was bright red. The few lucky individuals who managed to escape to the galleys anchored offshore crowded into a handful of rowing boats right from where we are sitting. Runciman claims there was such a plentiful supply of women on the market that the price dropped to a drachma apiece."

After dinner we strolled along the citadel ramparts. A Franciscan monk stood at the entrance to the small church along the walk. After greeting him in French, Dr. Moses engaged him in an animated conversation.

On our return trip, Dr. Moses signaled the driver to pick up a hitchhiking soldier, a North African. Sitting next to me in the back, he freely answered each of Dr. Moses's purposeful questions, speaking of his family, his girlfriend, even his plans for the future. As he was getting out of the car on the outskirts of Haifa, Dr. Moses held out his card, inviting him to drop by any time he found himself in Tel Aviv. "One must do what one can for the new immigrants," Dr. Moses declared virtuously.

The last time I visited Dr. Moses, he spoke pensively of his membership in the Blau Weiss, a Jewish nature club in Germany, where he was an instructor. "We wanted to imbue the youth with a sense of fair play and discipline without turning them into automatons." Leaning back in his seat, eyes half shut, he reminisced: "The boys had an uncanny sense of justice. First offenders would receive a warning, but on the next occasion they'd receive a good basting."

I stared at Dr. Moses, an embarrassed look on my face.

"Afterward, we again were the best of friends," said Dr. Moses. "There's nothing like a good lambasting." He stared at me. "Why, even T. E. Lawrence, under far more trying circumstances, mentioned the delicious warmth that enveloped him as he was whipped in Deraa."

"You make it sound like a gratifying experience."

"You are too theoretical," said Dr. Moses censoriously, and I, not wishing to compromise the cataloguing job, remained silent.

Dr. Moses's question "Can you fence?" took me by surprise.

"No," I said, not knowing what to make of his challenging look.

"In the university I was a member of a Jewish fraternity

where dueling was obligatory. At the slightest provocation one might be challenged to duel. We fought with sabers." Asking me to get up, Dr. Moses handed me a cane and, arming himself with a similar weapon, walked to the center of the large room, where, surrounded by the most precious glass-encased objects, he insisted that I stand close to him as he proceeded to instruct me in the fine art of dueling with sabers. The two of us—a bizarre sight among the four- and five-foot-tall glass-encased stuffed birds and the tall Egyptian pottery and figurines—fought a duel of sorts with walking sticks. I was stiff, awkward, and resentful, an easy target for his mockery. Despite his weak heart he swung the walking stick at me with great gusto . . . To my relief our fencing was interrupted by the housekeeper, who, not revealing any astonishment at our behavior, announced a visitor. "Now do you understand what I mean by discipline?" Dr. Moses asked, as he put away the walking sticks. The white drapes billowed like sails.

As I was leaving, Dr. Moses remarked: "We'll have to continue your education." I nodded mutely. By now, I sensed that any hope I had of ever getting the job cataloguing his library was fast eroding. A week later he took off on his annual trip to Europe, where he acquired antiquities. He was known to buy indiscriminately, picking up whatever struck his fancy.

PROUST

Friday evening, on a visit to my parents in Ra'anana, I read nonstop sixty-five pages of *Swann's Way,* perplexed as to why, heretofore, I had had so little success. I read with a growing exhilaration, aware that the insurmountable obstacle of reading Proust had vanished in the face of my persistence. That same night I was awakened by a dull pain in my right side. Was it to fix the reading in my mind? As I lay half-asleep in the dark, the dull pain grew in intensity. My father finally got dressed and set off on foot to fetch the village doctor. By the time he arrived, an hour later, I was writhing in pain. With one smartly delivered whack to my side, he diagnosed a kidney attack and administered morphine. When the pain had subsided, my first inquiry was whether he had read Proust. I was blissfully happy when he said yes—as might have been expected from a German-Jewish physician. I saw my parents exchange glances of astonishment when I remarked to him that the evening prior to the kidney attack I had begun to read *Swann's Way.*

ABC

Before ABC hired me, I was questioned about literature by Herr Popper. I must have provoked him, for he prolonged the inquisition as if determined to prove me inadequate.

To his elderly customers Popper personified the intellectual book dealer, at home in the hothouse atmosphere of the Viennese or Berlin cafe—how else to explain those deeply etched facial lines, the thin, disapproving, downward twist of his lips, and the restless eyes, two sparkling points of inquiry? Tall, lean, with a pinched, emaciated face, he hovered in the rear of the ABC bookstore on Allenby, to all appearances an ungainly and spiteful bird, remote, aloof, discontent: the nose, long, disdainful; the gray locks fastidiously combed over his overly large, paper-thin ears. Yet, Popper was transformed the instant he spotted a "serious" customer. Then, with a tentative smile he'd step forward, his prissy motions synchronized to an invisible metronome. One, two, three, halt . . . The unexpected laugh, a skittish laugh that conveyed no humor, served as a kind of release. Though he considered books merchandise, Popper nonetheless went through the motions of appraising each new title. If Spengler was mentioned, he'd let it be known that Toynbee was in fashion. The elderly ABC clientele would head for Popper who, after expressing his joy at seeing them again, would immediately try to persuade them to purchase an expensive book. However, these stodgy Germans had no money (at least not for books) and, having come in for a tiny illustrated book on bees for their nephew or niece, quickly extricated themselves, to the dismay of Popper, who'd ingratiatingly repeat, "Danke, Herr Doktor . . . Danke,

Frau Doktor," as he walked them to the door, only to grimace the
moment their backs were turned.

With Bilha's assistance I found a huge, sunny furnished room in
the apartment of an elderly couple in northern Tel Aviv. The only
drawback was the overly large oil painting of an eagle perched
on a mountaintop. I couldn't bring myself to ask the owner to
remove the painting, which dominated one wall, since he was the
artist. Still, the room was a decided improvement over Jaffa.
Bilha and I now lived only a few blocks apart. On several occasions, looking out of the window, I saw her walk past.

On his return from Europe, Dr. Moses stopped by the ABC
bookstore. Popper, all aflutter, sold him several pricey art books.
Moses shot me an inquiring look . . . To this day I don't under-
stand why I failed to walk over to greet him. After he had left,
Popper ambled over to inform me with a wide grin that Dr.
Moses had expressly requested that I deliver the books.

"Sure," I agreed.

Popper smiled lewdly. "Well, since you appear to know him
so well, I suggest you do it after hours."

"Certainly not."

"In that case I'll have the delivery boy do it," Popper said
primly.

"Suit yourself."

Two months later I spotted Dr. Moses's obituary in the
Jerusalem Post. I had missed an opportunity to see him for the
final time.

With his Germanic face and military posture, Dr. Walter
Moses was a replica of George Grosz's caricature of the archetypal
German. I think, in his mind, the duel we fought with wooden
canes was meant in earnest. I now regret that I didn't attend his
funeral. He never did get to see the completed museum, on
grounds that encompass Tel Qasila, an ancient mount dating back
as far as the twelfth century B.C. The museum compound con-
sists of eleven pavilions, of which one, a striking circular glass
structure, houses his incomparable glass collection, the largest in

the Middle East. His numismatic collection is located in another building.

BILHA

On two occasions, at night, from behind the cluster of trees on the slight elevation facing the apartment building, I—the jealous lover, like Proust's Swann—eyes glued to Bilha's window, spied on her movements. Once I caught sight of Dr. Berlowitz. The dignified-looking elderly gentleman arrived by taxi, carrying a huge bouquet of flowers. The taxi waited until Dr. Berlowitz, minus the flowers, emerged some twenty minutes later. What prompted him to visit? What occasioned the flowers?

Despite my notation "Tonight was the second time that I stood on the rise facing the house, staring at her window," I attempted to convince myself that I wasn't in the least jealous. "Observing her lean out of the window, I concluded that she was waiting for him. When I left an hour later, she was still alone."

A week later, when I ran into her at the Niza, Bilha with a wan smile of chagrin said that her lover disclosed that he was in love with the wife of his best friend. She mentioned how desolate she felt to find herself mixed up in this triangle, while I, feigning utter indifference, wondered, Why is she telling me this?

FELIX ROSENHEIM

There was a Khamsin on Friday, the day Rosenheim, carrying several packages he had picked up at the post office, absentmindedly left his briefcase containing his journal on a bench on the promenade. The hot, dry winds from the east shrouded the city in a haze, draining it of its color. By the time Rosenheim became aware of the absence of his briefcase, he was in the bookstore. With a frenzied look on his bespectacled and gnarled face, he raced back to the promenade and spent the remainder of the morning erratically traipsing back and forth in search of it, filled with despair at the enormity of the loss—though he still clung to the hope that whoever found the battered, yellowed briefcase containing the thick journal would, after examining its worthless contents, leave it at one of the cafes. When I saw him the following day he wasn't certain if he had left it on a promenade bench or somewhere else. By now he was already devoting every available minute to jotting down what he could recall of the last months—a momentous period in which he had lost his companion of many years, a woman he trusted, loved, and relied upon; severed his friendship with Rosenkranz, a close relationship of over twenty years; and stopped seeing Micha, the young Israeli poet he was inordinately attached to. "I cannot bring myself to discuss what happened," Rosenheim said mournfully. "It diminishes the significance of the occurrence." He did, however, refer to one occasion less than a month before his companion's death when, late one evening, the four of them—the last time the four were to be together—were strolling along the boardwalk, Rosenheim and Micha trailing Rosenkranz and Rosenheim's then already ailing companion. Suddenly hearing a startled cry, Rosenheim looked up to see his companion on the ground. Racing to her side, he recalled a pained look of remorse on Rosenkranz's face. Had Rosenkranz confided something to Rosenheim's companion? Filled with a premonition, Rosenheim attempted to help his friend to her feet, all the while blaming himself for the accident—a blame that struck me as puzzling and inappropriate.

Of Rosenheim's mini circle of friends, Rosenkranz stood out in that he was the only one before his breakup with Rosenheim to openly challenge me. Which was why, trying to overcome what I naively believed to be a problem of communication, I decided to seek him out—to visit him unannounced. I must have sat for over an hour on a bench outside the ramshackle one-story frame building in which Rosenkranz lived, waiting for him to return from work. I could see his surprise when he caught sight of me. Reluctantly he invited me into his long and narrow one-room apartment. Clearly, he was perplexed by my visit. For the first time ever, I seemed to have caught him at a disadvantage.

I was struck by the neatness. Seeing the blanket tightly drawn across his bed, I was reminded of a cot in an army barrack readied for inspection. Rosenheim, trying to explain his friend to me, had equated Rosenkranz with a massive boulder, unyielding, intractable. On our way to a cafe, passing an elderly beggar, I was surprised to see Rosenkranz press into his hand an excessive amount, at least ten times what I'd given. After a few hours together, in which my attempts to break down the division between us met with little success, we parted. I was no wiser than before. In parting, Rosenkranz remarked in German that I must be glad to escape—by that I took him to mean that I was glad to escape his probing of my inconstant speculations. Earlier, as if duty-bound to convey his dictum, he stated that a discussion between two people should evolve into a deeper understanding of oneself and the other. To which I replied that the surest way to obstruct any exchange was to dissect and scrutinize it. "It's impossible to pin you down on any subject," he complained. "Why would you wish to?" I responded mildly. To which he replied: "I don't know what you are about."

When I dropped by to see Rosenheim the next day, he was already apprised of my visit to Rosenkranz. "You mustn't take Rosenkranz too seriously. He had no right to attack you as flexible and evasive. Rosenkranz is self-critical. He's only attacking himself."

Months later, during the period when Rosenheim was desperately attempting to recover the missing material of his journal, I stepped into a jitney cab on Allenby to find myself in the company of a transformed, even jovial Rosenkranz and an equally effervescent Micha. I'd never seen Rosenkranz so animated . . . so verbose. Gone was his customary animus. What had happened to that massive self-absorbed boulder? I asked myself as we chatted of everything under the sun without once mentioning Rosenheim's name. From their easy banter, I concluded that the exuberant Rosenkranz and his radiant-looking companion were passionately in love. It explained the falling out with Rosenheim and the latter's reluctance to speak of it.

I didn't mention my encounter to Rosenheim, who, immersed in recollecting as much of the missing material as possible, day by day appeared to recover his former ironic self. After all, one pro-pitious by-product of his struggle to recapture his past was the added introspective speculations . . .

By now, looking back, I can hardly separate Rosenheim from his journal. Wasn't it a substitute for life?

BILHA

After a year in the army as a language instructor, due to the scarcity of teachers, Bilha was exempted from further duty as long as she didn't change her occupation. However, the moment she expressed a desire to study law, the army claimed that she, still unmarried, owed them a year's service. When she appealed the army's directive, she secured a final six-month deferment, which gave her time to figure out how to circumvent what was bound to be an intolerable year in the company of eighteen-year-old recruits. Yet, after going through her list of acquaintances and friends, hoping that one of them might be of help, she was forced to admit defeat. One thing only could save her—marriage. And that, given the short time left to her, was highly unlikely. As for me, by that time I was no longer in her apartment or in her thoughts.

It was Dr. Berlowitz who, having invited us to dinner, deli-cately broached the possibility of my assistance, after first declar-ing that he had seriously contemplated marrying Bilha himself. "Yes," he repeated, as if to nullify my look of doubt. But, even though he had been a widower for over twenty years, he wasn't able to lay his hands on the documents to convince the authori-ties. He eyed me thoughtfully, as if the idea had only just then occurred to him: "Of course, you—" He chuckled at the very absurdity of the idea, while planting it firmly in my mind. "You, however . . . you might do it." Bilha's face was inscrutable. Why not? I thought. It appealed to my every negative impulse. How could a rebellious young man, a writer-to-be at that, resist such a tempting offer? A marriage in name only. A favor to a friend, that's how I'd regard it. No repayment. That was the one condition I'd insist on. Nothing in return. Isn't that the iconoclastic act of a writer-to-be?

By now the marriage preparations remain a dim memory. The lawyer Bilha had hired, a seedy, disreputable individual, was on hand to orchestrate the wedding. I simply did what I was bid. That's to say, I lied persuasively. On the way to my wedding, sporting my best jacket and a necktie, I stopped to see Rosenheim, the only one to whom I had confided my intentions. Without success he had tried to dissuade me. "It's an unwise decision," he declared. "You'll regret it." Now we simply shook hands.

Wasn't it apparent to the witnesses and the officiating rabbi that the ceremony was a sham? Couldn't they detect it on my face? Furthermore, the absence of our families and friends should have been a dead giveaway. The only indications that a wedding was to take place were the pastries from a nearby bakery, the pile of paper plates, and two bottles of domestic wine on the white-linen-covered sideboard. The presence of our lawyer didn't particularly improve matters. The officiating elderly rabbi must have suspected something was amiss, for he inquired of the lawyer for the whereabouts of our families and friends. The lawyer was an old hand at this. Never at a loss for an explanation, he maintained that we intended to celebrate that evening with them in Ra'anana. Once the lawyer had rounded up the necessary number of witnesses—he brazenly solicited them in front of the nearby Mograbi cinema—the openly mistrustful rabbi proceeded, but in a perfunctory, almost grudging manner, while Bilha and I stood under the chuppa held over our heads by four unsuspecting strangers. Stealing sidelong glances at Bilha, I tried to read on her determined face my own perplexing designs. What on earth was I really trying to accomplish? The odious lawyer handed us a glass of wine, then placed a wrapped glass at my feet for me to step on. As we were leaving, he winked conspiratorially at me—with that wink making everything odious and shifty explicit.

Catching me by surprise, the elderly man who came by the cafe to sell cigarettes, one of the several witnesses the lawyer had corraled for our wedding, would regularly approach me at the Niza and politely inquire after Bilha: "And how is your wife?"

"She's well, thank you," I would reply, suddenly overwhelmed by the awareness that I was married.

"Please convey my regards."

It was months before I paid Bilha my first visit, disconcerted to find that the furniture in her apartment had been rearranged—was it to eradicate any lingering recollection of my stay? Looking around, I could see no evidence of another man's presence. True, my photo was gone from the aquarium, but so was the aquarium, which apparently had shattered, sending a tidal wave of goldfish as far as the corridor.

For over a year, until our divorce, I lived a stone's throw from Bilha's house. We'd see each other periodically. On each visit to her large, austere apartment, while disinterestedly on the lookout for changes, I'd try to behave as if I'd never lived there. I was determined that nothing in the apartment spark a Proustian recollection. Only once, shortly before our divorce, did Bilha unexpectedly signal her availability, when, just out of the shower, for a split second she stood undressed in the bathroom's open doorway down the hall as I, after ringing the doorbell, hearing her call out, "The door's unlocked," let myself in. I don't know if there was any deliberation to my instantaneous response. Did I feel that I was safeguarding the writer-to-be's future when, instead of following my inclination and heading toward her, I stepped into the living room instead?

Munich

Hotel Schlicker. Room 125, the only room available. Austere. View of inner courtyard. A streaked washbasin with hot and cold water that could have been included in one of Joseph Beuys's exhibitions. Bathroom and toilet down the hall. No shower. In the corridor the floorboards creak. In the lobby, an elderly man was talking a blue streak to a bored-looking desk clerk. I heard him say: "Er war ein alter Kriegskamerad von mir. Wir haben uns gedusst. In '44 hat ein Scharfschuessen ihn verwundet . . ." At breakfast the young German woman wearing a T-shirt advertising in bold letters PLATO'S RETREAT, a renowned New York sexual hangout in the seventies, attracted no attention.

Reluctant to ask the desk clerk for directions to Dachau, I walked to the S-Bahn station at nearby Marienplatz, intending to take a train to the main railroad station, not realizing that the S-Bahn trains, albeit heading in the opposite direction, stopped in Dachau. In less than twenty minutes we arrived at the somewhat ram-shackle Dachau railroad station. The local bus, marked Lager, awaiting the train looked equally antiquated. In addition to half a dozen tourists and a handful of locals, all definitely old enough to have weathered the war, the passengers included a class of high-school students and their teacher on their final day in Munich.

The bus shook and vibrated as it rumbled down the broad main street lined with unassuming low houses and stores, stopping frequently to let the locals off. The Dachau camp, its final stop, was the destination for everyone else.

Pointing to the infamous gate that still bears the ironic-sounding precept "Arbeit Macht Frei," the high-school teacher informed his students: "Das war eine Todesfabrik!"—That was a death factory! His voice—a welcome, unequivocal voice of condemnation—was free of qualifications, free of any concern but outrage. It's a voice I had expected to hear more frequently. Walking aimlessly from one site to the next, I kept glancing at the somber individuals diligently reading the multilingual signs, which also listed the precise number of dead entombed there, as if by gauging their muted response I might explain my own inexplicable detachment. Standing at one of the several burial sites, I felt numb, distanced, emotionally untouched by what was in evidence, even though, for all I knew, members of my family were entombed here. Everything was so tidy. Only in the bookstore, as I leafed through an illustrated book on Dachau, did I feel a sudden upsurge of emotion. It wasn't the photographs of the camp, which I had seen countless times, but faces that provoked my response. To think that everything on display would be so sterilized, so carefully scripted, so drained of all possible emotional content that I had to turn to an illustrated book to respond emotionally!

In the smallish crematorium housing two gas ovens I met Kirk Brafford, a fellow New Yorker, who shared my misgivings on hearing a German guide assure a group of German-speaking visitors that the gas ovens were never utilized. I later established that it was the gas chamber and not the ovens that were never employed. The deadly gas chamber disguised as a *Brausebad,* shower room, was erected in 1942 but never utilized, since it was more convenient to send the thousands selected for extermination by gas to Hartheim Castle near Linz.

As we stepped outside, I was made conscious of the many birds twittering in a small cluster of trees nearby. It was a bucolic scene out of an eighteenth-century novel. A cleaning lady, by herself on a wooden bench next to the toilets, was placidly knitting while taking in the sun. Idly I wondered if in the early forties there might have been birds in the trees. The inmates would have appreciated the sound of birds—if only as a reminder. In his memoir *What a Beautiful Sunday!* Jorge Semprun, who was incarcerated in Buchenwald, provided the answer. He stated that the acrid, poisonous stench of burning corpses drove the birds away.

Everywhere in Germany I was woken by songbirds and church bells in a kind of exquisite, Schumannesque coupling. Until recently I considered the declaration "Arbeit Macht Frei" above the concentration camp gates as more malevolently ironic than a solemn avowal. I now understand that the intent was primarily utilitarian. For, given the small number of German and Croatian guards in the concentration camps, the misleading signs were essential to the smooth operation of the facilities. In the death camps especially, the signs were intended to allay the apprehension of the new arrivals. Only the most prescient, seeing the signs that promulgated German virtues such as hygiene and work, would have anticipated gassing within the hour.

Evening, I attend a brass-quintet concert with Kirk Brafford. Several of the musicians were his friends. Later, dinner at Tre Colonne. Never had an Italian atmosphere been more welcome. The owner seemed to know the musicians. I was seated next to Dorotea, a med student, and her friend, an architectural student. I inquired if they too were conscious of what I considered an almost willed sharpness. Everything appeared to be so brittle . . . the surfaces, the faces, conversations. Yes, Dorotea agreed. At some point one is made aware of it. One's parents are. One's friends. One is as well. Well, she added, I have an English boyfriend. And my three sisters are going out with Englishmen or Americans.

Jorrit de Boer—guest professor of nuclear physics—drove

me back to my hotel. He was being put up by the university in a villa, once the home of an affluent Jewish businessman. During the war it was occupied by the SS; subsequently it housed several families of concentration-camp survivors. They built a makeshift temple in the garden. "It's still standing," he said, smiling. I tried unsuccessfully to determine what he was telling me by that cryptic smile.

In the Marienplatz square, a crowd of German tourists circled a fire-eater, closely watching as he was about to swallow fire, when a drunk weaved in and, holding an unlit cigarette in his outstretched hand, in a slurred voice requested: "Feuer, bitte!" The fire-eater tried to shoo him away, but the man kept insisting "Feuer, bitte!" while the stony-faced tourists watched and waited.

In the Glyptothek, the reclining archer, one of the remarkable Dying Warriors, braces himself with one hand as the other grasps the now missing lance thrust deep into his abdomen, as he dies with an extraordinary serene smile upon his self-absorbed face. Each of the warriors invites a multiple interpretation— something the ancient Greeks must have appreciated. For at the moment of their dying, the facial and bodily motions of the warriors mirror sexual ecstasy.

Unlike the high-minded nineteenth-century art in the new Pinakothek, the collection in the old Pinakothek contained a great many Dürers and Cranachs, including the latter's *The Golden Age.* And finally an opportunity to see one of Dürer's self-portraits.

Caught in a sudden downpour, I took shelter at the Cafe am Dom. Everything around me resembled a stage set—it reminded me of how I, in writing *How German Is It,* wished to evoke in the "innocent" reader a fantasy of Germany.

Every building along the route of Hitler's march up Residenzstrasse to the Feldherrenhalle has been restored. On Prinzregentenstrasse a streamlined .22-caliber pistol in a store window caught my attention. Given the context, even something as innocuous as a target pistol took on a fresh meaning.

Dutiful visit to the Hofbrauhaus. Massive, noisy interior, packed with families consuming the huge quantities of beer and sausages the colossal muscular blond barmaids, deftly balancing the enormous trays of beer in one hand, had brought to their tables. I remembered Madeleine Gins's reaction, after she and Arakawa were taken to the Hofbrauhaus by a museum curator who, having selecting a table, jovially informed her that she was sitting on the precise spot Hitler used to sit. For a moment, she said, she thought she'd keel over.

"Ist das der Englische Garten?" I inquired.
    "Ja, das ist der Englische Garten."
    "Danke."

From where I sat in the palace garden, idly watching two men in shirtsleeves, both shop owners in that row of elegant stores, play bocci, the former army museum, a vast majestic-looking ruin, was plainly visible. The glints of gold on the scorched dome were offset by foliage wildly projecting out of the building. In front of it, a bronze horseman, one of the princely Wittelsbachs, faced a low, almost unobtrusive World War II monument. Only the incised words SIE WERDEN AUFERSTEHEN, "They will rise again," on the smooth marble exterior gave any hint of what it was. A few steps led into the sunken cryptlike interior, in which a recumbent steel-helmeted Wehrmacht soldier—representing a continuum of bravery and obedience—lay faceup on a low marble base. At his feet were a bouquet of wildflowers loosely tied with a blue ribbon bearing the words "Unseren Gefallenen Kamaraden." To our fallen comrades.

As I left the monument, an exhausted collarless German shepherd limped past, trailing blood . . . On a grassy slope nearby, a homeless man, the first I'd spotted in Munich, was stretched out, reading a newspaper, his few possessions at his side, looking as if he didn't have a care in the world.

The chic stores facing the palace grounds were empty. The two bocci players were still at it. In passing, I could hear the pleasant click of the metal balls colliding as I followed the collarless dog to the main avenue. No one gave the bedraggled animal, a dog straight out of a Günter Grass novel, a second glance. I concluded that the gods must have intended this spectacle for my benefit. They decided: a German shepherd trailing blood will appeal to him—something to use in his next novel. But all along I kept wondering, Is this not inconsistent with what Germans feel for dogs? Clearly, it has to be a message beamed at me!

Back in New York, I ran into the sculptor Julius Tobias, who lives in my neighborhood. As a bombardier, he participated in a continuous, devastating seven-day air raid on Berlin. When I questioned him about it, he said that somewhere he still had a list of other targets, which included a raid on Schweinsfurt. On his twenty-sixth mission his B-17 lost two engines to antiaircraft fire. As they headed for the nearest sanctuary, Switzerland, they were barely staying aloft. A straggler, they presented an inviting target. "As a rule, the German fighter attacks came from the rear," Tobias said. In all, they were attacked by ten fighters. "We shot nine out of the sky—the final plane turned tail." There's nothing the least bit boastful about his statement. "Nine?" I asked, sensing exaggeration. "Are you sure?"

"That's what the gunners claimed," he said crisply.

By now they were flying low, while the crew, to lighten the load, frantically jettisoned everything not bolted to the plane. Julius recalled the pilot telling him to aim their Norden bombsight at a farmhouse they were approaching. Explaining that he didn't have the heart to kill a civilian, he aimed it at a lake instead. It's this final detail that I find so psychologically compelling—with a crash landing imminent, the pilot still had the presence of mind to ask Julius to kill a German.

I asked him if at any time during the flight he was aware of the scenery below.

"From the nose of the plane one had a magnificent view of the landscape below." Searching his memory, he added, "The flights consisted of long, long stretches of boredom punctuated by moments of intense fear."

"Did you ever attend a reunion with the crew?"

"No."

When I visited Wieland Schulz-Keil, whose long-contemplated wish to film Malcolm Lowry's *Under the Volcano* was finally reaching fruition, I hadn't expected him to allude to *How German Is It* by reiterating what to my ears had become a familiar German refrain—namely, that nowadays there was a widespread tendency to overinterpret everything German through the limited prism of the Hitler years. After all, the Hitler years were only a short period in a long history. Was it the expression on my face that caused Wieland to justify himself by stating: "After all, I carry a German passport"? When I referred to the stringent, hard-edged attitude that seemed to predominate in Germany, he noted that as Hochdeutsch was being introduced, all former regional differences—the various softer, melodious dialects, even the regional dishes—were vanishing. "One simply cannot be chummy in Hochdeutsch," he said. To illustrate the changes taking place in Germany, he recounted how a recent major exhibition of prewar life in Prussia excluded everything military and warlike one had come to associate with Prussia, whereas a far smaller exhibition on the Jews in Prussia highlighted the entries in the diaries of Jewish soldiers to emphasize their patriotic fervor. Sentences declaring how happily they'd sacrifice their lives for their country were commonplace.

PART TWO

The prominence of German Jews also says something about their place in culture, about the milieu in which they worked, which mixed, perhaps uniquely, hospitality and hostility—and perhaps both were needed for this extraordinary achievement . . . The German has a veneration for learning, a yearning for greatness, a lingering insecurity. German Jews shared these traits and found further sustenance for them in their own distinct past. Jews did not foster talent; they hovered over it, they hoarded it, they nearly smothered it . . . The rise of German Jewry is one of the most spectacular leaps of a minority in the social history of Europe.

—FRITZ STERN

Who can read without emotion the history of those [Jews] who to the point of suicide maintained the claim that they were better Germans than those who were driving them to their death?

—GERSHOM SCHOLEM

THE WRITER

Berlin

A month prior to our departure for Berlin in 1986, I stepped into a shallow hole dug for a fencepost alongside the pavement and fell, fracturing my left ankle. When I informed friends of the accident, they laughed in disbelief, as if to imply that this couldn't possibly have occurred by chance. When I informed the Deutscher Akademischer Austausch Dienst (DAAD), which had invited me to spend six months in Berlin, of my mishap, they promptly urged me to come the following year. By now I was convinced that the gods had arranged this visit.

In 1987, a year later, I traveled blindly to the walled-in city, quite unprepared to dismantle the wall I had erected within myself. The Berlin I became acquainted with has little in common with the Berlin of 2002, where construction proceeds at a feverish pace—though, given the magnitude of the project, no one yet has an inkling of the outcome. Cities expand and drastically alter, but few do it as purposely and as rapidly. Looking at the panoramic photos of the day-by-day dramatically changing Berlin skyline, with its thousands of active construction sites, one is tempted to speculate on the outcome of this supreme endeavor. In order not to undermine the city's celebrated symbols such as the Schauspielhaus, the Gendarmenmarkt, the Altes Museum, the Pergamon Museum, and the Rathaus, Hans Stimmann, Berlin's former architectural czar, favored a background architecture that would blend in, not the distinctive designs that would challenge Berlin's central integrity. "We must bring this city back so that when we look in the mirror, we will know that it is our face," Stimmann declared emphatically. "Berlin must look like Berlin."

Of the notable exceptions to Stimmann's restrictive and conservative rules of design regarding height and a consistent wall along the street—parameters that favor the construction of large blocks with courtyards at their center—Daniel Liebeskind's Jewish Museum is unique, in that it appears to flaunt its modernist contradictions while remaining attached to Berlin, like a prematurely born infant attached to a respirator. Uprootedness prevails. Liebeskind brandishes his unquestionable genius—a disconcerting accomplishment that forever stamps him as the other. People come to visit it prepared to be stunned. Do they ask themselves: "How Jewish is it?"

I wrote *How German Is It* in the late seventies without any particular desire to visit Germany. Though I tried to present an evocative and plausible picture, I didn't think it mattered that my descriptions of everyday life in Germany be accurate in every detail.

A day after our arrival in Berlin a DAAD employee, a ruggedly handsome blond man in his forties, came to the apartment to check if we needed anything. To Cecile's bewilderment, the two of us in no time were mired in a dispute over a question of design. I maintained that our hallway showed every indication of having been altered, presumably in the fifties, while he stubbornly insisted that it was unchanged.

In the vicinity of our neighborhood the plain, unadorned three- and four-story public housing constructed in the fifties, a period of burgeoning optimism named the *Wirtschaftswunder,* is still eminently serviceable. The small, curtained windows, framing little knickknacks and plants, provide a reassuring view of everyday life. The metal plaques bearing the year of construction on the public housing furnish an additional service—they memorialize. What? An admirable consistency. Decency, hard work, a kind of obstinacy—and *Heimat!* Here and there, as if to disprove that the city's charm had been expunged, an appealing tranquil square with a fountain, such as Viktoria-Luise-Platz, where I frequently breakfast at the Montevideo, stands out.

In the fifties, many of the former quintessential Berliner apartments being rehabilitated were divided into two. We occupy the more preferable spacious front of one, with its high ceilings and parquet floors. The tenants in our five-story building are a representative group of youngish couples, a few aging gays, and the middle-aged owners of the ground-floor antique store. Within walking distance are the vast Tiergarten, the former Italian and Japanese embassies, the giant department store KaDeWe with its Breughelesque upper-floor food emporium—a lavish display of every single region's wurst and cold cuts, really a jubilant political advertisement leveled at a then deprived East Germany.

It's possible to walk for hours without a glimpse of the Wall, actually a double wall with the deadly *Todestreifen,* death strip, in between. Though Berliners adapted themselves to the ubiquitous Wall the way the one-legged adapt themselves to a prosthesis or crutch, the everyday aura is misleading.

Yet, didn't the presence of the Wall save everyone in Berlin from having to ponder the awkward period preceding it?

In a then recently published collection of photos by Friedrich Seidenstücker (1882–1966), I was struck by several snapshots taken in 1946 of an attractive young couple, both under twenty, deep in conversation next to a relatively unscathed monument in the Tiergarten. It's hard to appreciate that less than a year had elapsed since the Russian battle for Berlin. She's modishly dressed, in a short-sleeved top with matching pleated skirt. There's not a trace on their youthful, serene faces of that inordinate fear that enveloped the city as Soviet troops battled their way to the center, a short distance from where the couple are seated. It's a warm day, and his shirtsleeves are rolled up. In another photo, the same couple is perched on a low metal guardrail beneath the damaged torso of Venus, their backs to the hollow shells of decimated buildings at the far end of the park. The two are completely absorbed in each other. In the second photo, the intimacy is intensified as the young man, smiling, leans toward her to catch what she, shielding her mouth with one hand so as not to be overheard, is saying. The still-standing-tall Siegessaule, victory column, which somehow survived the war, looms in the background.

In another evocative photo, Seidenstücker snapped a neighbor, a placid-looking man in his fifties, relaxed on a lower balcony, taking a midday snooze in the sun. Timelessness prevails. Nothing could be more pleasantly tranquil. In yet another shot, a gardener is reseeding the devastated Tiergarten. What makes these photos singular is that they do not strike one as photos of a defeat. True artist that he is, Seidenstücker not only documents the shattered city and its people without a trace of self-pity; in seeking out the familiar, he detects amid the ruins a charm one wouldn't suspect to be there . . .

In the municipal office where I've come to register, the civil servants who were about to leave, one by one, dutifully make the rounds, walking from desk to desk, to shake hands with the eight or more remaining clerks. Mystified, I observe the solemn handshaking wondering if it was a widespread office ritual.

I was surprised by the vast number of books on every aspect of the Third Reich, Hitler, and World War II. Was anyone actually reading them? A great many focus on that critical moment of defeat, *Stunde Null,* zero hour, with illustrations depicting a mind-numbing devastation—although, so many years later, might these pictures also serve as a measure of Germany's postwar resilience and industriousness? At first glance, I was left with the erroneous impression that everything about the past was being revealed.

To satisfy my curiosity, I bought as many wartime diaries as I could. As a rule, not contemplative, but factual journals by diplomats, lawyers, journalists, calmly, stoically detailing the downward progression of the war. Engrossing, packed with information, they evade one essential: any reference to the fate of the German Jews or, for that matter, to the European Jews in general. Evidently, that other war, which had commenced so openly for all to witness and culminated in mass extermination, proved to be a dilemma for the dedicated diarists from the very beginning. At most, a writer would confine himself or herself to a fleeting sighting. For instance, in *Als Berlin Brannt,* the author, Hans-Georg von Studnitz, a well-traveled German diplomat, in 1944, on spotting from his train compartment a passing train packed with skeletal Jews, confines himself to one single (empathetic?) comment: "Ein erschüttender Anblick"—A horrifying sight. To question further where they might be headed or infer from their emaciated appearance what horrors might lie in store for them is evidently beyond him. In other diaries, this predicament doesn't even arise. Spectators, bystanders, reluctant participants, former neighbors, not to mention individuals who in one way or another benefited, however slightly, from the expulsion of the Jews, evidently cannot bring themselves to refer to the Jews in their personal diaries. What was it—apathy, indifference, or acute discomfort—that nothing, not even the disclosures at the war's end, could undo?

In that final gasp of the war as Nazi Germany was disintegrating, as selected groups of Jewish inmates feverishly dismantled and destroyed the incriminating evidence of mass gassing in the by now vacated death camps before themselves being summarily dispatched, long columns of barely surviving inmates were marched by maniacal guards and their Kapo cohorts hither and yon, across the devastated landscape of Poland to the overcrowded concentration camps in the near vicinity of Berlin, Hamburg, Munich, and Hanover. Primo Levi, the most prescient witness of this dark period, in a remarkable essay, "The Gray Zone," refers to the men and women on these death marches that only a handful survived as *Geheimnisträger*—bearers of secrets. Clearly, the secret he's referring to was the intimate and secret knowledge of their own horrifying demise. It's straight out of Kafka. Paradoxically, our world still swarms with *Geheimni-*

sträger. Now, however, the secrets these aging witnesses, these former participants, withhold are secrets not of their own demise
but that of others long gone.

How well does one need to understand Kafka to absorb this?
Doubtless he's widely read. He may, for all I know, be admired as
a preeminent German writer—a classic. But isn't there something about Kafka, the inventor of the unexpected, whose arguments were always, indubitably, directed against himself, that's
antithetical to German literature? Something of which the
Germans may actually disapprove? Doesn't Kafka, who'd be the
first to provide reasons for his own demise, whose nonendings
serve as a tantalizing culmination, pose a threat to the German
universe? Alone the equivocal ending of *The Trial*—"It seemed as
if the shame would outlive him"—seeks to disallow a reader's
withdrawal into a safe retreat.

A Berlin bus driver wordlessly indicated his displeasure with the
way I positioned my ticket on the smallish metal tray by pointedly straightening it before he stamped it—all the while glaring
furiously at me. What German lesson was being communicated?

Living in Berlin, one is compelled to become German defensively.
At first, as a visitor, an outsider, a writer, I welcomed the artificiality imposed by the unprepossessing, nondescript Wall. Packed
with asbestos, like the consequence of some misdirected socio-
logical experiment, it arbitrarily dodged in and around streets—
dividing, I was soon to discover, not just a territory but the very
German language and its identity. Soon, however, I began to
resent its existence, not only as a disfiguring impediment, but, for
a novelist like myself, as something that curbed rather than
encouraged the imagination.

Joachim Sartorius presents me with a copy of his translation
of Drieu La Rochelle's late journal, *Récit secret.* I vaguely recall
that during the war André Malraux, who sided with de Gaulle, as
if to demonstrate that class ties transcend political divergence,
continued to meet with the pro-Nazi Drieu, who committed suicide at the end of the war. Alastair Hamilton, the English transla-

tor of Drieu's *Secret Journal,* notes: "Drieu associated Jews with a certain type of subversive modernity which he considered incompatible with his own romantic belief in tradition . . ."

Seeing me cross a deserted street against the light, an offended motorist on a cross street stopped in midtraffic to upbraid me at the top of his lungs. "What business is it of yours?" I yelled back, my voice matching his in loudness. Surprised by my furious rebuttal, he sounded aggrieved: "You're wearing an eye patch . . . your eyesight is impaired. You might get hurt!"

Here and there, one can still come across unmistakable neoclassical "Nazi" buildings, which the younger Berliners dismiss contemptuously—whereas I find them arresting. Am I insensitive to the past horror they represent? Their highly charged, aestheticized reality reminds me of Speer and Hitler's architectural "partnership." Hitler's idealized, utopian view of a future presupposed a world free of Jews, whom he identifies with internationalism, democracy, and pacifism. Noteworthy is Hitler's consistency. To the end Hitler remained convinced of his sacred mission and faithful to his twin passions: his architectural vision, really a form of self-glorification, and his pledge to bring happiness to the world by eliminating the Jewish bacilli that threatened to engulf the very nations and people he intended to subjugate. The architectural models, such as Speer's model of Berlin, which occupied an entire room, substantiated, if only in miniature, his grandiose "Germania" project. As late as 1945, Hitler would leave the safety of his bunker to visit the nearby chancellery cellar, where two model makers had worked round the clock to complete a scale model of Linz, which was to supplant Vienna as the future cultural capital. As Hitler studied the model of Linz, which by then had been flattened by Allied bombers, was he still capable of fantasizing a different outcome to the war, one in which Linz's reconstruction and the ultimate displacement of Vienna remained a distinct possibility, or was he by then so absorbed with diminutive architectural details that all other factors became irrelevant?

In quest of inconsistencies, I determined that close to the war's end, German city planners who had moved to areas in Bavaria deemed relatively safe were still painstakingly drawing up plans for the postwar reconstruction while keeping Berlin informed of their timetable. For the planners, it was a way to avoid the fighting; for the authorities in Berlin, it was a means of sustaining the vast pretense that the war wasn't lost. To my surprise, I found that a few outstanding modernist structures, such as Erich Mendelssohn's architectural gem in Potsdam, the Einstein Astrophysical Observatory, completed in 1921, had survived the war.

Visitors to the tranquil cobblestoned courtyard of the former army headquarters on Bendlerstrasse can contemplate the somber memorial to Claus von Stauffenberg and his fellow officers and the wall where they faced their executioners the night of June 20, 1944, following their failed attempt to kill Hitler—an occurrence that is now a keystone of Germany's "usable past." Stauffenberg's last words, "Lang lebe das heilige Deutschland," are in dispute. Equally telling, though it doesn't possess the same valiant ring, is General Rommel's puzzled query: "Was there no captain with an army pistol available?"

I keep persuading myself that everything I see, every conversation I have, is potential material for future use. But is that so? Most exchanges are oddly dissatisfying; it's as if an unseen caution prevails—on my part? on theirs?

The heated dispute that was triggered in 1986 by the historian Ernst Nolte's essay "The Past That Will Not Pass" is still being waged in the papers. People who customarily pay little heed to scholarly debates closely follow the clash of left- and right-wing historians and intellectuals. I'm nonplused by the thinness of Nolte's arguments, such as his claim that the invasion of Russia by Germany was a preventive measure.

   If Nolte and other conservative historians were to prevail, I fear the Holocaust may yet come to be regarded exclusively as a Jewish, not German, issue, for which a Jewish, not German, explanation must be sought.

Ryszard Kapuscinski, a Polish writer I admire, explained in an interview that he couldn't find a way into the book he was writing about Emperor Haile Selassie of Ethiopia until he had interviewed the man responsible for the emperor's dog, Lulu. Daily, as I diligently read several German newspapers and periodicals, I keep looking for a similar loophole.

It's the equivocal content in Anselm Kiefer's mythologizing paintings that I find compelling. The enormous canvases convey a spectrum that haunts history. Is there such a thing as Germanness? Do the paintings lay siege to a Germanness? To this day the huge canvases evoke uneasiness. For how is one to interpret these dour ruinations of the past, especially in view of the fact that American Jewish art collectors esteem Kiefer above all other German painters?

What draws me to the seedy hotel I frequently pass? I keep asking myself as I stop each time to scrutinize it, as if intending to make use of it in my novel. The dozen or so airline, credit-card, and travel-agency endorsements at the entrance to the unprepossessing six-story hotel match, sticker for sticker, the ones glued to the wide windows on the enormous Mercedes touring bus that several times a week pulls up at the entrance to disgorge a group of fatigued elderly German travelers who've come to experience Berlin. Why do I feel that everything, from the dark wood-paneled hotel lobby to the daily menu posted outside the rustic restaurant, presented to these visitors a reassuring authenticity—call it *Heimat*?

The artists, critics, and writers I encounter, most in their thirties and early forties, scarcely differ from the ones I know in New York. Nearly all have lived in Berlin for years and years. Their measured, down-to-earth concerns and commensurate priorities are identical to those of artists elsewhere—though by 1987, despite the increased number of cultural institutions, not to mention the additional funding, I sense that the Berlin artists and writers seem weighed down by an incommunicable mental fatigue.

What's left of the German Jewish community? Their former presence supplanted by a diffused and attenuated memory, the German Jews, who strove so mightily to be German, have left a curious dissonance in the malleable German imagination. Yet, there's evidence aplenty of their remarkable past: in the Wertheim and Kaufhaus des Westens department stores, once owned by Jews; even the notorious Wannsee villa in which Heydrich's conference on their elimination took place was once the residence of an affluent Jewish family. Many Germans find it inconceivable that a German Jewish working class ever existed, so determined are they to identify their former fellow countrymen as successful physicians, lawyers, art historians, businessmen, or publishers. In a discussion with a German lawyer, when I mentioned that my uncle Phoebus had been an amateur boxer, he shook his head in disbelief, declaring: "You must be mistaken."

One side window in our apartment gave out on the Hinterhof, a quintessential Berlin courtyard from which the cheerful, crisp voices of several young hairdressers eating their lunch at a folding table below while loudly discussing their weekend affairs with a pleasant absence of animus were a welcome daily distraction as I pecked away on the rented typewriter.

Berlin was the center from which Germany's twin wars, the military war against the Allies and that other insidious war—not alluded to by Speer—were conducted with equal dispatch and bureaucratic zeal.

The city housed the key institutions, with the SS Head Office for Race and Settlement furnishing the detailed classification of undesirable human beings, while hundreds of secondary offices administered the vast network of concentration and death camps, responsible for everything from the scheduling of the one-way transports, the staffing of SS brothels, and the distribution, controlled by Speer's ministry, of Zyklon-B, a gas that had a shelf life of four months, to determining the number of calories inmates were to receive.

The menu in the well-designed Art Deco dining area of the new Museum of Fine Arts lists a few delectable Turkish dishes alongside the German ones. I kept glancing at the Turkish waitress, who spoke a fluent if accented German. Her foreignness was such a welcome sight.

On the occasion of President Reagan's visit, Berlin's police were placed on high alert. In their white helmets and padded uniforms and riot gear they resembled outer-space warriors in a Hollywood spectacular. I spotted a number of elderly German tourists eagerly chatting up the cops on Nollendorfplatz. Was this bonding to convey their disavowal of the longhaired, disheveled left-wingers protesting Reagan's visit to Berlin?

Though violence was in the air, I hadn't anticipated the clash when it occurred that afternoon to be so unrelenting. As I watch the cops advance on the protesters, I mentally try to compare them to cops elsewhere, in France, China, the U.S. After isolating a group of about a dozen young men and women, leaving the encircled protesters no avenue of escape, the cops in unison proceed inward, swinging their long truncheons with methodical rage. I keep reminding myself it's twentieth-century crowd control.

In the Kleist Park square, fronting the former People's Court, where Roland Freisler, the infamous *Blutrichter,* the hanging judge, shrilly dispensed death sentences to anyone deemed a threat to the nation, a dozen enlargements of the district's late 1930s police ledgers were displayed on easellike structures. Each ledger page (of which several were defaced by incensed viewers) listed the address, floor, and apartment number of every Jewish family or individual residing in the district. A notation in the final column indicated the individual or family's "departure" by suicide or removal to the east.

Cecile and I spend the evening with Klaus Wagenbach, the

publisher and writer, whose expertise has contributed vastly to the study of Kafka. After dinner he proudly shows us, one by one, his extraordinary collection of Kafka first editions. I had no idea that so many of Kafka's stories first appeared individually in meticulously designed, oversized slim volumes. A Kafka scholar, Wagenbach turned up invaluable information, including hitherto unavailable school reports and family photos, as well as photos of Kafka.

At a party a senior editor at Klett-Kotta, once publishers to the Prussian court, in all seriousness declared Ernst Jünger to be one of the three preeminent German writers, the other two being Thomas Mann and Kafka. To my mind, there aren't two more antithetical authors than Kafka and Jünger. When Kafka introduced the word *Ungeziefer* ("vermin"), he didn't do it innocently. When he named his character K., he did so to deprive K. of his precursors. For K. concealed not only his identity but, more significantly, his origins. Did Kafka knowingly exclude Jewish characters from his fiction to avoid the stereotype they'd unintentionally convey?

Most likely Ernst Jünger's metaphysical reflections on the annihilation of the Jews wouldn't deserve much attention were it not for the willful avoidance of that exacting topic in the manifold published diaries of World War II by Germans of all backgrounds and convictions. Jünger's comments become significant since, alas, he's one of the few to refer to the extermination of European Jewry. Stationed in Paris from 1941 to 1944, a captain whose fluent French made him an attractive dinner guest in French social circles, the admired World War I hero's religio-philosophical mulling over the widespread killings, tempered by a steely self-discipline, illuminates the inordinate degree to which the Jews occupy his fantasy. The only intimation in Jünger's diary that he's unsettled is an intermittent entry that he's not sleeping well. But instead of the sociopolitical scrutiny that would have exposed the widespread collusion, the shameless self-interest in the rounding up and annihilation of Jews, Jünger prefers to contemplate Jewish traits, Jewish archetypes, as well as the sacrificial role of the

Jews, in order to buttress his cosmic rationalizations. Engrossing himself in Jeremiah, the chronicler of the Judean expulsion to Babylon, and in *The Jewish Wars* by Josephus, the first-century historian who chronicled the Roman conquest of Jerusalem, Jünger appears to be seeking a historical and mythological parallel for the genocide.

An admirer of Josephus, Jünger's evaluation of the Jewish historian is revealing: "It's remarkable how little Jewishness adheres to this author, though he was a priest and leader of his people. It appears that Jewishness may be more difficult to jettison than other national and ethnic traits; however, in the rare case where it is achieved the individual soars to exceptional heights."*

Clearly, nothing will induce Jünger to examine the effect of the mass killings on the society—or to ponder the ultimate consequences for Germany. In a final summary in April 1945, maintaining his customary intellectual distance, Jünger comments elliptically: "King Ahasuerus, also, couldn't exterminate the Jews. It always leads to a cutting and with that to a strengthening, a sprouting afresh from the old trunk. A converted people lack this hardened persistence through the centuries . . . Was our persecution the last birth pang before the appearance of the second Messiah, the intercessor, with whom the age of the spirit is to begin? It's impossible that such a sacrifice won't bear fruit."†

However, once the war is over, Jünger appears to lose all interest in the further contemplation of the Jews—as far as he's concerned, they no longer warrant more thought. The distinguished author, whose postwar diaries reflect as before his insatiable curiosity in human affairs, appears to have said everything there's to say on the subject of one of the most challenging and virulent episodes in history. I consider it an intellectual and moral omission.

Klaus Stiller, the novelist, who works for Radio HIAS, doesn't conceal his aversion to everything East Germany represents. Like

---

*Ernst Jünger, *Das Zweite Pariser Tagebuch*, in *Sämtliche Werke*, vol. 3 (Stuttgart: Klett-Cotta, 1998), p. 197.

†Jünger, *Die Hütte in Weinberg* (former title: *Jahre der Okkupation*), in ibid., p. 415.

the majority of German autobiographical novels, his well-written *Weinachten: Als wir Kinder den Krieg verloren* is exculpatory. Listening to him disparage German leftist writers, I can only conclude that he must be assailing their lack of national pride. By mocking Hitler in his intriguing novel *H,* Stiller appears to be trying to salvage what Andreas Huyssen referred to as Germany's "usable past." At a party in Stiller's huge, undivided Berlin apartment, a young woman approached me and, after cheerfully introducing herself, proceeded with a compulsive forthrightness to explain that after she had overheard someone in the kitchen mention that there was a Jew at the party, she decided to seek me out, since her mother was half-Jewish. Guilelessly, she rambled on, remarking that her mother had informed her that the Jews invariably smile whenever they touch upon their misfortune. To my relief, my conversation with the next person I met, a former East Berlin architect, was on a topic more to my liking—architecture. His brother, he explained, was chief of an architectural brigade in East Germany. Given the valuelessness of the currency, East Germany had become a barter society. In order to survive, each day one of the seven or eight members of the architectural group would scour the city in search of anything, really, that might be useful for future barter. One could survive in East Germany only as long as one was a member of a group—people one could rely upon—though from what was revealed after the collapse of the East German government, this trust seemed often misplaced.

The Berliners on the street, wearing loose sporty cotton jackets with exaggerated wide shoulders, look relaxed and somehow jaunty. Unlike the elderly, who are generally quick to reveal their resentment, the young appear laid-back. I watch groups of *Freunde,* arm in arm, three, even four, abreast, lightheartedly stride through the city with the grace of an infantry regiment.

During dinner in a new "French" restaurant near Kreuzberg, a sudden inexplicable sickening odor forced us to withdraw to the tiny bar near the kitchen, from where I was able to observe a well-dressed young woman diner on her knees, wiping up after her dachshund had vomited on the tiled floor the succulent tidbits she'd been feeding it under the table. No one seemed the least surprised that she—after all, a diner—would be made to clean up the mess without any assistance from the restaurant staff. Having been given a pail of water and other essentials, she stoically scrubbed away—it might have been her own floor at home—without any trace of resentment, while the staff never once looked in her direction as they went about their business.

Klaus Stiller cannot refer to Jews without an involuntary twinkle of his eyes. I can only conclude that for many people Jews must still be such an oddity.

In our lively neighborhood, in addition to a sprinkling of gay bars and boutiques there are a considerable number of antique stores. The pile of German books I've acquired grows taller and taller. When Joachim Sartorius said that he'd arrange for me to see any German movie of my choosing at the Arsenal, I promptly requested a favorite, *Ich liebe dich, ich töte dich,* only to be informed a week later that Uwe Brandner's film was unavailable. No one seemed to know what had become of the Bavarian film-maker who along with Wenders, Fassbinder, and Geissendorfer belonged to the cooperative Filmverlag der Autoren in the 1970s. Years later, a German film producer told me that Uwe was living in Munich, but he wasn't writing or producing movies. "He's a loser," the producer stated flatly. To my dismay, the dismissive, often indiscriminately used word "loser" is making inroads in Germany.

In the open-air flea market located on the Strasse des 17. Juni, I search the largely predictable piles of bric-a-brac for pre–World War I Baedekers. Their maps were so faultless that in that war's Russian and French campaigns German officers preferred them to their own. Though the collector's passion at the flea market transcends ideology and nationalism, I resist the impulse to buy anything bearing Hitler's likeness or a swastika. They now serve a fetishistic purpose. The Egypt Baedeker I'm looking for is hard to come by. So is the one for Moscow. One of the dealers, an amiable man who reminds me of the antiquarian dealers elsewhere, promises to see if he can lay his hands on either one.

One major drawback to the attractive design of the new housing along the Landwehr Canal is an evident lack of privacy for the tenants. Unlike the scruffy young leftists who moved to Berlin in the sixties, the inhabitants appear well dressed. How soon before they'll begin to displace the now aging revolutionaries?

At the KaDeWe, a salesman, upset at being asked by a passing shopper for directions to the toy department, indignantly complains to a colleague: "What does he take me for? Am I information?"

The model trains at the KaDeWe are beautifully crafted, expensive adult toys. I watch closely as the technician rearranges the miniature countryside, shifting a cluster of trees, a water tower, and a fire station to make room for yet another railway track. Since the tiny station signs are in German, it follows that the diminutive figures realistically grouped on the station platform are identified as such—even though the true setting for this edenic landscape is the imagination. How to explain the gratification one experiences observing the realistic model train speeding over a bucolic landscape that's crisscrossed with a myriad of tracks?

The huge Tiergarten on a blistering summer's day . . . Here and there, nude Berliners seated on the grass were luxuriously soaking in the sun. On their startling white bodies every tiny defect stands out. A young Turk on a bicycle like a windup toy slowly circles a reclining naked young woman immersed in a book. No one interferes. No one objects to his fixed rotations. Like everyone else, she, the alluring target of his gaze, pretends not to notice. Otherwise, the idyllic scene, which includes a number of boisterous nude men playing handball, is oddly, even disturbingly, asexual.

Mallary, our niece, comes to visit. Born in Berlin, she hadn't been back since my brother-in-law Norman and his wife, Barbara, moved to London. Norman's recently published *The Berlin Wall,* dedicated to Mallary, is based on his firsthand observations as the Wall was being erected. As a British correspondent all doors are thrown open to her. Refreshingly unconstrained, she views this as an opportunity for a vacation, not an article. As a working journalist she's promptly invited to visit Spandau, and then, courtesy of the British army, given a helicopter ride over Berlin . . . She'll stay in our apartment during our vacation in Italy.

A majority of the former German Jewish community were united in their fervent wish to be one with Germany, yet, as the Judaic scholar Gershom Scholem, fellow Berliner and a close friend of Walter Benjamin, acknowledged: "A person living in a liberal Jewish, German assimilationist environment had the feeling that those people were devoting their entire lives to self-delusion." That may indeed be so. Yet, despite the poignant truth that "when the German Jews thought they were speaking to Germans they were speaking to themselves," as students of the Enlightenment their achievements—to take one example, Erich Auerbach's *Mimesis,* which he wrote in Istanbul during the war without the aid of libraries—are such that, in my opinion, they came to mirror the best of what is Germany.

Cecile's photos show a very distinct and personal Germany—a *Heimat* perspective that borders on the clinical. The people in the photos appear to inhabit a model city—one that will be replicated in miniature for the children to enjoy.

Italy

Our flight to Rome on an East German airline jet entailed a circuitous hour-long bus trip to the forsaken-looking East Berlin airport guarded by edgy East German militia. Their assertive vigilance testified to a kind of paranoia about a West they do not know or comprehend. Our Russian-made plane would return to Berlin directly after we touched down, a fellow passenger informed me. The crew, he said, had never set foot on Italian soil. Indeed, as we prepared to disembark, I saw our blond stewardess wistfully fingering her silk scarf as she gazed at the lively Rome airport through the plane's window—her doleful expression revealing her innermost thoughts.

On the flight I read Calvino's story "Smog." Calvino proceeds with a careful dentistlike prodding of a sensitive terrain, while trying to avoid inflicting pain. I recall, during one brief encounter with him at Arakawa's studio in New York, his matter-of-fact statement: "I treat the personal in a most impersonal manner, whereas the impersonal becomes personal." Coming from Berlin, what immediately struck me in Rome was the absence of constraint . . . True, the cumulative weight of history seems to inhibit rather than further inventiveness. In the end, for the Italian writer, every idea is refined and subsumed in the past.

Our hotel is within walking distance of the Colosseum. The elegant Italian owner grows miniature trees on the roof and traps wild birds, which he domesticates in an aviary. Today he showed me his bonsai trees—as many as two dozen of varying ages and degrees of health. The lowest shelf, his hospital, contains the ailing trees. Though any kind of tree could be transformed into a bonsai, aesthetically, the Japanese, he explained, aspire for an exterior triangle formed by the apex and outer branches or an oval or umbrella shape, whereas the Chinese tend to disregard these strict rules.

I described Berlin to him. I spoke of the German attention to order, the attachment to laws and rules, and the apparent Italian disregard of the same, but I could tell that he was uninterested. Germany left him unmoved. I mentioned that while walking in the vicinity of Rome's main railroad station I came across a six-story neoclassical building on which Mussolini's helmeted visage, so familiar to me from the postage stamps I used to collect as a boy, was mounted between each of the elongated windows on all the floors. There must have been no fewer than thirty reliefs of Mussolini. He burst out laughing. "He was killed along with his mistress . . . strung up by his feet from a tree or lamppost, as befits a dictator down on his luck. Given our contempt for history's losers, why bother to destroy those affectations of the past?"

In the Forum, the reliefs inside the Arch of Titus depict the bowed, defeated Judeans, bent under the weight of the treasures from their destroyed temple. The Romans had selected the hardiest and best-looking young Jews for the triumphal march into Rome. The others were killed, used as slave labor or as participants in Roman games. Josephus went to great length to describe the internecine fighting of the besieged that pitted three groups against each other: the Jewish warriors from the mountainous north who had fled to Jerusalem; the Jewish aristocracy and its followers, not willing to cede power to the new arrivals; and lastly, the religious group, who, paradoxically, were willing to negotiate and compromise with the Romans at the gate.

In Rome I feel as if nothing is immutable—at least, nothing that as visitors we're likely to encounter. There's always ample room for negotiation—for compromise. We're surrounded by levels of decay, levels of inhabitation, a kind of permanent state of bedlam. As I observe people in animated conversation, I infer an almost sensuous attention to details . . . the speaker seems to make a genuine effort to win over his or her listeners. The eloquent gestures only add to the ceremonious exchange.

In the Esposizione Universale di Roma, referred to by all as EUR— the vast and ambitious project undertaken but never completed in Mussolini's lifetime—the mammoth, eye-catching Colosseum, a cube-shaped structure with nine enormous arches on each of the six levels, is a kind of symmetrical overstatement, reminding one of Mussolini's bluster and quasi-comical posturing.

"Look behind you!" Cecile warned me as we stood waiting in line for an espresso. Turning, I caught sight of a menacing face— and if further proof was needed, his jacket was draped strategically over one arm, a technique favored by pickpockets, thereby shielding what the man's other hand was about to undertake. With an exaggerated bow, I stepped aside, inviting him to take my place: "Prego, Signor." As I walked away, his fixed stare reminded me of the look of an attack dog about to leap at his quarry.

The bus to the Catacombs of San Callisto traveled along via Appia, passing through one of Rome's ancient gates. The age-old narrow road was clogged with traffic. Not particularly eager to view human cadavers, I felt only relief when, approaching the Catacombs, I could make out from afar the ubiquitous sign CHIUSO on what I took to be the entrance.

At the hotel owner's suggestion, we set off for a resort town south of Rome. The six-sided hotel overlooked the Mediterranean. Since it was late in the season, a day after our arrival a mass exodus emptied the busy resort as if people were escaping the plague. Overnight the street below, buzzing with activity at our arrival, looked abandoned. To my delight, two days later, only eight of us were guests in the hotel.

The inelegant, awkward-looking exterior of the twenty-four-year-old hotel belied the appealing, cozy interior. On our floor the tiles were blue; on the floor below they were green; below that, yellow. In sections the tiles were chipped. But the hotel was aging gracefully. One had to be careful descending the marble steps, since they were slippery and had a sharp edge to them. With the guests gone, the staff could relax in front of the TV in the lobby. It was the end of the season. Everything, including the appealing open-air cafe, was being shut down.

The following day the sky was overcast and the sea more turbulent. The only other hotel guest having lunch was a pleasant middle-aged lady immersed in a book. The restaurant staff remained closeted in the kitchen until the arrival of a German woman who had spent the entire month at the hotel. She smiled at no one in particular. She spoke Italian with the waiter and the cook—and, I soon determined, with any hotel staff willing to chat.

To my dismay, the kiosk no longer carries the *Frankfurter Rundschau* or the *Frankfurter Allgemeine*. How am I to follow the windup of the historical debate? I observe a gray-haired man trying to read a newspaper, battling the wind. The wind here is soft—it caresses one. For some reason, the Italian refuses to fold his paper and make things easier for himself.

In one section of the deserted roof, paved with red brick, the hotel laundry hangs to dry in the Mediterranean sun. I watch the blue bus heading for the top of Circo Antico. Below, the nearby villas are boarded up for the winter and the tennis courts deserted. My headaches come irrespective of the season, of the weather, of the time of day . . .

Each day something else has been removed. First it's the easy chairs on the terrazzo, then the beach chairs and umbrellas, except for half a dozen left for the remaining guests.

Having been informed that there will be no electricity after nine, we order breakfast at eight. By nine-thirty no power. The rooms won't be cleaned until late this afternoon. No elevator. Silence.

We set off on foot to retrace the walk we took yesterday, but miss a turn. The boarded-up villas look unfamiliar. There are roses blooming in the well-kept gardens and the fruit trees are heavy with lemons. In one garden, the three wicker chairs drawn around a low round table with a mirrored top in which the overhanging trees were reflected give the impression of a stage set awaiting the return of the performers, who any moment now will spill out of the deserted-looking villa. Here and there, one of the larger trees I've seen only in Italy appears to be dying. The streets are evocatively named—via Calypso, via Nauticas, via Odissea—whereas the villas are identified only by their street number, which is set above a metal disk or tile in the wall on which a dog, teeth threateningly bared, is depicted as a warning to intruders.

Andrea, a dealer of antiquities in Zurich, lent us her book of Piero della Francesca's paintings. The German woman refers to her as "the Swiss lady"—though from the way she says it, it's meant to cast doubt on Andrea's extraction. A large, statuesque woman, Andrea wears loose-fitting, expensive dresses. Everything she does indicates an expansiveness, a largesse. She has a house near Sicily. Antonioni shot *L'Avventura* on a nearby island. The film crew used her house.

"Did you meet him?"

"No."

"Did you meet Monica Vitti?"

"No."

In her sixties, her round face is free of wrinkles. She smiles easily. Her former husband, a German who had fought and was wounded at Monte Cassino, by marrying her became a Swiss citizen.

After her husband left her, Andrea traveled to India. She described how a blind man, while holding her hand, depicted the triangle in her life: her husband, her father, and her narcissistic mother. "In the next life you'll be reunited," he promised.

Sunday. Today, a strong wind. The waves are high. Afternoon, the sun vanishes behind the clouds. With surprising efficiency the boats are being hauled away to their winter storage. In no time, all that's left in the harbor are the bright yellow inflatable motor dinghies bobbing up and down in the water.

Cecile, wearing her goggles and cap, is steadily swimming back and forth. Thirty, forty laps.

I listen to Andrea chat with the cook, the barman, the man in charge of the steadily disappearing beach chairs, sensing the drollness of what she's saying and their humorous response. Her Italian is melodic. Still, there's something childlike about us as we repeatedly express our pleasure: "Belle, molte belle." It's unavoidable. Every move, every gesture, every remark signifies our role.

Back in Rome . . . Each year more Roman walls, pillars, and busts are brought to light. The omnipresent windswept pines soften the architectural profusion of ancient stone and marble. One's eyes dart from the Renaissance to the baroque back to the Roman period. What matters is the staging, the spectacle.

By now, Berlin will be gray and cold.

Return to Berlin

I asked a journalist about her unusual first name, Hartmut. "It's a typical Nazi name" was her immediate response. "My father was a small-time Nazi," adding with a thin smile, "He was absolutely contemptible. I despise his craven embrace of power, his petty small-mindedness, his lack of imagination." Wasn't this what I had all along expected to hear?

For ruined buildings, for pockmarked walls one has to visit East Berlin. I brace myself to confront the East German officials who peer suspiciously at one from behind their tiny cubicle windows. Their accusing stares induce a sense of culpability; one is made to feel vaguely guilty . . . of what? That's immaterial. At the Berliner Ensemble we see a correct but wooden performance of Brecht's *Galileo.* Stores are empty. People are wary. No one smiles. As we stand in line at a bookstore (given the size of the store, only so many people are permitted inside at one time), I become aware that people speak in low voices, avoiding eye contact. After a twenty-minute wait, it's our turn to enter.

As soon as I raise my camera to take a shot of a derelict factory courtyard, an elderly woman, indignation writ on her wrinkled face, comes tearing at me, shrilly screaming, "Verboten!" For these aged semiretired ladies—quite a few are employed as museum guards—even minimal authority must be a kind of aphrodisiac.

Klaus Stiller has, until last week, when he went to meet a German translator in East Germany, not set foot in the other Berlin for twelve years. He encourages me to read Alice Miller's provocative essay on Hitler's fear of having Jewish blood. Again, the odd involuntary smile. "Hitler feared that he might be part Jewish."

. . .

Back in our neighborhood, I return the rented Adler typewriter and, having made the final payment, request a receipt for the six monthly payments. "You were given a slip each month you came by," the salesman points out reprovingly.

"Yes, but I'd like a receipt for the total."

His jaw jutting out irately: "That's against the law."

"All I require is a receipt for tax purposes."

The salesman I've been dealing with for six months is adamant. Realizing that this was about to become a battle of wills, I request a copy of the rental contract I signed. "Or is *that* against the law?"

The clerk reluctantly makes a copy—behaving throughout as if I've somehow checkmated him.

On the day I am to give a reading, troubled that a German audience is bound to overinterpret what I say, I feel a need of something to uplift my spirits. Wishing to step out of this constricting atmosphere, I'm overcome with an unaccountable longing for French paintings. I'd give anything to see a Manet . . . I'll even settle for a Delacroix. In the end, I listen over and over again to Blondie's "Accidents never happen in a perfect world . . ." To my pleasant surprise, the audience is immensely friendly and receptive.

We're invited to a show at a transvestite club before a late dinner at the gallery owner's apartment. I think up an excuse to avoid the transvestite entertainment. On another occasion we're invited for drinks in a brothel. To encourage us to come, I'm assured it's a real whorehouse. For similar reasons I make up an excuse not to attend what I expect will possess a contrived Fassbinder-like garishness.

It's easier to describe the divided city by what it lacks. By what's absent. After years of living within the walls, normal, everyday existence by itself is a virtue. I hadn't anticipated the canals with their tree-lined walks . . . Reading Walter Benjamin's *Berlin Chronicles,* I try to envisage the former landmarks to which he refers. It's as if Benjamin is traversing a by then unreachable past to obtain a better sense of the present.

The former Japanese embassy, thoroughly gutted and modernized, has been transformed into a glitzy building that bears no trace of its past. By comparison, the nearby partially destroyed and neglected Italian embassy evokes an elegiacal, tranquil mood . . . Doubtlessly it'll be next to lose its incomparable character.

Changes are taking place on our street. A new boutique. Handbags and shoes. The owner is new to the business and hasn't yet mastered the art of running a store. Like the owner of Motz bookstore, my favorite store, he has an academic background.

Stiller, an involuntary grin lighting up his usually somber face, informs me that his father had taught him to shop the Jewish way. Apparently, his father, a physician and passionate amateur filmmaker, preferred to purchase his equipment from Jews. He learned to bargain, Stiller explains. He quite enjoyed it. Stiller's grin challenges me. To my knowledge, German Jews would consider bargaining as profoundly un-German. They'd rather die than bargain. What's Stiller trying to accomplish? I can only conclude that there's something abhorrently compulsive underlying Stiller's statement. Is he at all cognizant of what he's saying?

Is the reality I daily encounter identical to that which engages the German writers? Why does it fill me with such dismay?

On a desultory walk in Wannsee, after asking a passerby for directions to the nearest cafe, we follow his directions down a pleasant tree-lined street. We stop to look at what once must have been a grand private villa at 56/58 Am Grossen Wannsee only to realize on reading the metal plaque on the gatepost that it was the site of the infamous Wannsee Conference. In this cozy neighborhood with its boat clubs along the lake, the villa, like all else, conveys an atmosphere of exemplary *bürgerlich* respectability. It's far easier to picture the occupants planning their leisurely weekends, instead of dedicated civil servants endeavoring to overcome bureaucratic snags as they plan to transport an inconceivable number of European Jews by rail to their death.

At a dinner celebrating the engagement of an American friend and his German girlfriend in her L-shaped Berlin apartment, the guests included a rare-book seller who piqued my curiosity when he spoke of traveling each year to Israel in order to purchase German libraries brought there by Jews who had fled Germany. It occurred to me, as he expressed regret about the general poor condition of many of the bindings, that in place of the now dead German Jewish owners, their most prized possessions, the lovingly acquired complete editions of Heine, Goethe, Schiller, would be returning to their place of origin—their *Heimat*.

On a Sunday jaunt to the Grunewaldsee, Cecile and I were greeted by the sight of bare-chested men romping with their oversized pets, loudly summoning them by what were decidedly non-German names. It was a chaotic, Breughelesque scene as huge Dobermans, German shepherds, and smaller but feisty terriers excitedly dashed to retrieve sticks thrown into the lake. To my surprise, not a single dog owner was to be seen disciplining his or her dog.

On our way to the Forsthaus Paulsborn, an old inn, we stopped at a nearby *Jagdschloss* to spend an hour looking at an exhibit of Old Masters on loan from the museums. As we were leaving, I inquired if a German or a foreign architect had designed the attractive *Schloss*. In response to my innocuous question, the bored custodian promptly declared: "There were no Germans when this *Schloss* was designed. These distinctions didn't matter then. Even you," he said, peering closely at me, "could have been one of us."

"You mean to say that when Dürer traveled to Italy to study art, and in fact on his return revealed an Italian influence, there were no boundaries? No distinctions?" The custodian threw up his hands, all too readily capitulating: "I'm self-taught. You mustn't take what I say seriously."

The 750th anniversary—something both East and West could celebrate. East Berlin, with an endless parade that I watch on our black-and-white TV. Nothing would have led me to suspect that in less than two years the uniformed East Germans would be out of a job. West Berlin, with concerts, performances, and many special exhibitions. At four a.m. the Kudamm is still jammed with West German tourists aimlessly walking back and forth in pursuit of elusive pleasures. One potential diversion, the slim and spindly young prostitutes in thigh-high plastic boots, mini trousers, and little else, parade up and down, stopping obligingly to discuss their sexual menu and price list whenever a prospective client approaches. The heavily applied makeup lends their juvenile features a doll-like semblance that's anything but erotic.

The history is in our bones. (Christian Meier)

A good-looking Ethiopian who is a male nurse in an old-age home told me that a majority of the elderly daydream of the Hitler days and still cast blame on the Jews for everything that has transpired. "How do you get along with them?" I asked. And he, with a beatific smile on his pitch-black face: "They simply love me."

After a two-hour session with the photographer in our apartment, the photos, when I get to see them days later, seem an accurate assessment of my uptightness. I hardly recognize myself.

At night I dream of people I haven't seen in years. People who don't have the remotest link to Germany. They simply pop up. Though some of the dreams are turbulent, I remain unconcerned by the intensity.

As Cecile and I walk around the deserted Olympic Stadium, I recall Leni Riefenstahl's aestheticized cinematic treatment of the Olympic Games. A partially effaced swastika on the huge cracked bell on the ground level reminds me of how Leni Riefenstahl and Alfred Speer, she by means of her films, he with his architectural effects, successfully staged fascism as the supreme enticement.

On a subsequent visit, for a soccer match between France and Germany, the Olympic Stadium is packed with rowdy Berlin youths screaming derisively "Bagett fresser!" at the French players. In this setting, the past spectacles so solemnly and reverently filmed by Riefenstahl now appear outlandish and laughable.

The owners of the antique store in our building mentioned that in August each year they visit New York.

"That's the hottest month. What do you do there?"

"We buy furniture."

"Art Deco?"

"Oh, no. We only acquire furniture that was taken there by the German refugees. There's so little of it left in Germany. Most of our good prewar German furniture was destroyed. Now there's a huge demand for it."

When Nicole Zand, a reporter for *Le Monde,* came by to visit me, she shook her head disapprovingly on seeing the stack of books on Germany and genocide beside my desk. "Don't go that way," she warned. "It'll destroy you."

THE SCRIBES' DILEMMA

Uxmal: Yucatán, Mexico

> When Cain killed Abel, murder became a new element of
> consciousness, a then constant expectation which puts its mark on
> individual experience and social institutions alike. Analogously,
> the prospect of genocide is now also inevitable and common: there is
> no way of avoiding it, and the variations of its past history include
> everyone, all of humanity, in its future.
>
> BEREL LANG

Sunset at the compound. There were birds thrashing about in the
bamboo thicket. The gardener in blue overalls, oblivious to all
else, dexterously removed leaves and waste out of the L-shaped
pool with the aid of a tiny net fixed to a long metal pole. His
broad face was virtually indistinguishable from the faces of his
progenitors in countless Mayan murals and tablets. The group of
travelers relaxing at a nearby table spoke Italian and English,
while their hands, in accompaniment, expressed a more univer-
sally understood communication. The two young American
women reclining on lounge chairs at the edge of the pool, their
voices too low for me to make out what they were saying, took
turns focusing the large binoculars on the exotic, brightly plumed
birds that swiftly darted from the line of trees towering above the
attractive enclosure. Toward the center of the pool, on a pedestal,
a replica of a Mayan figurine, a proud-looking androgynous fig-

ure, was cemented into place. Smaller figurines were on display in the wall niches along the open walkway to the rooms. One could hear the steady hum of air-conditioning even though it was only February. The ruins were tantalizingly nearby. But thus far, though elated to be so close, we hadn't taken a step in that direction. In my mind, already leaping ahead, I was savoring Uxmal's proximity.

By deciphering the Mayan script, recent scholarship had stood the former interpretation of the Mayans as peaceable and their cities as ritual centers virtually on its head. What the texts revealed was an unrelenting rivalry over boundaries and lineage honors between combative city-states.

The prime purpose of warfare was to obtain sacrificial victims, whose blood, drawn from the tongue, the earlobes, or the genitals, was offered to the gods as sustenance. The calamitous bloodletting, first documented in A.D. 200, persisted for well over a thousand years. On special occasions, determined by the Mayan calendar, even the king and queen would participate in these blood rites before the assembled nobility. On murals, on vases and pottery, and in sculpture, torture was plain to see. A recently uncovered mural depicted warriors sacrificing their victims as a patient line of scribes who were taken prisoner stand waiting to have their fingernails extracted, plucked like so many flowers. This ordeal was followed by a methodical breaking of all fingers. Since writing was an instrument of power, these luckless scribes, whose duty it was to extol the power of the enemy ruler, were being singled out for special attention.

What nations tend to conceal and deny was depicted as a central function, virtually a necessity of the state.

That first evening, a moonless night, Cecile and I carefully made our way to the pyramid and from there, in pitch darkness, followed a broken stony trail to the "nunnery," where the son-et-lumière show was taking place. The palace with its vaulted chambers was illuminated. A silent audience seated in two rows at the edge of a sunken plaza intently watched the slide show on the far side, while a taped voice poetically evoked the glorious

Mayan history, which dated back to 600 B.C. The dramatic voice of the commentator referred to the harmonious interrelationships of the buildings and the Mayan concern with death and the underworld—but no mention, not a word, of the society's ferocity and unmentionable cruelty.

The next morning we set off to the ruins hours before the tourists from Cancun were due to arrive in their chartered buses. At that early hour Uxmal, enveloped in mist, was breathtakingly beautiful. It was built and rebuilt as many as five times, but to the visitor the hundreds of years of history were somehow compressed into one illuminating experience, the unique layout imparting a transcendent calm. The question remained, how to relate these awe-inspiring structures in one of the most beautiful of Mayan sites to the unappealing torture of captives and the perpetual bloodletting? I saw a self-assured Mayan guide in high-laced shoes rapidly scramble down the steep, narrow pyramid steps without a pause, and tried to glimpse something of that, to me, unfathomable history in his uncanny agility and composure.

Toward the end, when the Mayans retreated eastward to the coast, the danger looming ahead had acquired greater specificity. Tulum, overlooking the Caribbean, was one of their last redoubts, their final city. From its heights they could observe the occasional Spanish galleon and thus contemplate the power of the new gods as well as their own inescapable decline. Given the human capacity for self-deception, I assume that to the last climactic event the Tulum scribes, witnesses of finger mutilation and decapitation, dutifully recorded only their ruler's everlasting invincibility.

AFTERWORD

In 1974 my parents came from St. Petersburg, Florida, to spend a week with us in Northampton, Massachusetts. Now, looking at the black-and-white photos Cecile and I took of us picnicking in the park, sitting in their hotel room and in our tiny fourth-floor apartment overlooking City Hall, I cannot contain my astonishment at this revealing look at my family, who remain at once so distant and yet so very near. Though I recognize myself in the photos as I would in a mirror, somehow my ever critical writerly perception fails to live up to the tenderness, unity, and generosity my parents impart. In this, their final visit, they had come to bid us goodbye. In the close-ups, my father looks far younger than his eighty-three years. Months later, when Cecile and I flew to St. Petersburg to spend several days with them, the last time we were to see them together, my father inquired why I had neglected to send any of the photos. I remember making some excuse and still recall the look on his face—not accusatory, but puzzled. He was trying to understand my reasoning. Referring to my mother's illness, he stated, "It would be nice if we'd have one more year together." It seemed, at the time, such a modest request. Three months later my parents died within weeks of each other. Some time later I dreamt of meeting my father, who casually informed me that he intended to become a

219

photographer. He even went so far as to describe the kind of photos he intended to take. As I jotted down this dream, I commented that I had found it painful and, as a result, for days postponed entering it in my notebook. In a subsequent dream, I ran into my dead father again. I was delighted to see him. We embraced. When I resumed walking in the direction of home, he remained at my side. After a while, I turned to him and asked: "Where are you going?" And he, instantaneously, with his customary smile, replied: "Why, to you, of course." His answer was entirely consistent with his loving behavior to me. It's my question, "Where are you going?," that I find so disconcerting.

Recently, speaking with William Farley, a West Coast filmmaker, who was about to make a film about his father, I mentioned my failure to send my parents the photos I'd taken on their visit—and how puzzled I was by this action. "You can always rectify the matter by showing the photos to your father now," he suggested. I've taken William Farley at his word.

Acknowledgments

The author gratefully acknowledges the generous support of the Lila Wallace–Reader's Digest Foundation. In addition, the author wishes to thank the Deutscher Akademischer Austausch Dienst (DAAD) for its invitation, enabling him to spend six months in Berlin.

Some of the names in this account have been changed.

A NOTE ON THE TYPE

This book was set in Adobe Garamond. Designed for the Adobe Corporation by Robert Slimbach, the fonts are based on types first cut by Claude Garamond (c. 1480–1561). Garamond was a pupil of Geoffroy Tory and is believed to have followed the Venetian models, although he introduced a number of important differences, and it is to him that we owe the letter we now know as "old style." He gave to his letters a certain elegance and feeling of movement that won their creator an immediate reputation and the patronage of Francis I of France.

Composed by Creative Graphics, Inc.,
Allentown, Pennsylvania

Printed and bound by R. R. Donnelley & Sons
Harrisonburg, Virginia

Designed by Soonyoung Kwon